D0615725

THE TRUTH ABOUT HOMOSEXUALITY

The Cry of the Faithful

JOHN F. HARVEY, O.S.F.S.

The Truth about Homosexuality

The Cry of the Faithful

IGNATIUS PRESS   SAN FRANCISCO

Cover art by Georgia Oliva
Cover design by Roxanne Mei Lum

ISBN 0–89870–583–5
Library of Congress catalogue number 95–79890
Printed in the United States of America ⊗

To the memory of
Father Richard Murphy, O.M.I.

Dedicated teacher, canonist,
priest, religious, friend

CONTENTS

FOREWORD

Few people in the United States have dedicated themselves more generously or wholeheartedly to the pastoral care of homosexual persons than has Father John F. Harvey, O.S.F.S. I am exceedingly grateful that he has again contributed to the growing body of important literature both for those working specifically in this field and for a broad reading audience who may have little understanding of the issues or the persons involved.

Father Harvey has long directed our Courage program in the Archdiocese of New York, a program he himself founded. It is a program that has proved vitally helpful to enormous numbers of individuals in need, a program that has my total support and for which I am deeply grateful.

I pray that this new work of Father Harvey's will be given the serious, prayerful attention that it deserves.

✠ John Cardinal O'Connor
Archbishop of New York
June 1995

PREFACE

Several years ago I asked myself whether I should write another book on the moral and pastoral aspects of homosexuality and homosexual behavior. My experience as guest editor of the 1993 *Journal of Pastoral Counseling*, published by the Graduate Department of Pastoral and Family Counseling of Iona College, New Rochelle, New York, convinced me that I should do so. The topic discussed in the 1993 journal was "Homosexuality: Challenges for Change and Reorientation". It is a collection of essays opening up new ways of looking at the homosexual condition and related behavior. I realized more strongly than before that the topics discussed should be presented to a larger reading public than the learned readers of the journal.

In this book, then, you will find two distinct kinds of writing. The first kind is concerned with the history and progress of the Courage movement in the United States, Canada, and Great Britain and with additional moral arguments in favor of the magisterial teaching of the Roman Catholic Church. The second kind is concerned with opening new vistas of hope in the pastoral guidance of persons with an apparent homosexual orientation. (Please note that I refuse to label a person "homosexual"; even if he has the orientation, there is something more fundamental about the person. The Church "refuses to consider the person as 'heterosexual' or 'homosexual' and insists that every person has a fundamental identity: the creature of God and, by grace, his child and heir to eternal life".[1]

[1] Congregation for the Doctrine of the Faith, "Letter to Bishops of the Catholic Church on the Pastoral Care of Homosexual Persons" (PCHP), Oct. 1, 1986, no. 16.

The first two chapters are a preliminary statement of the question. Called "The Cry of the Faithful Seeking the Truth", chapter one sums up the collective experience of Courage leaders and members in America and elsewhere, namely, that our Catholic people need instruction on the nature of homosexuality and its related behavior. Living in a culture that assumes individuals are "born" gay and should simply accept the active homosexual lifestyle, individuals who have homosexual inclinations are confused. Must they give in to these inclinations to be "happy", as so many therapists advise? Is there any hope that an individual can work his way out of this condition through therapy, group support, and prayer?

Chapter two, "The History of Courage", describes the expansion of the Courage movement to include the parents, relatives, and friends of Courage members. This latter group is called "Encourage". Parents whose sons and daughters refuse to accept Catholic teaching on homosexual behavior find support and consolation at Encourage meetings. They love to come to the annual conventions of Courage, where they can converse with members.

In chapter three, Father Jeffrey Keefe carefully examines questions concerning the origins of the homosexual condition; and in chapter four, I consider whether it is possible for an individual to change his sexual orientation. Thanks to the research of Father Keefe, it can be safely said that we do not have proof that the condition of homosexuality is the result *primarily* of genes or prenatal hormones; indeed, the evidence he offers, along with that of Maria Valdes and Dr. Richard Fitzgibbons, indicates that psychological factors are prepotent in the development of a homosexual orientation. From many years of research and counseling, I share their view.

Chapter four discusses how Courage leaders encourage persons with the homosexual orientation to try to move out of it, while recognizing that some are either not able or not willing to make the considerable effort the process of change requires. The difficulty is particularly evident for individuals over forty who have been involved in sexual addiction and who desire only to lead a chaste life. Chapter five deals with how one can lead a Christian life of chastity in these circumstances.

In Catholic teaching the central consideration is the objective morality of homosexual activity, already expounded in my book *The Homosexual Person*. Here, in chapter six, I further nuance the argument from divine tradition and Holy Scripture with special emphasis on the *essential* connection between the teaching of the Church on the nature of human sexuality and marriage and her teaching on homosexual behavior. The teaching on marriage is found in many places, including the Second Vatican Council's *The Church in the Modern World*, numbers 47–52, and in the *Catechism of the Catholic Church*, passim. At the same time I do not neglect the question of the subjective freedom of a person with homosexual tendencies.

Because my primary focus in this book is to give pastoral guidance to persons with homosexual orientation, I discuss a variety of related problems in chapter seven, "Pastoral Perspectives". One of these problems demanding careful scrutiny is the question of so-called gay rights, which I consider at some length with the help of Catholic legal scholars and philosophers. Chapter eight, then, is a response to the gay rights movement, which continues advocating the homosexual lifestyle as an alternative to marriage.

Having followed the literature on same-sex unions, I read the late John Boswell's *Same-Sex Unions in Premodern Europe* (New York: Villard Books, 1994), and I thought it necessary to respond to his argument. I do so in chapter nine, where I also address other issues. For many years I have noted the lack of serious study on women with homosexual inclinations. In chapter ten, therefore, after some general reflections, I present a group of Catholic women, most of whom are members of

Courage, and all of whom are striving to lead chaste lives. Their personal accounts speak for themselves. It is encouraging that these women derived personal insight from writing their personal histories. By reading this chapter, other women may be inspired to seek spiritual guidance and sound therapy so as to change their lives, if possible.

In Appendix I, Richard Fitzgibbons, M.D., with whom I have appeared on many panels, explores the interplay of emotions in persons with homosexual tendencies and the importance of spirituality in the healing of the person. His insight is the result of many years of clinical experience. His analysis of anger in his clients is fascinating.

In Appendix II, Maria Valdes, Ph.D., explains her method of therapy and her creative use of biofeedback in helping her clients to move out of the condition of homosexuality. Over a period of twenty-five years, she has had a phenomenal success in this endeavor, but I want her to tell her own story.

I know that what has been written by my esteemed associates and myself is a contribution in an ongoing conversation with other professionals, spiritual directors, and the members of Courage. We seek more insight into the multiple factors involved, not only in the genesis of the homosexual condition, but also in helping people move toward heterosexuality.

ACKNOWLEDGMENTS

I thank John Cardinal O'Connor, Archbishop of New York, for his constant support of the Courage program and for the Foreword that he graciously wrote for this book. I am grateful to Father Benedict Groeschel, C.F.R., who describes in the Introduction the role he has played in Courage from before its beginnings until the present writing. Through fifteen years he has stood with me in our joint effort to encourage persons with the homosexual condition to lead a truly chaste life. Time for research and writing would not have been available were it not for the two-semester sabbatical funded by the Oblates of Saint Francis de Sales and by Allentown College of Saint Francis de Sales. Special thanks to the Very Reverend Richard Reece, O.S.F.S., former Provincial Superior, and the Very Reverend Daniel Gambet, O.S.F.S., President of Allentown College.

In planning the content of this volume I relied upon the contributions of Father Jeffrey Keefe, O.F.M. Conv.; Richard Fitzgibbons, M.D.; and Maria Valdes, Ph.D., all of whom have for many years counseled men and women with the homosexual condition. I have depended upon Sister Mary Cronin, Daughter of Mercy, to do the indices and the late Mrs. Terry Kutyn, business manager of Saint Francis of Assisi Parish, Springfield, Pennsylvania, and Maria Messina, secretary of Courage (New York City), to seek permission from publishers and authors for the use of their materials. Finally, I thank many others who remain anonymous, particularly the women who share with us (in chapter ten) their struggles to overcome the homosexual condition by lives of Christian love and chastity.

I also thank the following authors and publishers for permission to reprint material:

Gregory Baum, S.T.D., for excerpts from "Homosexuality and the Natural Law", in *The Ecumenist*, series 2, vol. 1, no. 2 (1994), published by Sheed & Ward, Kansas City, Missouri.

Andrew Comiskey, for excerpts from *Pursuing Sexual Wholeness*, published by Creation Lake, Strang Communications, Lake Mary, Florida, © 1989.

William Consiglio, for excerpts from *Homosexual No More*, published by Victor Books, an imprint of Scripture Press, Wheaton, Illinois, © 1991.

Fleming H. Revell Company, a division of Baker Book House, Grand Rapids, Michigan, for excerpts from John Stott, *Involvement*, © 1994.

Free Congress Foundation, Washington, D.C., for excerpts from George Rekers, "The Formation of a Homosexual Orientation", in *Hope for Homosexuality*, © 1988.

Lawrence Hatterer, for excerpts from *Changing Homosexuality in the Male*, published by McGraw-Hill, New York, © 1970.

Christiane Hudson, for excerpts and paraphrase from her letter to *The Catholic Times* (London), March 24, 1995.

The Institute on Religion and Public Life, for excerpts from Robin Darling Young, "Gay Marriages: Reimaging Church History", in *First Things* (November 1994), pp. 43–48.

The New Republic, for excerpts from Brent Shaw, "A Groom of One's Own", in *The New Republic* (July 18–25, 1994), pp. 33–41.

Notre Dame Law Review, for excerpts from Richard F. Duncan, "Who Wants to Stop the Church: Homosexual Rights Legislation, Public Policy and Religious Freedom", in *Notre Dame Law Review*, vol. 69, issue 3 (1994), pp. 393–445. Copyright 1994 by *Notre Dame Law Review* and excerpts reprinted with permission. The author and publisher bear responsibility for any errors that might have occurred in editing or reprinting.

Notre Dame Law Review, for excerpts from John Finnis, "Law, Morality, and 'Sexual Orientation' ", in *Notre Dame Law Review*, vol. 69, issue 5 (1994), pp. 1049–76. Copyright 1994 by *Notre Dame Law Review* and excerpts reprinted with permission. The author and publisher bear responsibility for any errors that might have occurred in editing or reprinting.

Michael Pakaluk, Ph.D., for quotations from "Homosexuality: Challenges for Change and Reorientation", *Journal of Pastoral Counseling*, Iona College, New Rochelle, New York, 1993.

Leanne Payne, for excerpts from *The Broken Image*, Crossway Books, Wheaton, Illinois, © 1981.

Jeffrey Satinover, M.D., for excerpts from "Psychotherapy and the Care of Souls", in *New Techniques in the Treatment of Homosexuality* (1994), pp. 82–89. National Association for Research and Therapy of Homosexuality (NARTH), 16542 Ventura Blvd., Suite 416, Encino, California 91436.

INTRODUCTION

Benedict J. Groeschel, C.F.R.

As I read the manuscript of this book, with its rich and multifaceted approach, I recalled a conversation with Terrence Cardinal Cooke in the summer of 1979. This kindly and gentle pastor was also a very dynamic man who tried to look after every pastoral need in the complex Archdiocese of New York. On a bright, sunny day we were sitting by the edge of the sea at Trinity Retreat. Out of the blue the Cardinal said, "We have to do something for Catholics with homosexual orientation, to help them lead a chaste life." I knew this servant of God only too well. This was no idle thought but something that had been on his mind. I gulped. I was already too busy with a very demanding schedule. As if by inspiration I answered, "What about contacting John Harvey, the priest who wrote the guidelines for confessors on questions of homosexuality?" He looked me straight in the eye and said, "Get hold of him and see if he can do something." That something has since grown into the Courage movement.

Recently I attended a Courage meeting in Toronto and was very impressed by the quality and the numbers of members of Courage and Encourage, including the number of priests who were working as Courage chaplains. It would seem obvious to me that any bishop should consider it a real advantage for a diocese to have a loyal and dedicated group of Christians like these people, who have made a definite and often painful decision to observe the gospel of Jesus Christ.

Many times, organizations, even religious ones, can be self-serving. People enjoy the prestige, bask in the sunlight of recognition, seek their own comfort in this role or that. Depending on the nature of the organization, this may not even be wrong, although Christ warns his disciples against such motives when he says, "Let the greatest among you become as the youngest, and the leader as one who serves" (Lk 22:26). Although we often forget this point, the Christian should avoid using the Church of the crucified Savior in any self-serving way. When one attends a Courage meeting or, in fact, any one of the so-called Twelve Step groups (such as Alcoholics Anonymous or Sexaholics Anonymous), it is clear that they are implicitly not self-serving in this undesirable way. These groups call people to change, to conversion, to what the Scripture calls *metanoia*—a radical reversal of their ordinary way of acting. These groups are born out of a desperate choice, either to change or to be destroyed by some compulsion. For me they represent one of the higher forms of activity in our troubled times. Along with a number of other explicitly Christian groups, Courage supports this need for change by a direct appeal to the teachings of Christ and by total dependency on his grace. Since the official teaching of the Catholic Church as reiterated explicitly by her highest authority has called homosexually oriented members of the Church to a chaste life, how can anyone be opposed to Courage? Candidly, I don't know. But inasmuch as there is such opposition, at times direct, but more frequently subtle and indirect, an *apologia* for all programs encouraging chastity for homosexual persons was needed. This book not only serves that purpose but also provides an excellent summary of the most solid thinking available at the present time on living chastely with homosexuality.

This effort is clearly going against the tide. We live in an age of hedonism, self-indulgence, and self-gratification, when most institutions—religious, cultural, educational, and governmental—have sold out to selfism. Most churches do not preach what the Master sent his disciples to teach, but what people want to hear; universities do not communicate what students need to know, only what they want to know; the media provide only what the most indulgent want to hear and see. The Cross has all but disappeared from the effective presentation of Christian spirituality. Christians struggling with homosexual inclinations may say, "Why bother?" So may some of the clergy and religious who are supposed to give an example of loyal dedication to Christ's teachings.

It is so easy to disguise this denial of principle (and even belief) under the veil of compassion that people begin to believe their own distortions. The argument for exempting homosexually oriented people from the law of God goes something like this. It is true that, like the rest of us, homosexually oriented people hurt. They have often been wounded in the past by misunderstanding and prejudice. The thought of leading a life of sexual abstinence seems completely unattractive and unattainable. Like many other people who do not easily follow the gospel teachings, they want to belong. Besides, many homosexually oriented people are intuitively religious and often are generously responsive to others' pain. Why not meet them halfway, especially when anyone knows that there are only certain moments when compulsions can be successfully reversed? One often hears at A.A. meetings that someone "has to hit rock bottom". This means that a genuine attempt at conversion awaits the proper time. As a student of Saint Augustine, I would be inclined to think this is true. For this reason some pastoral people motivated by compassion or at least by a desire to be of help make the mistake of approving directly or indirectly homosexual relationships and activities. Often, in social situations, it is difficult not to appear approving when one is only trying to be thoughtful and courteous. After all, we are all sinners, and none of us would appreciate being reminded of this fact in a social situation.

In response to the expressed needs of many homosexually oriented people, a whole movement toward acceptance of homosexuality as normative has begun. This acceptance may range from "don't ask, don't tell" (which is often simply courtesy) to pseudo-marriage ceremonies performed in churches. It is worth mentioning that the media are largely given over to efforts to make the homosexual lifestyle an accepted part of the American scene.

However well intentioned this approval is, it sidesteps two very critical moral issues. The first of these is addressed to all serious believers, namely: Is approval for the sake of being nice and helpful actually enabling someone to run along the road to moral and spiritual disaster? Recently I read a review of a biography of Robert Mapplethorpe, a well-known photographer who died of AIDS. According to his biographer, he led an extremely dissolute life replete with serious pathological compulsions, such as sadomasochism. He apparently induced others to follow him in even more bizarre behavior. Strangely, he started in life in a devout Catholic family with obviously concerned parents and successful siblings. The spectacle of such a ruined life ought to warn us of the dangers of enabling, dangers that A.A. has been pointing out for years.

I recently viewed the Gay Pride Parade during a prayer vigil alongside St. Patrick's Cathedral and saw an incredible display of self-defeating and self-depreciating behavior. By no means do all homosexually oriented people approve of such goings-on, and obviously parades are going to bring out the exhibitionists of one kind or another. They are supposed to do that. But when one considers the ruin of human lives, the persistent spread of AIDS by promiscuous sexual activity, and the psychological conflict one observes in the gay scene, the haunting question comes, "Can I approve of behavior that so frequently leads to destruction?" This question is sidestepped by many in an effort to be politically correct, but it still remains, and the hoopla of parades and demonstrations does not make it go away. The grim reminders of the AIDS epidemic were in constant evidence at this parade, but covered up with the most incredible projection and denial of the inescapable fact that promiscuity of any kind is self-destructive. Everyone from Moses to Shakespeare, from Saint Paul to Mother Teresa has reminded our forgetful race of that fact.

The second moral issue is even more basic, namely, should we pretend to be able to alter objective moral standards because some people are unable to live up to them at a particular time in their lives? If in fact an individual cannot live up to the gospel reflected in the teachings of the Church, should we change that teaching? This question pertains not only in the case of compulsive behavior (such as alcoholism) but also when moral laws are very difficult to observe because people must live with obvious, inescapable temptations. A good example is the Church's teaching on artificial contraception. Although compulsions and contraception are very different, the common element is that individuals may not actually be here and now capable of the motivation necessary to overcome such needs and drives. Saint Augustine speaks of this situation when he writes, "I was sick at heart and in torment, twisting and turning in my chain in the hope that it might be completely broken. . . . I kept saying, 'Let it be now, let it be now', and by the very words I moved to a resolution. . . . I shrank from dying to death and living to life" (*Confessions* 8.9). Suppose someone had come along and told Augustine that fornication was not wrong, at least in his case. He had a good excuse. He lived faithfully with a woman he respected, and she respected him. Social convention did not permit them to marry, or they certainly would have. Why not change the law? After all, his mother, Monica, with much admonition, had allowed the two of them to live in her house in order to see to it that their child was raised in the Catholic Faith. Is it not compassionate, more Christlike, to go along with what cannot be changed? This kind of thinking is prevalent in most churches in the English-speaking world.

There are many serious objections to this kind of compassion based on pragmatism and relativism. These objections have been thoroughly enunciated recently by Pope John Paul II in *Veritatis Splendor*. The most obvious (but not the most fundamental) objection is that such thinking precludes the possibility of moral conversion and true Christian discipleship. Apart from the radical denial of truth, such thinking leaves the person lost in a swamp without a map. It is a most dangerous compassion. Once, a young man who had given up the fight to live chastely and had decided to have a live-in homosexual relationship made two requests of me. He said, "Don't reject me, and don't agree with me. If you agree with me I will never get out of this."

The experience of Saint Augustine and his final grace-filled triumph over sexual need and sin lead into the main theme of this book. The possibility of overcoming profound compulsive needs is clearly demonstrated by a great number of personal testimonies and by the very existence of Courage, Exodus, and similar organizations. Anyone working with any of these organizations has heard over and over again the accounts of people who were once deeply committed to a homosexual lifestyle and who forcefully rejected the notion of the Church that conversion was necessary. Frequently, after conversion, these people express considerable hostility or at least dissatisfaction toward those who had encouraged them previously in the thought that they could put active homosexual relationships together with devout Christianity.

Father Harvey and those who have assisted him in writing this book have discussed with eminent clarity the various issues involved. This clarity itself stands in sharp contrast to much of the literature on the indulgent side, which is muddled and lacks any intellectual rigor.

Most of the people who read this book will do so for very

practical reasons. They will be looking either for guidance in their own struggles to lead a chaste Christian life or for ways and means to assist others who have come to them for support and pastoral care. Those who seriously study this volume will find in its pages not only good advice, wise counsel, and intelligent discussion but also the bright light of hope, which comes to those who are courageous enough to believe that the gospel works even in our own confused and paganistic society.

The ultimate reason for assisting any person with a compulsive or morally dysfunctional lifestyle is to assist that person in the struggle for virtue—in this case, the virtue of chastity, which is an aspect of temperance. The natural virtue of chastity guides persons in all their sexual needs and expressions so that they may lead a well-ordered, temperate life in this world without hurting others and themselves. This is the concept of moral responsibility that is the common goal of such groups as Sexaholics Anonymous and Homosexuals Anonymous. However, a Christian group like Courage has yet another quite distinct goal, and that is the attainment of the Christian moral virtue of chastity, which is directed toward living the life called for by the gospel. The goal is not only a well-ordered, temperate life, but also the eternal life promised by our Lord Jesus Christ to those who struggle to follow him faithfully. The ultimate goal of any genuine Christian movement is not simply a well-ordered life but a life of commitment and sacrifice leading to the eternal destiny of divine love. This is the life to which the Holy Spirit calls the disciples of Christ. Unless this goal is clearly stated and the means of grace are consistently employed, the use of the name "Christian" is only a self-deception.

In the Sermon on the Mount, Christ enjoins a sexual morality more demanding than that of the founder of any other world religion. Christ equates an accepted lustful desire with the act that is its object. In Matthew 5:27, Christ demands interior chastity as well as temperance in behavior. This demanding teaching is thoroughly consistent with all his other precepts because he requires inner adherence to the law he proposes. The law of Jesus is not satisfied if we merely avoid hurting our enemies; we must love them. We must not merely be faithful to religious duties, but we must pray within the depths of our hearts. The integrity and uncompromising spirituality of Christ's moral teaching are always stumbling blocks to those who wish to be half-baked Christians and to those who just want to be nice. The following passage from the writings of the distinguished Catholic Scripture scholar Rudolph Schnackenburg puts the case for chastity very well. It seems to me this is the final word in the conflict over the morality of homosexual acts and many other things. This powerful analysis serves as an eloquent opening to a book that is not merely about homosexuality but also about the disciples of Christ who are struggling with that particular challenge to the gospel life:

> So then we must let the words of Jesus stand in all their severity and ruggedness. Any mitigation, however well intended, is an attack on His moral mission. But how Jesus judges those who fall short of his demands is quite another matter. His behaviour towards the disciples gives us an object-lesson on this point. He took back even Simon Peter, who denied him three times and yet was the leader of the circle of twelve, after Peter had bitterly repented his actions, and He confirmed him in his position as the chief of the disciples and the shepherd of the sheep (cf. Luke 22:32; John 21:15-17). Admonition and mercy are found together. It is the mercy of God which always comes first. It comes definitively into history with the person and works of Jesus. But Jesus also longs to awaken the ultimate powers for good in those laid hold of by the love of God and saved from eternal ruin. They should now thankfully do the holy will of God in its totality, unalloyed. If in spite of everything they again succumb to human weakness and wretchedness, God's mercy will not fail if they turn back in penitence.[1]

[1] *Moral Teachings of the New Testament*, 3rd ed. (London: Burns & Oates, 1982), p. 88. Cited in B. J. Groeschel, *Reform of Renewal* (San Francisco: Ignatius Press, 1990), p. 116.

A word of respectful gratitude must be said to Father John Harvey, who has effectively and modestly worked with homosexuals seeking a chaste lifestyle for almost half a century. He has had more than his share of opposition, rejection, and misunderstanding on all sides. Being a real disciple of Christ, he never quit. He has never even thought of quitting. He was and remains way ahead of his time. I wish also to acknowledge the members of Courage, who include some of the most dedicated Christians I have ever known. The members of Encourage and the priests who are chaplains of Courage deserve a great deal of thanks for persevering in a work that many misunderstand and some disparage. Courage proves again the truth of the powerful words of Saint Paul, "Where sin abounded, Grace did more abound" (Rom 5:20).

THE CRY OF THE FAITHFUL
SEEKING THE TRUTH

Since 1989 Courage has become more widely known as a result of our annual conferences and the advertisements in the Catholic press. During the same period the Courage office in New York City has received hundreds of letters from all over the United States, including Hawaii, seeking information about the work of Courage and the locations of Courage groups in twenty dioceses of the United States, six in Canada, and one in Great Britain. People want to know whether their diocese is willing to form a Courage spiritual support group to take care of the needs of a son or daughter. They are aware of various homosexual organizations, such as the Gay Men's Health Crisis, Dignity, AGLO in various dioceses, and Communidad in Los Angeles, but they are not satisfied with what these groups teach concerning the morality of homosexual activity or how they can persuade a son or a daughter to get out of the gay scene. Are there counselors who can help late teenagers to understand their situation and begin to relate to the other sex? More often than not, Courage is contacted by parents seeking help for their child rather than by the individual himself.

Most faithful Catholic parents are primarily concerned with the spiritual aspects of homosexual behavior. Generally speaking, their son or daughter is not going to church and has no intention of giving up the gay lifestyle. Often the son or daughter has sought advice as to what his parents should do next, supplying them with information from gay organizations. Meanwhile, Courage sends these parents a bundle of information, but usually we are not able to recommend a nearby Courage unit, because there are none in the vicinity.

Forming a Courage Unit

This naturally raises the question of how a Courage unit can be formed in a particular diocese. It is not an easy venture, for a variety of reasons, which I can discuss as I develop the theme that there are many Catholic men and women who could profit by a spiritual support group like Courage but either do not know it exists or do not know any priests who would be willing to get the group started. While many priests and religious know that Courage exists, still little is done to spread its message. Why is this so?

I can think of a number of reasons for the *apparent* lack of interest among our priests. The first is the overwhelming impact of the media culture favoring the homosexual lifestyle. Like others, priests are affected by the media culture. They may believe that chastity is impossible for a person with homosexual orientation and that it is better for him to settle down with one lover than to be involved in promiscuity. The priest may be inclined to accept a compromise position on the morality of homosexual activity, seeing the magisterial teaching merely as an ideal that relatively few can attain. I run into this position frequently.

Another reason for the relative inactivity among priests is that they feel overburdened by the responsibilities they already have in their parish or school. There is a critical shortage of priests, and when a bishop asks the pastor of a one-man parish to take on the responsibility for a Courage unit in his locality, the priest is likely to say: "What—one more thing?" He thinks Courage is a good idea, but he does not have time for it.

There are other reasons. One priest feels that only "experts" can handle questions of homosexuality; another is afraid that if he is the only priest working with persons of homosexual inclination, he will be categorized as "queer". Others do not believe that the Church's teaching is truly binding on the homosexual person; they regard it as only an option, an ideal. Still others repress any serious reflection on the problem.

Some of these reasons can be considered. I have learned to set up a team in an individual diocese, thereby avoiding possible gossip about *one* priest director. I have persuaded some older priests to work with Courage, because the members of Courage need kindness and affirmation. The most serious roadblocks, however, are those priests who oppose the certain teaching of the Church, thus failing properly to teach the young.

The situation would indeed be gloomy were it not for the determination of many lay persons who seek help from the diocese to get a Courage unit started. In this regard I learned a lesson from an English bishop to whom I went for advice, as I was trying to set up a Courage unit in South London several years ago. The bishop said: "Father, in this country when you want to get something done, you don't go to the bishop first. Rather, as a priest, you discern in your flock the need for a spiritual support group. With a few laymen you trot off to the chancery, speaking to the authorities there about this need. You volunteer to give the group spiritual direction. The bishop says 'yes', and now the group exists with the bishop's approval."

Actually, this was the method by which Courage was established during the summer of 1994 in the diocese of Westminster, England, where it is called "Encourage". This method is also being used in the United States. We listen to the "cry of the faithful", urging individual laity to find a priest, asking him to be the spiritual director. He, in turn, goes to the bishop of the diocese to get approval, so that if anyone inquires of the chancery, he can be informed of the bishop's approval. As one diocesan official informed me, the laity have a right to organize spiritual support groups for the practice of virtue; and pastors, including the pastor of the diocese, the ordinary, have the duty to listen to the spiritual needs of their faithful.

If in every diocese there are individuals with homosexual tendencies desiring spiritual guidance to overcome serious temptations to impurity and to lead a truly chaste life, then it is the duty of the ordinary and of all priests in the diocese to appoint competent personnel to provide such help. Granted that, in some small dioceses or very rural ones where there is a severe shortage of priests, it may not be possible to provide such personnel. Usually in such situations the ordinary may be in communication with other spiritual support groups who hold firmly to the Catholic doctrine that homosexual activity is always immoral.

Local units of Exodus International and Sexaholics Anonymous are populated with Catholics who want to lead a chaste life, and still other struggling Catholics in such regions should be informed of their existence. But, if at all possible, a Courage group should be set up, because the faithful treasure their Catholic identity, seeking the benefits of the sacraments of penance and the Holy Eucharist and the clear teaching of the Church.

Because in so many cases, as I know from hundreds of letters from all over the country, bishops and priests have been silent on the need for positive help for our fellow Catholics, struggling persons have felt deserted by the Church. By and large this segment of our faithful has been ignored, while ironically in several dioceses homophile organizations have arisen with the claim of helping Catholics with homosexual orientation to be integrated into the Church. Their literature delivers an unclear message from which is absent due emphasis on the truth that homosexual activity is always immoral and that persons are able not only to be chaste but also in some instances to get out of the condition.

A Typical Scenario

Let me present a typical scenario in which the names of the diocese and of individuals are omitted in order to protect the anonymity of the participants. Since our purpose is to promote Courage for the sake of the people who request it, I wish to avoid negative criticism of a diocese or of individuals with whom I happen to disagree.

In the fall of 1994 I was invited to speak with an Exodus group, several of whose members were Catholic. Both the leader of this Exodus group and at least three Catholic members wanted to see Courage established in the diocese. Already there was in the diocese a spiritual support group, but the three Catholics did not believe it was giving the clear message of the Church on the immorality of homosexual activity or an effective program for the practice of chastity according to one's state of life.

I was invited to speak not only to the Exodus group but also to some priests who might be interested in starting a Courage unit. Telephone contacts were made with approximately ten priests for an all-day workshop in a parish rectory. I came prepared for such a workshop, but the only priest who showed up was the pastor who was my host. I had a meeting with two Catholic laymen and a woman from the Exodus group. We planned a strategy for the next year. Previously I had consulted with a learned canonist to ascertain how one could reach the ordinary of this diocese, and he told me that the Catholics who wanted a Courage unit should first find a priest who would be willing to be their spiritual director.

At the chancery the priest would represent the individual Catholics desiring a Courage group. (Individual members might want anonymity.) The chancellor, in turn, would take this petition to the ordinary, who would give his approval, or at least permission for a Courage unit in his diocese, since he would recognize a legitimate spiritual need for a support system in full agreement with the authentic teaching of the Magisterium.

But suppose the other Catholic support group for persons with homosexual inclinations would object to the ordinary that they already have his approval and that there is no need for a second group like Courage, which is known to be so "rigid". My canonical advisor said that this would make no difference. The ordinary may not refuse the request of a group of Catholics forming a support system in order to live fully the teaching of the Church concerning homosexual behavior.[1]

So much for good canonical advice. There are, however, several difficulties. The first is finding a priest, preferably priests, to lead the group. The second difficulty is to get persons who need the Courage program to come out of the woodwork. They do not trust the homophile group already in the diocese, thus resigning themselves to a very difficult life, trying to be chaste all alone, "white-knuckling it", or they may lapse back into a lifestyle of active homosexuality—an occurrence all too common.

Since I have a file of persons who have written from this diocese, I have written to ask them to contact our network person, who is willing to make himself known to others interested in starting a Courage unit. I am happy to report that, as of December 21, 1995, a new Courage group is in the process of formation with the approval of the diocese.

---

[1] See canons 210, 215, and 223, no. 2, which states that "ecclesiastical authority has competence to regulate the exercise of the rights which belong to the Christian faithful." It is conceivable that a particular bishop could have convincing reasons that would cause him to forbid the exercise of the rights given in c. 215. However, he would have to make those reasons known to the group, and recourse could always be taken against his decision. See also the corresponding canons from the *Code of Canons of the Eastern Churches* (C.C.E.O.) promulgated in 1990, which would be applicable in situations dealing with bishops of the Eastern churches. See C.C.E.O. 13 and 18, which are equivalent to the above canons of the Western code.

Spreading the Message through Annual Conferences

Despite the difficulties involved in starting a Courage unit in a given diocese, the leaders of Courage in the United States and Canada are not dismayed, as was evident at our annual conference in the Archdiocese of New York during the summer of 1995. Indeed, all six previous conferences had been marked by the same enthusiasm. Each conference brought together more than a hundred participants from all over the United States and Canada, with the latest attracting about 150. The three days are filled with informative, inspiring, and challenging presentations by men and women who have a message of hope for the participants. Many related aspects of the homosexual condition are discussed: the emotional components of homosexual orientation, the possibility of change, questions of hatred and forgiveness, emotional overattachments as the enemy of true friendship, conversion testimonials, a Jewish theology of homosexual behavior, female homosexuality, and so on.

More important than these discussions are the informal conversations at all hours of the day and night, during meals, early in the morning, and late at night in which members of Courage and the parents of persons who claim to be homosexual exchange ideas, sharing with each other in a supportive, loving fellowship and later continuing their friendships by mail or phone. This is particularly true of members and parents who come either from the boondocks of America where Courage does not exist or from areas where the kind of help offered under Catholic auspices is strangely silent about the need for celibacy as the first step toward true interior chastity.

But there is another aspect of the annual conferences, and that is communal prayer. Besides the daily Mass, time is set aside for the Church's Morning Prayer, Evening Prayer, and Night Prayer, all carefully prepared by Father Kazimierz Kowalski. On Friday and Saturday evenings there is perpetual adoration of the

Blessed Sacrament; and on Saturday evening, a healing service. Opportunities for the reception of the sacrament of penance are made available through the generosity of the priests present at the conference. The laity in particular express their appreciation for the religious services in their evaluations of the conferences. They want to preserve their Catholic identity.

Each annual conference is like a giant advertisement, because it is covered by the local Catholic press in New York City and on Long Island and by the National Conference of Catholic Bishops News Service. The 1994 conference, in the diocese of Brooklyn, was covered by CNS and also in the English edition of *L'Osservatore Romano* (Aug. 31, 1994, p. 8).

Silence within the Church

Courage, however, in all its chapters needs to become better known through the work of its members. It is simply tragic that so many young Catholics with homosexual orientation do not know where to turn when they recognize the conflict between their desires and the teachings of their Faith. All they hear from those near them is to "accept" their condition and to settle down with a steady lover. This usually does not happen, because by and large the male with such tendencies tends to be promiscuous, at risk of becoming HIV-positive. This leads to the question: *Why is there so much silence within the Church on the issue of the immorality of homosexual activity?*

For example, do organizations like AGLO, Communidad, and other Catholic gay and lesbian outreaches *proclaim* the teaching of the Magisterium and *promote* sexual abstinence as Courage does? These are tough questions that we all need to face. How we resolve them will influence both the temporal and spiritual welfare of many Catholic young people. There is, then, an urgency in making Courage better known to the faithful as a genuine help for the development of interior chastity and as a preventive measure against becoming HIV-positive.

Is it not strange that the closest allies to Courage in reiterating the Church's teaching on homosexual behavior are Exodus chapters (Protestant) and Sexaholics Anonymous (secular in name but religious in teaching)?

Our bishops, moreover, are confronted in many large dioceses by strong political homosexual movements aiming to change the civil laws in order to place the homosexual lifestyle on the same level as marriage. (See chapter eight, "A Response to the Gay Rights Movement".) Within the Church many men and women with homosexual orientation demand the "right" to receive the sacraments while actively living in a homosexual lifestyle. They insist that the Church approve gay rights bills, adding that such laws will exempt Catholic schools from having to employ openly gay teachers. The same sorts of pressure are exerted upon pastors in areas of any large city to accommodate parishioners with homosexual orientation.[2]

I should like to paraphrase the thought of some of these pastors: The official Church teaches that homosexual activity is always immoral; however, learned theologians believe that some exceptions ought to be made to this position, considering the fact that in the circumstances of life some individuals are not able to remain chaste. That is what hundreds of our flock tell us as pastors. They feel they were born this way, and all they ask is to be allowed to have a steady lover. They have been living with their lover, who comes to church with them. Both are trying to lead good lives, being faithful to one another, and each of them deep down in his conscience has resolved the conflict he sees between the official teaching of the Church and his manner of living by consulting the writings of theologians. There they have learned that the official teaching is the

---

[2] In my pastoral experience this phenomenon of pressure is very common.

ideal, which, unfortunately, not everyone can attain; so, in practice, one settles for less than the ideal, striking a middle ground between the ideal and promiscuity, living with only one lover in a marriage-like relationship. After all, they say, the official Church teaches that contraception is always wrong, but the majority of married Catholics ignore this teaching. As the Church comes to understand sexuality better, she will revise her positions on both homosexual and contraceptive behavior. Both teachings are reformable, as we have been told by learned theologians.

This line of thought is not unusual. In Greenwich Village, New York, there are large numbers of Catholics, both young and old, who frequent the Metropolitan Community Church, which considers itself to be *the* church for homosexual people. There are also Catholic priests from religious orders and other dioceses who celebrate Mass in Protestant churches. Under these circumstances what can a pastor do? How can he advocate sexual abstinence?

In practice, the response which many beleaguered pastors give by their policy, if not in words, is to remain *silent* on the central moral issue of homosexual activity while concentrating on other aspects of Christian living. They may urge homosexual persons to full participation in parish life, not only in liturgical celebrations, but also in all social concerns, including the care of the sick and those with AIDS. But the main issue remains unresolved. It is like letting an individual remain in good faith concerning one part of his life, because you think that the individual will not accept what you say, and then he will be in bad faith. One can understand this predicament without agreeing with the silent irresolution.

It seems to me this is what many pastors do in areas where there are many persons with homosexual orientation. It is similar to the response of many clergy during the years after *Humanae Vitae*: just do not talk about contraception or homosexual behavior from the pulpit or in formal catechetics! Recently I saw a news clip in *Crux of the News* (Oct. 3, 1994, p. 3) that illustrates this strategy of selective reference. The National Association of Catholic Diocesan Lesbian and Gay Ministries proposes as its aim the fulfillment of the U.S. bishops' 1976 statement *To Live in Christ Jesus*, quoting the following statement: "Homosexuals have a right to respect, friendship, justice . . . [and an] active role in Christian community", while omitting the sentences immediately following: "Homosexual activity, however, as distinguished from homosexual orientation, is morally wrong. Like heterosexual persons, homosexuals are called to give witness to chastity, avoiding with God's grace behavior which is wrong for them, just as nonmarital sexual relations are wrong for heterosexuals."[3]

Another reason for stressing the rights of the homosexual person while soft-pedaling the question of acts is the unspoken fear that if priests and teachers were to give the full Catholic teaching concerning homosexuality from the pulpit or in formal catechesis, they would lose many persons struggling with homosexual desires. In an obvious comparison with homosexual behavior, a priest said that if priests were to preach the immorality of contraception, it would empty the churches. This fear has led some pastors in several dioceses where Courage has already existed to form an alternative to Courage. They argue that the "rigid" program of Courage does not appeal to the vast majority of persons with homosexual inclinations. In place of the specific program of Courage, designed to help the individual to live a life of virtue with emphasis upon interior chastity, these pastors substitute a welcoming Sunday liturgy followed by a social where various questions, including homosexuality, are discussed. In these gatherings the primary accent is not on a specific exposition of Catholic magisterial teaching on sexuality in general and

---

[3] *To Live in Christ Jesus*, no. 52, in *Pastoral Letters of U.S. Bishops* 4 (1984):182.

homosexuality and homosexual behavior in particular, but rather on the development of a sense of community, of belonging in the parish, a chance to be with others of the same sexual orientation. Discussions tend to be of an informal nature on a wide range of subjects, including homosexuality in its social, political, and religious aspects, and AIDS. Through these meetings it is hoped that homosexual persons will continue to come to church, gradually growing out of the active homosexual lifestyle.

But there are a number of difficulties with this approach. (1) It avoids the public proclamation of the Church's teaching on sexuality and marriage, while privately in pastoral counseling it tends to stress so-called pluralism in moral theology—meaning the opinions of learned and dissenting theologians on the "practical" impossibility of sexual abstinence among homosexual persons. (2) It does not give a specific program of ascetical practices to help an individual to practice chastity in his state of life (as Courage does in its Five Goals). (3) It does not promote the regular reception of the sacrament of reconciliation as a most efficacious means of overcoming the strong temptations many persons experience almost daily. (4) It does not deal with the fundamental moral and spiritual issue in the life of the homosexual person, namely, the need to reform one's way of thinking, feeling, and acting so as to move as far away as possible from the homosexual mind-set and to practice Christian virtues, particularly chastity, in imitation of Christ.

If the pastors in several dioceses who have presented such programs were to remedy these defects, they could form an alternative program to Courage. But there is no evidence that such remedies are being developed.

Such programs may attract larger numbers of people than some Courage units in a given diocese, but do they change the interior lives of these people? While Courage is still few in numbers, compared with Dignity, it continues to grow, increasing in numbers throughout the U.S., Canada, and now Great Britain. More important than numbers, one witnesses people changing their way of living, learning to be chaste.

To come back to the fear of losing our people, has not the Church in Western Europe and the United States already lost many persons by not giving the full truth about difficult issues, like contraception and divorce and remarriage? The Omaha Conference on *Humanae Vitae* in 1993 pointed to the tragedy of silence within the Church for the collective failure to proclaim the teaching of the Church on contraception. Surely, it is not a time to be silent on the moral issue of homosexual behavior.

To be sure, we need to place these questions within the full context of Catholic teaching in the *Catechism of the Catholic Church* and in *Evangelium Vitae (The Gospel of Life)*. Suppose, however, for the sake of the argument, many would leave the Church if they were fully informed on the issues of contraception and homosexual behavior. In this unlikely event, the Church would have to accept their departure, even as Christ did not try to stop those who left him because they could not accept his teaching on the Holy Eucharist (Jn 6). Christ has promised to take care of his Church (Mt 28) by being with us until the end of time. Our Holy Father says: "It is in the saving Cross of Jesus, in the gift of the Holy Spirit, in the sacraments that flow from the wounded side of the Redeemer (Jn 19:34) that believers find the grace and the strength always to keep God's holy law, even amid the greatest of hardships."[4]

Need for Spiritual Support

On the specific issue of homosexual behavior Courage attracts those who have a strong conviction that they need spiritual support to avoid the kind of behavior that separates them from God

---

[4] *Splendor Veritatis (The Splendor of Truth)* (Vatican Library translation, Vatican City, 1993), no. 103.

through serious sin. These are potential members of Courage looking for the truth and not finding it in their part of the country. I should like to quote, or in some cases paraphrase, several recent letters:

"I am a forty-eight-year-old confirmed bachelor who has never married. For many years I have struggled with strong homosexual feelings and desires, and it has not been easy. Nevertheless I have totally rejected homosexual behavior and have followed the teachings of the Catholic Church." He goes on to say that he will be glad to help me set up a Courage unit in a particular diocese, adding, "It is desperately needed by homosexually oriented people who desire to live chaste lives and to reject the so-called 'gay agenda'."

Another writes, "I am interested in how a homosexual person can 'come out' of homosexuality. It troubles me as a Catholic that no such kind of organization as yours that says homosexuals can change and were not 'born that way' exists in the archdiocese of _____. Please send me information." He asks for information on videos and books that explain the origins and treatment of homosexuality, adding that the bookstores he has visited are "blatantly prejudiced in favor of homosexuality and against homosexuals who want to come out and live as God made them—heterosexual. . . . Even most of the clergy of the Church in this area are either ignorant of or in favor of homosexuality."

Another writes, "I am and have been striving to live according to Church teachings regarding being gay, and I must say that I have met with not only ridicule but disbelief as well. And that from clerical as well as lay. In fact, I almost went over the edge when I was told that offering the sexual side of me to the Lord (in trying to remain celibate) was indicative of my dire need for professional help. That from a vowed religious."

Another, previously in Dignity, writes, "I have had no success in locating any Courage group in _____. I have been so desperate whereas I have had to go outside the Catholic Faith to get help. But I need to regain my Catholic heritage and to have a support group of Catholics who want to live a celibate life. Can you help me to locate a contact in _____?"

Another, to whom we sent information on Courage, writes, "I have read all the brochures and pamphlets, and I have been applying the Twelve Steps in maintaining celibacy and acceptance to my homosexual condition. I am very familiar with the Twelve Steps, as I have been a recovering alcoholic for a few years, and I follow the program of A.A. very closely."

All of the above letters come from one archdiocese that does have a gay and lesbian outreach program and whose ordinary, in saying Mass for the group, exhorts its members to be celibate. Why are the writers of these and other letters on file from this archdiocese so dissatisfied with what the archdiocese has provided for them, and why do they ask for Courage instead? I suspect that one of the reasons is the way the archdiocese (and other dioceses as well) describes its form of help to persons with homosexual orientation. The archdiocese uses the terms *gay* and *lesbian*, connoting that the most important quality possessed by those calling themselves "gay" or "lesbian" is their sexual orientation. It also implies that this condition is permanent, with little or no chance that an individual can come out of it. Finally, it implies that homosexual orientation is a natural variant of human sexuality.

This is not a mere matter of terms. When an individual says, "I am gay" or "I am lesbian", he is revealing how he understands himself: "I am this way, and I see life from this perspective of gayness. True, the Church says that I may not engage in genital acts, but I can live with the one I love without sexual intercourse. It will be very difficult. Some theologians say that gayness is a gift, another way of loving. In our diocese we have a gay and lesbian outreach, and I go to the meetings, and I have found many friends. They feel the same way I do. We go to a special

Mass together, and I notice other couples going to Holy Communion together. At last I have people who understand me, and the priests are so supportive."

Such a way of thinking and feeling is not in accord with the reality of sexual desire; usually it will break down. An individual attracted by another member of the same sex in an emotional and physical way will be severely tempted to go beyond kissing and hugging to some form of genital activity, usually involving mutual masturbation and oral sex. Unwittingly, one places himself in the occasion of an objectively grave sin. Thus, religious counselors and priests involved in gay and lesbian support groups should have second thoughts on their approach.

This is not the same as encouraging persons with homosexual tendencies to form chaste friendships, not just one but at least several, not just with other homosexual persons but also with heterosexual persons. As a matter of fact, the more such men and women seek friendships with "straight" men or "straight" women, the more they will free themselves from homosexual ways of thinking and feeling.

Of course, all this presupposes that one regards homosexual orientation as an "objective disorder".[5] In the literature advertising gay and lesbian groups this is not mentioned. One bishop, in a statement of support for a gay and lesbian group, said, "While affirming the inviolable dignity of a gay or lesbian person, and the goodness of their stable, loving, and caring relationships, I cannot endorse homosexual genital expression."

While this statement could be interpreted to mean that one should form many chaste friendships with other homosexual persons, that is not the way it will be understood by someone desirous of an intimate relationship. Probably, it will encourage intensive emotional attachments to one significant other, and it will very often place both persons in the occasion of serious sin.

[5] Congregation for the Doctrine of the Faith, "Letter to Bishops of the Catholic Church on the Pastoral Care of Homosexual Persons" (1986), no. 3.

In fact, this is the opinion of several distinguished Catholic psychiatrists and psychologists with whom I have consulted. It is also my pastoral experience. However well intentioned the above prelate may be, he needs to clarify his position or risk continuing to mislead the faithful.

It is noteworthy that the Society of Catholic Social Scientists sent a letter to the American bishops on November 28, 1994, in which they expressed their concern "with a trend in U.S. ministries which flatly contradicts Catholic doctrine on homosexuality".[6] They outline ambiguities and contradictions, using scientific research in order to show the erroneous assumptions upon which these statements and activities are founded. They list five fallacies:

1. False statements are being made about homosexuality being biologically determined.

2. Catholic homosexuals are being told that change in sexual orientation is never possible.

3. The term *gay* is being used to describe people of a homosexual orientation who do not identify with the gay sociopolitical position.

4. A separate "gay spirituality" is being encouraged, and gay ministries tell us that a person who suffers from the homosexual disorder has special "gay gifts" for the Church.

5. Catholics are being informed that the homosexual condition is not disordered.

---

[6] "Recent Trends in Ministry to Homosexual Catholics".

2

THE HISTORY OF COURAGE

In *The Homosexual Person* (pp. 119–74), I described the beginning of the Courage movement in 1980, tracing it up to 1986 and comparing the spiritual support system of Courage with Alcoholics Anonymous and Homosexuals Anonymous. The format of Courage meetings, the goals of Courage, together with the kinds of topics discussed, are noted with some detail. In this chapter I should like to describe the development of Courage from 1986 through 1995.

In the spring of 1987 Courage established a unit in Vancouver, British Columbia. This was the second group in Canada, Toronto having been the first in 1986. By this time the New York office of Courage was becoming a clearinghouse for information on the pastoral approach of Courage toward homosexuality. Besides requests for information from priests in different dioceses, we also began receiving many inquiries from anxious parents, not only in the New York area but also from all over the country. I say "anxious" parents, because most of them were concerned about their adult children who had already rejected the teaching of the Church on homosexual activity, and these parents sought help from Courage. Eventually this led to the formation of Encourage, a support group for parents and relatives of such adult children.

For these reasons we decided to print a newsletter, which has become an effective means of communication with the other units of Courage as well as with others interested in the Courage movement. On the last page of the *Newsletter* are found the addresses, phone numbers, and names of leaders of the various Courage units in the United States and Canada. Now published four times a year under the editorship of Father Don Timone, each issue contains at least two brief articles, one on Holy Scripture and one on contemporary issues. In the summer 1994 *Newsletter*, for example, I comment on same-sex unions and their advocacy by the late John Boswell (*Same-Sex Unions in Pre-Modern Europe*, Random House, 1994).

The Growth of Courage

In 1989 the New York office sponsored the first annual national conference of Courage at the Cardinal Spellman retreat house in Riverdale, Bronx, New York, with slightly over a hundred attending. The theme was the possibility of change of sexual orientation. Dr. Elizabeth Moberly, Maria Valdes, Ph.D., and Dr. Joseph Nicolosi presented papers on the origins of the homosexual orientation with the possibilities of changing a pattern of thinking and feeling that may have been there from the early years of childhood. The members of Courage and parents of homosexual people gave a very positive response to the three psychologists.

No longer would Courage be known as an organization concerned exclusively with sexual abstinence; now it would give serious consideration to encouraging individuals to move out of the condition itself, but it would not make working for such change an obligation. Courage was now more than "Harvey's halfway house" (as my Protestant friends had called it). This broadening of our vision, however, was not without adverse criticism from a few members leaving Courage.[1]

[1] In the subsequent national conferences since 1989 we have taken care each year to have at least one major presentation on the topic of change of

Gradually it became clear that there was no incompatibility between two kinds of members in Courage, namely, (1) those who want only to get out of the gay scene, while dedicating themselves to a life of celibacy—this group is mainly composed of older men who very often have suffered from compulsive drives in the past and who have seen the need for a support system—and (2) those who want to gain control over their sexual drives with the hope of learning how to move toward heterosexuality and, possibly, marriage. These are usually younger persons. Both kinds of members attend weekly meetings in New York City, with the group seeking change having at least two extra meetings per month with Father Don Timone, who began this spiritual direction over a year ago. Most of these younger members also receive psychotherapy, while Father Timone seeks to help the members integrate spiritual truth with psychological.

Another way in which Courage has grown is in the response given to women. During the last two years the Brooklyn and New York chapters have begun to attract women in sufficient numbers to form a separate women's group. Previously, the few women in the six groups have gone to one of the units, but naturally they have desired to have their own meetings as well; thus, in January 1994, Courage women from the metropolitan area of New York decided to meet in the Brooklyn diocese once or twice a month with a spiritual director while continuing to go to meetings with the men. I shall say more about the women in Courage in chapter ten.

One other facet of the growth of Courage needs explanation. We have acquired legal protection for the name Courage as the result of a legal challenge from Courage Center in St. Paul,

---

orientation. Other counselors and I work very closely with therapists who, unlike the leaders of the American Psychiatric Association or the American Psychological Association, believe that one can move out of homosexuality.

Minnesota, which is a charitable institution working with the handicapped. With the help of a competent patent lawyer who handled the whole issue very skillfully we reached a compromise agreement. Since the basic area of their fund soliciting is in Minnesota, Wisconsin, Iowa, and North and South Dakota, they agreed to allow us to use the name Courage in the other forty-five states. In those five states Courage is known as Faith in Action. We are now trademarked in the other forty-five states in the United States and in five dioceses in Canada.[2] The legal costs were covered by an anonymous donor.

Meanwhile the Courage movement has continued to grow slowly but surely. By the end of 1995 Courage had 26 units in the United States and Canada and one in London, England. Several other units are on the drawing board, with invitations from certain dioceses during 1996. I have said Courage has grown *slowly*. Some bishops and priests either remain unconvinced of the need for a spiritual support system for Catholics with homosexual tendencies, such as Courage, or they desire a group that will be more acceptable to homosexual leaders in the large cities.

As mentioned in chapter one, Courage is described as "rigid" by its critics, and so they deem it necessary to describe the Catholic outreach to homosexual persons in language more acceptable to them. In the title of such a Catholic organization the terms *gay* and *lesbian* are used instead of the term *homosexual*. Great stress is placed on the dignity and rights of the homosexual person, but little is said about the immorality of homosexual activity or the need for a program concerned with

---

[2] The official document reads "United States Patent and Trademark Office Reg. No. 1,793,097. Service Mark Principal Register Courage".

After stating the location of the Courage office in New York City, the description reads: "For Association Services, namely, promoting the interests of Catholic laymen and women who aspire to live chaste lives in accordance with the Roman Catholic Church's Teachings on Homosexuality, by establishing and directing support groups in class 42 (U.S. CL 100)".

the practice of chastity. This avoidance of the issue of the morality of homosexual activity fits in perfectly with media propaganda in favor of the alleged rights of homosexual persons while raising the question whether Church leaders in America make the issue of such activity an important moral teaching.

With happy exceptions, I do not believe that the Church in America has provided a positive spiritual program for persons with homosexual orientation. Since I have dwelt upon this point in chapter one, suffice it to say that we clergy need both to encourage and direct persons with homosexual inclinations to a chaste life in following Christ. Clerical indifference and murky messages will not inspire Catholics with these difficulties to move away from the occasions of sin where they may be now. We need to do more to help such persons and their families.

There are bishops who are seeking clergy to help them start a Courage unit in their diocese. More than one bishop has told me, "I can't get a priest to give spiritual direction to a Courage group." As I write, I keep in touch with a lay leader in a diocese where men have asked for a Courage unit. He has only recently found a priest. Members of Courage themselves wonder why many pastors simply refuse to put a notice in their parish bulletins with a hot-line number for Courage. Many individuals whom I have counseled in New York City and elsewhere complain that in their parishes there is no provision for individual pastoral counseling or referral sources for spiritual support systems that would help the individual to lead a chaste life.

In contrast, professional homosexual organizations abound with their seductive teaching. One naturally asks why this real spiritual need of Catholics in this struggle is so far down on the list of social activities in many of our large dioceses. Meanwhile, many Catholic youth become entrapped in the homosexual lifestyle, and some of them will die of AIDS. Rightfully we are compassionate to the persons with AIDS, but why do we not support Courage and other support systems advocating sexual abstinence as the most effective way to avoid becoming HIV positive?

Parents and Relatives of Persons with Homosexual Orientation

In 1986 Courage had not yet organized any group of parents who had sons and daughters who claimed to be "gay", although I was already involved in counseling couples who were deeply concerned with the attitudes and behavior of their son or daughter. I referred such parents to Homosexuals Anonymous, a Christian nondenominational group that works with persons desirous of changing their orientation, and also with their parents, relatives, and friends. Since 1987 Courage has formed similar support groups in Massachusetts, Toronto, Philadelphia, and New York. At first such groups were called Courage Anonymous, but in Philadelphia the group came to be known as Encourage, and the other groups adopted the name. Encourage is located in the Family Life Office of the Archdiocese of Philadelphia and in Staten Island, New York.

This is a very important point, because it can lead to a better recognition of the fact that homosexual development takes place within the family and that members of the family can help an individual who chooses to change his orientation, or at least to control his behavior. Our knowledge of parents of children who claim to be homosexual comes mainly from the work of Protestant writers, like Barbara Johnson and Alan Medinger of Regeneration, in Baltimore, Maryland.

In her first book, *Where Does a Mother Go to Resign?*, Barbara Johnson expresses the agony and complexity of parents when they become aware that their son or daughter claims to be gay. Shock, anger, confusion, embarrassment, and a sense of hopelessness fill their minds and hearts. The parent asks: What did I do wrong? Where can he go to get over this? Why did this happen to me? He was such a model child. What the parents need at this point is to work through their emotions under the guidance of psychologists and spiritual counselors who agree with parents that homosexual activity is immoral. This talking out of one's feelings, leading to new understanding, requires some sort of spiritual support group for parents, spouses, and families of persons with these difficulties. That is why Encourage can be so helpful.[3]

Barbara Johnson advises other parents in the same situation she has experienced to love the son or daughter unconditionally:

> This unconditional love is what you must communicate to him. You love him, but you must hate his sin, because it hurts him. . . . Keep your love flowing to your child in every possible way you can demonstrate it. This will prevent stagnation and bitterness from settling in your heart. It will assure him of this unconditional love you are showing him which will remind him of God's love for him.[4]

From my counseling of such parents over the last ten years I should like to add a few pointers. (1) One must avoid labeling the child or teenager but instead get a professional diagnosis from a clinical psychologist, because so often teenagers claim to be "gay" when they are not really so. (2) Do not be dismayed when a child is reluctant to share with you his feelings. Children are afraid of rejection. (3) If your child tells you he is gay, avoid harsh and hurting words, even though you become the object of his anger and bitterness. (4) Turn to the Lord in your powerlessness, giving your child over (no matter what his age) to the care of the Lord. (5) Try to understand the emotional factors found in the genesis of homosexuality by reading Elizabeth Moberly's *Homosexuality, A New Christian Ethic*. (6) If your child is an adult,

---

[3] Addresses of some Encourage units: Pennsylvania: Family Life Office, c/o St. Charles Borromeo Seminary, Wynnwood, PA 19096; Canada: 412 Queen St., Toronto, Ont. EM5–1T3; Massachusetts: 415 Lowell St., Methuen, MA 01844.

[4] *Where Does a Mother Go to Resign?* (Minneapolis: Bethany House, 1979), pp. 134–35.

you may receive from him advocacy literature in favor of the homosexual lifestyle and against the "narrow-minded" Roman Catholic Church. Do not be disturbed by such literature. If possible, consult with a priest who believes in the teaching of the Church and do not argue with your child. Oftentimes siblings will side with your child. This is very hurtful for father and mother, but simply ask the Lord to give you strength. (7) Get in touch with the Encourage group nearest you. You will profit spiritually and emotionally from this encounter. (8) In order to gain a deeper understanding of celibacy read *The Courage to Be Chaste* by Benedict Groeschel, C.F.R. Celibacy is a deep love for Christ expressed in love for one's fellowmen.

The Interior Life

Although Courage groups read the Five Goals at the beginning of every ordinary meeting, they have refined the means used to fulfill the Five Goals. This is evident from a careful perusal of the revised *Handbook* of Courage, 1995. Previous to this revision there was much controversy in several chapters concerning the relative importance of the Twelve Steps within the program of Courage. There were some who saw no difference between Courage and Sexaholics Anonymous or Sex and Love Addicts Anonymous. Courage was regarded as a Twelve Step program, in which at *every* meeting a member presented his perception of the way in which a particular Step applied to him, and others sought to express their identification with the Step and with the presenter. Prayer at the beginning and end, and the spiritual direction of the leader, usually a priest, were regarded as appendages to the core elements of the meeting.

While acknowledging their importance, others believe that the Twelve Steps should be placed within a distinctly Catholic context in which prayer and spiritual direction are stressed in the effort to integrate the spiritual and the psychological. There should also be flexibility in the content of the meetings, that is to say, not every discussion period should be given over to one of the Twelve Steps. This view was incorporated into the revised *Handbook*:

> Alternative formats to the Twelve Steps include the following: (a) Guest speaker: occasionally a speaker will be invited to address the group on a topic related to the goals of Courage. (b) A testimonial from one of the members, perhaps on a particular crisis that person is undergoing. (c) Celebration of Holy Mass.[5]

Groups should guard against the tendency to do away with the Twelve Steps altogether, substituting free-flowing discussion of issues related to homosexuality, because such open meetings usually deteriorate into a "discussion" club where one does not have to talk about his inner feelings. This is a form of denial. On the contrary, leaders of Courage groups should ordinarily insist that each participant speak about himself in terms of his response to the Step or topic presented.

In this way the Twelve Steps provide a framework within which each member can concentrate on his own personal development. Of course, this means that someone should prepare a Step, or a related topic, like unresolved anger in one's life, and that the other participants should bring to the meeting their own reflections on the material presented. The *Handbook* goes on to discuss the kinds of problems that occur in any discussion in group support meetings.[6]

Another way in which Courage has matured is in its relationship to other spiritual support groups, such as Sexaholics Anonymous (S.A.) and Sex and Love Addicts Anonymous (S.L.A.A.). As Courage leaders work with its members, it becomes clear that

[5] *Courage. A Handbook* (rev. ed. 1991), pp. 15–16. It should be noted that Courage obtained permission from Alcoholics Anonymous World Service, Inc., to reprint and adapt the Twelve Steps. Actually only number 1 is changed to read: "We admitted that we were powerless over homosexuality, and our lives had become unmanageable" (p. 13, no. 1).

[6] Ibid., pp. 16–18.

those who have been sexually compulsive need more help than weekly meetings can provide. We recommend S.A. in its original form, not the so-called reform group (S.R.A.), because S.A.'s understanding of the meaning of human sexuality is in agreement with ours, and because de facto those who go to both Courage and S.A. meetings testify to the help they receive at S.A. meetings. In other chapters I have heard of individuals who have derived similar benefits from S.L.A.A. What Courage, S.A., and S.L.A.A. stress is the important and irreplaceable value of sharing problems in the group, and deriving support therefrom, as well as giving it. In this regard we all give thanks for the original support group, A.A. In tandem with this relationship with S.A. and S.L.A.A. is Courage's communication with reliable therapists, not necessarily Catholic, though many are, who have helped individual members with deep-seated problems, and who—with the explicit permission of the Courage member—have helped the spiritual director to understand the individual on a deeper level.

Other ways in which Courage has grown interiorly, and which also emphasize its distinctly Catholic character, are the availability of the sacrament of penance before or after meetings, particularly before Mass on the week when Mass is celebrated; two days of recollection, one during Advent and the other in the month of May, which are open to Encourage members as well; and warm devotion to the Blessed Virgin Mother, with every meeting ending with the Memorare.

Perhaps the most significant development of Courage since 1986 has been the success of the seven national conferences (1989-95). The evaluation papers after each conference, together with voluminous correspondence, testify to the spirit of the members throughout the United States and Canada. People look forward to coming, saving their vacation money and time for the annual three-day meeting. These conferences are the joyful "cry of the faithful".

While the annual conferences have been the most effective publicity instruments of Courage, they do consume a significant amount of our financial resources. So far we have been able to continue them due to the generosity of the friends of Courage, several grants, and some very generous bishops.

Obstacles to Growth

Just as advertising in Catholic newspapers and periodicals has been an effective factor in the growth of Courage units, so also its lack contributes to the decline of a local unit. Unfortunately, this has happened in some dioceses where Courage is in such a dormant condition that it is practically nonexistent. Sometimes this may be due to the diocese trying to avoid conflict with homophile organizations similar to Dignity.

Another obstacle to growth is the lack of personnel to conduct the Courage meetings. In some places only one priest has been appointed to Courage, and often he is already overcommitted in his parish or school. He misses meetings, and then the members miss meetings. Surely, it would be better if a diocese were to seek several priests to act as a team to cover the weekly meetings, as is the practice in Brooklyn and Philadelphia.

Still another obstacle is the failure of leaders of chapters to follow the *Handbook* in the conduct of meetings. The leader engages in an extended monologue while not using the Steps, or he gives mixed signals to the members by handouts favoring a theology not in agreement with Church teaching. Fortunately, this is rare.

Conclusion

Courage has established units in twenty-six dioceses of the United States and Canada, but this is only the beginning of the movement. Through advertising and the good example of its members it will grow. Its Five Goals, formulated by the members themselves and listed below, are based upon the rock of Catholic truth about homosexual behavior, that it is always immoral, and that it is necessary to make use of the means that God gives to the person struggling with such tendencies. In our judgment, one of the most effective means is participation in our spiritual support system. We encourage individuals who struggle to remain faithful to the Goals of Courage so that Christ himself will help them lead a life of prayer. As a young lady said to me when I told her how hesitant I was to give a retreat to some men with homosexual orientation, "Father, you have nowhere to go, but *up*." She added, "Father, if you lead one person back to Christ, it will all be worthwhile." That was seventeen years ago. Courage is still going up.

Here are the Goals of Courage, written by the first members in 1982:

1. To live chaste lives in accordance with the Roman Catholic Church's teachings on homosexuality.

2. To dedicate our entire lives to Christ through service to others, spiritual reading, prayer, meditation, individual spiritual direction, frequent attendance at Mass, and the frequent reception of the sacraments of penance and of the Holy Eucharist.

3. To foster a spirit of fellowship in which we may share with one another our thoughts and experiences and so ensure that none of us will have to face the problems of homosexuality alone.

4. To be mindful of the truth that chaste friendships are not only possible but necessary in a celibate Christian life and to encourage one another in forming and sustaining them.

5. To live lives that may serve as good examples to other homosexuals.

3

KEY ASPECTS OF HOMOSEXUALITY

Jeffrey Keefe, O.F.M. Conv.

Oscar Wilde's sexual partner, Lord Alfred Douglas, poignantly labeled homosexuality as the love that dare not speak its name. Today few feel any need for a veiled reference. Homosexuality is spoken of openly, often at high volume. Books, scientific journals, journals of opinion, the popular media, the academic podium, and the pulpit energetically tackle the topic. In its latest three-year period of coverage, Medline, the computer catalogue of medical and psychological sources, lists over 2,100 entries concerned in some manner with homosexuality.

Much of the treatment of homosexuality, especially in popular media, is marred by error, by lack of precision and nuance. These shortcomings are difficult to avoid because sexual orientation is a complex condition that does not lend itself to general statements.

This chapter will focus on certain issues that frequently are carelessly skimmed over or treated in a simplistic manner, both by those compassionate toward the personal plight of homosexual persons and by those who react with fear and the kind of prejudice that stems from ignorance. As for prejudice, it should be noted that some prejudice stems from lack of information or from misinformation. Another sort of bias is more deeply rooted in personal needs and motives and is less likely to be altered by dispassionate discussion.

This chapter has five specific aims. The first aim is to present a schema of sexuality for fuller appreciation of the complexity of human sexual development. Secondly, the chapter will consider some of the relevant research from laboratory animal experiments and human biological studies that provides some basis for biological theories of human sexual development. Extended attention will be given to five recent studies afforded major coverage in the popular media. This publicity illustrates the pitfalls of print-media condensations and the even briefer TV news summaries of scientific journal articles. Thirdly, the chapter will treat some common life history patterns, garnered from therapeutic experience and clinical studies, that are the basis of psychodynamic theories of the development of psychosexual orientation. This section will be relatively brief because these findings are treated at length in other chapters (e.g., chapter four). A fourth aim is to show that the term *homosexuality* is itself an oversimplification. Finally, a fifth purpose is to comment on the question of homosexuality as a disorder.

Basic Factors of Human Sexuality

Human sexuality has both physical and psychological characteristics. Through empirical research and accumulated clinical experience several factors, physiological and psychological, innate and acquired, have been identified from the aggregate of interacting forces that constitute an individual's developing sexuality.

Physical Sexuality

Physical sexual history begins at conception and continues in a definite sequential pattern until birth. There are three principal stages in uterine sexual development, namely, genetic sex, gonadal sex, and sexual differentiation in the brain.

Genetic sex is determined at conception by the pair of sex chromosomes. The ovum or egg of the mother always provides an X chromosome. Depending on the single sex chromosome in the fertilizing sperm of the father, X or Y, the offspring will be genetically female (XX) or male (XY). Thus an individual is female or male in every body cell. However, genetic sex alone does not guarantee proper physical sexual development.

In humans the next phase of sexual development begins about the seventh week of fetal life. As yet, the rudimentary sexual tissues remain undifferentiated. These tissues will develop into female organs unless there is some physiological intervention. This outcome is called the Eve Principle, expressed in the biological axiom "nature prefers females". In genetic males the Y chromosome provides this intervention by producing a protein that covers or coats the tissues otherwise destined to become female sexual organs and initiates the formation of male sexual anatomy.

A third phase occurs in the second trimester of human fetal life, following sex organ development. In the male the now-formed testes produce the male hormone testosterone, which masculinizes clusters of cells in the hypothalamus, thalamus, and limbic systems of the "old brain", the brain structures humans share with lower vertebrates. Estrogen and progesterone, hormones produced chiefly by the ovaries, feminize counterpart sites in the female brain. This neurohormonal programming of brain cell clusters influences many later functions and behaviors, among them the reproductive cycle and nurturing tendencies in the female and aggressiveness as well as preference for rough-and-tumble play in the male.[1]

---

[1] Hormones actually have a fourfold psychosexual influence: masculinizing and feminizing plus demasculinizing and defeminizing processes. To avoid the confusing complexities of these combinations, discussion in this chapter will be limited to the masculinizing and feminizing influences of hormones.

In summary, there are three aspects of physical sexuality that develop before birth: genetic or cytological sex, gonadal or anatomical sex, and sexual differentiation in the brain. Of course, physical sexual development continues after birth, especially during early adolescence, when hormone function brings increased sexual drive and fosters secondary sex characteristics such as breast formation in females and beard growth and voice change in males.

Mental Sexuality

Psychosexuality, that is, sexualized consciousness, is a postnatal development. Psychosexuality is sexuality as it manifests itself in the mind. It is a pervasive and fundamental personality feature that includes three interwoven components. The first component is one's basic conviction of being male or female. The second component consists of behaviors and attitudes that are culturally associated with masculinity and femininity. The third component is an individual's erotic preference for male or female partners, or both.[2] These components, variously labeled in the literature, are core gender identity, gender role identity, and psychosexual orientation.

Core gender identity is the recognition "I am male" or "I am female." It begins to crystallize in the second year of life as the infant undergoes "psychological birth", which includes moving away from his symbiotic relationship with the mother and acquiring a dawning sense of being an individual.

Gender role identity is the subtly different recognition "I am masculine" or "I am feminine." The individual gradually attains the felt conviction that he or she matches or falls short of the gender role expectations of a particular environment. Gender role identity may vary on a fairly wide spectrum without in-

[2] R. Green, *Sexual Identity Conflict* (New York: Basic Books, 1974), p. xv.

fringing on core gender identity or orientation. Conversely, it may occasion a sense of inadequacy antagonistic to the other two constituents of psychosexuality.

The third eventual psychosexual component is orientation, preferential erotic attraction to members of the opposite sex, same sex, or both sexes in varied degree. This is the defining element of heterosexuality, homosexuality, or bisexuality.

Sexuality, therefore, cannot be viewed as a simple or single dimension. Freud noted that the physical and mental characteristics of sexuality, including orientation, may vary independently of one another "*up to a certain point* [italics added] . . . and are met with in different individuals in manifold permutations".[3] However, these characteristics also have a reciprocal or mutual influence on one another.

Biological Influences in Physical and Psychological Sexual Development

Complications may occur in any of the interacting physical and mental elements of sexual development. Scientific literature contains numerous reports of animal experimentation, usually with rodents, in which the normal hormone sequence in uterine development was manipulated by various techniques. Among these methods is castration of fetal males; another is injection of male sex hormones in pregnant females at the critical period prior to anatomical differentiation of fetal sex tissues, or just prior to the subsequent phase of masculinization or feminization of the fetal brain.

Experimental interference with normal hormone function prior to anatomical differentiation results in variously intersexed offspring, that is, animals genetically one sex but with the external genitals of the other sex. Such offspring illustrate the possi-

[3] S. Freud, *Collected Papers*, vol. 2., trans. Joan Riviere (New York: Basic Books, 1962), p. 230.

bility of an organism with one genetic sex but another gonadal sex. At times the newborn animals are hermaphroditic: that is, they have the sex organs that appear to match both sexes.

When sex hormone manipulation follows anatomical differentiation of male or female genital organs, the offspring may demonstrate the temperament and behavior typical of the opposite sex. Male rats treated with female hormones show nurturing behaviors toward newborn rats. The prenatal reduction of androgen levels in rodents produces "homosexual" mating behaviors. For example, prenatal or near-birth castration and the resulting androgen deficiency in genetic male rats result in these males later assuming the female receptive posture known as lordosis. Androgen excess in prenatal genetic female rodents conditions them toward adult mounting behavior typical of males. In these instances gender behavior does not coincide with basic gender. Many other experiments of sex hormone control produced atypical sexual development. These and similar findings became the basis for the prenatal hormonal hypothesis of human sexual orientation.

One problem with this hypothesis is that it equates sexual orientation with behaviors, whereas in humans sexual orientation is defined primarily by erotic arousal, which follows fantasy about a preferred sexual partner. Behavior in humans may or may not match orientation, a point we will develop later. Animal studies report only *observed* behavior, which is at best analogous to the behavior of humans. Sexual orientation in humans is a mental condition, which motivates behavioral choices; in animals sexual behavior is reflexive and stereotyped. To assume the same "mentality" in animals is an unwarranted inference.

These observations are not made to dismiss the evidence for prenatal hormone function in organizing masculine and feminine pathways in the human brain, but neither can we unconditionally transfer a rodent model of programmed sexuality to the far more complex and varied sexual life of humans. To do so ignores the evolutionary chasm between the animal and the human brain. "It is difficult to imagine that the gamut and plasticity of human sexual behavior can be reduced to factors as simple as this [prenatal hormone programming]."[4]

Another observation is appropriate here. Behavioral results from experimental hormone control in higher animals such as sheep and monkeys are less clear-cut than is the case with rats and guinea pigs. This fact probably is explained by the more advanced brains of these animals. Humans, of course, have the most highly developed neocortex of all species. Arno Karlen remarks that "humans almost seem to be an experiment by nature to see whether sexuality can be left minimally to programming and mostly to learning."[5] John Bancroft, M.D., researcher and author of several works on human sexuality, reviewed the evidence for hormonal programming, brain structure, and genetics in regard to sexual orientation and concluded "that the uniquely human phenomenon of sexual orientation is a consequence of a multifactorial developmental process in which biological factors play a part but in which psychosocial factors remain crucially important".[6]

For obvious reasons experimental manipulation of sex hormones cannot be carried out with humans. However, Mother Nature has provided some "experiments" of her own. These include chromosomal anomalies, XXY and XYY among others, and syndromes of endocrine functioning gone awry during prenatal development.

Over the years John Money has followed a substantial number of "human experiments", that is, persons who were born with ambiguous genitalia or who suffered some prenatal endo-

[4] W. Byne and B. Parsons, "Human Sexual Orientation: The Biologic Theories Reappraised", *Archives of General Psychiatry* 50 (1993):231.

[5] A. Karlen, *Sexuality and Homosexuality* (New York: Norton, 1971), p. 389.

[6] J. Bancroft, "Homosexual Orientation: The Search for a Biological Basis", *British Journal of Psychiatry* 164 (1994):439.

crine disorder that affected their physical sexuality in some other way. At one point he summarized the scientific research and clinical experience in the field of gender disorder with this comment: "Whatever may be the possible unlearned assistance from constitutional sources, the child's psychosexual identity is not written, unlearned, in the genetic code, the hormonal system or the nervous system at birth."[7] In a more recent review of biological influences on human sexual orientation, John Money sees prenatal hormone history as strongly implicated in the beginning and final outcome of sexual orientation. Yet he also notes a major difference in sexual development between rodents and higher animals: "In primates . . . the influence of prenatal and neonatal hormonalization is more susceptible to subsequent superimposed variations in social communication and learning." He continues to maintain that "there is no human evidence that prenatal hormonalization alone, independently of postnatal history, inexorably preordains either [homosexual or bisexual] orientation. Rather, neonatal antecedents may facilitate a homosexual or bisexual orientation, provided the postnatal determinants in the social and communicational history are also facilitative."[8]

Five Publicized Studies

Due to mounting pressure from several quarters for legal codification of civil rights of homosexual persons and for recognition of gay relationships as equal to heterosexual civil marriage, the general media have given increased attention to scientific studies concerning homosexuality. Some liberal factions favor the hypothesis that homosexuality is inborn, both to offset discrimina-

---

[7] J. Money, "Sexual Dimorphism and Homosexual Gender Identity", in *Perspectives in Human Sexuality*, ed. N. W. Wagner (New York: Behavioral Publications, 1974), p. 68.

[8] J. Money, "Sin, Sickness, or Status?" *American Psychologist* 42 (1987):397f.

tion and to promote social acceptance of homosexual lifestyles. Since 1990 five studies have been highly publicized. Newspapers and radio and TV news and talk shows often have presented these studies as unprecedented breakthroughs, and in various sensationalized ways, to suit the polemics of the moment.

Simon LeVay

In 1991 neurobiologist Simon LeVay published a report on the differences he found in comparing a particular brain structure in heterosexual and homosexual persons.[9] He studied one of the nuclei in the hypothalamus. The hypothalamus is located just behind the attachment of the two cerebral hemispheres. It is considered to regulate sleep, coordinate body temperature mechanisms as well as manifestations of anger and rage, and mediate sexual arousal.

LeVay undertook his study of the hypothalamic nuclei in humans as a possible site of influence on sexual orientation because previous studies of cell structures in rats and monkeys had implicated this area as promoting typically male behaviors. He noted also that previous research on brain tissues of humans of unknown sexual orientation showed that the second and third interstitial nuclei of the anterior hypothalamus (INAH) are larger in men than in women. LeVay hypothesized that these two areas could be involved in sexual orientation. For this reason one might anticipate a smaller nucleus in homosexual men as well as in women generally, since both groups are erotically attracted to males.

LeVay compared the postmortem brain tissue from forty-one subjects divided into three groups: six women, sixteen men presumed to be heterosexual, and nineteen known homosexual males. LeVay's study did not find any difference in size in the

[9] S. LeVay, "A Difference in Hypothalamic Structure between Heterosexual and Homosexual Men", *Science* 253 (1991):1034–37.

first, second, or fourth INAH. Thus he failed to duplicate or replicate the earlier finding concerning the second nucleus, which had been designated sexually dimorphic, that is, different in form or structure in male and female.

However, LeVay did find differences in size in the third INAH. This nucleus was twice as large in heterosexual men as in homosexual men, and twice as large in heterosexual men as in women, with no difference in the size of the nucleus between homosexual men and the presumably heterosexual women.

LeVay's conclusions from these anatomical differences actually were quite modest: "The discovery that a nucleus differs in size between heterosexual and homosexual men illustrates that sexual orientation in humans is amenable to study at a biological level. . . . Further interpretation of the results of this study must be considered speculative."

If indeed there is an essential relationship between INAH3, a tiny area of the hypothalamus, and sexual orientation, one must ask, as did LeVay, whether this difference in size of the nuclei is a cause or a consequence of sexual orientation. Or is it due to an as yet unidentified other variable?

It may be that differences in development of the brain contribute to sexual orientation. It is indeed likely that sexual preference and behaviors connected with orientation have some neural pathways later in life, because experience is encoded in the brain. It is, moreover, a biological axiom that functional change causes structural change. In short, provided that this difference in size of INAH3 holds up in future studies, we still have the old chicken–egg problem: Which comes first, the difference in size of a hypothalamic nucleus, or the differing orientations?

LeVay calls attention to the "apparently comparable" hypothalamic nucleus in rats, the size of which co-varies with typical male sexual behavior and which maintains its relative size from the perinatal period of development. He suggests that it is likely that the third nucleus in question is established early in life. Yet he is sufficiently cautious to note that the validity of comparison between species is uncertain. Once again, it is important to note that it is always a risky presumption to transfer findings from animal brain function to humans, particularly regarding higher thought processes.

Other academic critics, taking a closer look at LeVay's data, note that they show a broad overlap in the size of the nuclei in straight and gay men. Even granting that most at one extreme were gay and most at the other extreme were straight, one could not tell from the size of a random nucleus in the middle range whether it belonged to a homosexual or heterosexual man.

Laura Allen and Robert Gorski

Another study that gained the headlines was carried out by researchers Laura Allen and Robert Gorski.[10] They investigated the anterior commissure, a nerve fiber tract joining the temporal lobes of the brain and believed to allow the two hemispheres to integrate sensory data. Even though men have larger brains than women, this structure is typically larger in women. However, the anterior commissure was not known to be related to sexual behaviors.

Using almost two hundred autopsied brains, Allen and Gorski found that the anterior commissure is larger in homosexual men than in presumably heterosexual women, who in turn had larger anterior commissures than the presumably heterosexual men. The authors proposed that these differences in size may underlie differences in cognitive function and, in some global fashion, be associated with sexual orientation.

[10] Laura Allen and R. Gorski, "Sexual Orientation and the Size of the Anterior Commissure", *Proceedings of the National Academy of Science, USA* 89 (1992):7199–202.

Some scientists and gay advocacy groups saw this finding as another proof that homosexuality is inborn. Other commentators, however, raise the question whether the AIDS virus, which has an affinity for brain tissue, might be implicated in the finding. Still other researchers advised that assignment of causality to slight anatomical discrepancies is too facile for anything as complex as sexuality and sexual orientation. Finally, as in the LeVay study, there was wide variation in size within groups. The anterior commissure from some female brains was three times as large as others of the same grouping. It was the averages of the groups that showed differences according to sex and sexual orientation.

With any scientific finding there is always the need for replication, that is, confirmation by means of a comparable study to determine whether a finding of differences between groups, for example, is a genuine discovery or a chance event. Most scientific research studies require at least a .05 level of probability, which means that there is one chance in twenty that the result is a statistical fluke.

It is not unusual for a researcher to present an apparently new discovery that afterward is not confirmed by other studies or is discredited by them. The original study often gets considerable media attention, but any subsequent inability to repeat the results gets little or none. This inattention to follow-up studies that go counter to the original study is certainly the case for some studies related to sexual orientation. In 1984 Gladue and his associates reported a hormone response pattern in homosexual men that was intermediate between that of heterosexual men and that of women. The researchers concluded that the pattern was one of the "biological markers" for sexual orientation.[11] Subsequent

---

[11] B. Gladue, R. Green, and R. Hellman, "Neuroendocrine Response to Estrogen and Sexual Orientation", *Science* 225 (1984):1496–99.

independent research failed to detect this "biological marker" or duplicate this finding.[12]

Columbia University psychiatrist William Byne cites other instances of replicated research that failed to confirm original findings related to sex differences.[13] One of these studies in fact had found sex differences in the *first* INAH. So now the literature contains studies indicating sex differences in three of the four hypothalamic nuclei, but only one of these findings has been corroborated in a subsequent study. Another study reported a "striking" morphological sex difference in the brain purportedly related to visio-spatial functions.[14] Twenty attempts at confirmation failed. Typically, such follow-up studies rarely rate much (if any) media attention, while the initial report remains "entrenched in the scientific literature where it is unlikely to be dislodged for years".[15]

Perhaps the most entrenched mistake about orientation is the claim that 10 percent of the population is homosexual. The frequently cited 10 percent comes from the 1948 Kinsey study. Ten percent of Kinsey's subjects reported that they were exclusively homosexual for at least three years between ages sixteen and fifty-five.[16] But who were his subjects? Twenty-five percent of the volunteers for Kinsey's study consisted of male prison inmates, ex-convicts, and sex offenders, so that overall it was hardly a representative sample of the American male population. In 1978 Paul Cameron conducted a survey with better sampling procedures and concluded that 4 percent is closer to

[12] S. Hendricks, B. Graber, and J. Rodriguez-Sierra, "Neuroendocrine Responses to Exogenous Estrogen: No Differences between Heterosexual and Homosexual Men", *Psychoneuroendocrinology* 14 (1989):177–85.

[13] Byne and Parsons, "Human Sexual Orientation".

[14] Christine Di Lacoste-Utamsing and R. Halloway, "Sexual Dimorphism in the Human Corpus Callosum", *Science* 216 (1982):1431–32.

[15] W. Byne, letter to the editor, *New York Times* (Sept. 19, 1991).

[16] A. Kinsey, W. Pomeroy, and C. Martin, *Sexual Behavior in the Human Male* (Philadelphia: W. B. Saunders, 1948).

the mark for long-term homosexual preference, even including bisexuals.[17]

Cameron's study received no attention from the general media; 10 percent remained a scientific canon for another fifteen years. A more recent study of male sexual behaviors from the Alan Guttmacher Institute concludes that 1 percent of American males, ages twenty through thirty-nine, are exclusively homosexual in orientation, while 2 percent have engaged in some homosexual behavior in the past ten years.[18] Critics of this study point to the reluctance of homosexual men to admit their orientation, despite the interviewers' promise of anonymity, and that such studies underreport the actual percentage. In any case, various studies over the past seven years in the United States and some European countries set the percentage range of male homosexual and bisexual orientation between 2.5 and 4 percent, and of lesbian persons at least a percentage point lower.

J. M. Bailey and R. Pillard

Another much reported study that focused on male homosexuality is the twin study undertaken by J. M. Bailey and R. Pillard.[19] They recruited a pool of fifty-six homosexual males who also were identical twins, plus fifty-four homosexual men who had fraternal twin brothers, and an additional fifty-seven homosexual males who had adoptive brothers. The sexual orientation of the 171 co-twins and adoptive brothers was ascertained by contacting them directly or by relying on the information obtained from the homosexual person who was recruited initially.

[17] P. Cameron, "A Case against Homosexuality", *Human Life Review* 4 (1978):19.

[18] J. Billy, T. Koray, W. Grady, and D. Klepinger, "The Sexual Behavior of Men in the United States", *Family Planning Perspectives* 25 (1993):52–60.

[19] J. M. Bailey and R. Pillard, "A Genetic Study of Male Sexual Orientation", *Archives of General Psychiatry* 48 (1991):1089–96.

Bailey and Pillard found that 52 percent of the identical co-twins were also homosexual, 22 percent of the fraternal co-twins, and 11 percent of the adoptive brothers. Since identical twins share the same gene pool, and fraternal twins share only the similar genetic makeup of any two brothers, it first would appear that the higher concordance among identical twins and the sizable rate of homosexual fraternal co-twins compared with genetically unrelated adoptive brothers do support the conclusion that there is a genetic contribution to male homosexuality.

Once again the researchers themselves are more conservative than media reports of inborn homosexuality. They propose that groups of genes may predispose an individual to homosexuality. They also caution that the several genetic influences act in concert with biological, psychological, and social environment.

Findings of higher rates of homosexual orientation among identical twins do not rule out prenatal and environmental influences in the development of such orientation. If homosexuality were simply hereditary, one would expect both identical twin brothers to be homosexual whenever one is, the reason being that identical twins possess the same genetic program. The nearly half of identical twins who do not share the co-twin's homosexual orientation suggests that environmental factors are at work in psychosexual development.

An ancillary finding of the study concerned the non-twin brothers of the homosexual twin subjects. Of the non-twin brothers 9.2 percent were rated as homosexual. The adoptive brothers' rate of homosexuality was 11 percent. Since biological siblings and fraternal twins share the same proportion of genetic material, the expected homosexual rate for non-twin brothers, presuming genetic influence, would be closer to the 22 percent rate of fraternal twin brothers. As they stand, these figures support a stronger influence of environmental factors over genetic factors in promoting homosexual orientation.

Further, the higher incidence of homosexuality in pairs of

identical and fraternal twins could support an argument for nurture as well as nature. The reason is that twins usually are raised in tandem in a more closely matched environment than ordinary siblings.

An earlier study by Pillard as senior researcher did show a comparable 22 percent of non-twin brothers of homosexual men who were themselves homosexual.[20] The wide divergence of results in these two studies, 22 percent versus roughly 9 percent, makes one wonder how representative of the general populations the samples of these studies were.

Arguably the most important question arising from scientific findings that bear on homosexuality is whether it is a direct consequence of inherited and/or prenatal hormonal programming, or whether these hereditary factors, insofar as they exist, interact in turn with activating environmental influences such as social learning. The fact that nearly half the interviewed identical co-twins were heterosexual, even though they shared the same genetic code, supports the conclusion that whatever cumulative genetic and constitutional factors exist, they predispose toward rather than predetermine sexual orientation.

Dean Hamer

Mid-1993 brought another genetic study of male homosexuality. Dean Hamer and his associates published a study that proposed that some male homosexuality is linked to a small stretch of DNA on the X chromosome.[21]

These researchers first recruited seventy-six homosexual men and traced their families for incidence of homosexuality. The

[20] R. Pillard and J. Weinrich, "Evidence of Familial Nature of Male Homosexuality", *Archives of General Psychiatry* 43 (1986):808–12.

[21] D. Hamer, Stella Hu, Victoria L. Mangnuson, Nan Hu, and Angela M. L. Pattatucci, "A Linkage between DNA Markers on the X Chromosome and Male Sexual Orientation", *Science* 261 (1993):321–27.

pedigree studies showed a much higher than expected incidence of male homosexual persons among the subjects' brothers, maternal uncles, and male cousins through their mothers' sisters. This pattern among maternal relatives led the researchers to investigate the X chromosome, which males receive exclusively from their mothers. They reasoned that "if the X chromosome contains a gene that increases the probability of an individual's being homosexual, then genetically related gay men should share the X chromosome markers close to that gene."[22]

The research team compared the X chromosomes of forty pairs of male siblings who acknowledged homosexual orientation. They found that thirty-three of the forty pairs shared a common set of gene markers near the tip of the long arm of the X chromosome. Hamer concluded that this finding "produced evidence that one form of male homosexuality is preferentially transmitted through the maternal side and is genetically linked to chromosomal region Xq28".[23] This area, Xq28, incidentally, contains hundreds of genes, so that scientists still will need to find the relevant gene(s) should this study hold up by replication.

The fact that seven of the forty pairs of homosexual brothers did not show this chromosomal linkage raises some questions. If the Hamer study identifies a genetic basis for homosexuality, how is it that seven of the forty brothers' pairs did not show this genetic pattern? Dr. Hamer offers some explanations: "Perhaps these men inherited different genes or were influenced by nongenetic physiological factors or by the environment."[24] His data support the presence of genetic factors in some but not all homosexuality.

A noteworthy point is that the study did not use a control group. Control groups are so essential to research design that

[22] Ibid., 323.

[23] Ibid., 325.

[24] S. LeVay and D. Hamer, "Evidence for a Biological Influence in Male Homosexuality", *Scientific American* 271 (1994):49.

Ruth Hubbard, a former biology professor at Harvard University, wondered that a top journal such as *Science* would have accepted the study.[25] As a consequence we know nothing of the presence or absence of the reported markers in the heterosexual brothers of the subjects of the study.

Dr. Hamer, perhaps prodded by criticism from "the unbendable Ruth Hubbard", as he called her, included in a subsequent study a group of heterosexual men who had two homosexual brothers. He and some members of his former research team undertook to replicate the findings of the original study. The data showed that 22 percent of the heterosexual brothers shared the same genetic markers on Xq28 as their homosexual siblings. This finding complicates conclusions regarding purported homosexual genes that somehow were overruled by other factors in the lives of the 22 percent of heterosexual brothers who shared them.

The main part of the newer study repeated the earlier scanning of the X chromosome of homosexual brothers for genetic linkage. The subjects of this research study by Hamer and his associates were homosexual brothers in families unrelated to the original study's pool. The results indicated that roughly two-thirds of the homosexual siblings shared DNA markers in the Xq28 region. The remaining third did not.

Still another part of the study was the investigation of thirty-six pairs of lesbian sisters for gene markers. The findings showed no common genetic patterns in homosexual sisters. Thus, whatever the genetic sources of female sexuality might be, they have not as yet been discovered.[26]

An independent attempt to replicate Hamer's original findings was carried out by George Ebers, a Canadian geneticist.

[25] Ruth Hubbard, "False Genetic Markers", in *New York Times* (Aug. 2, 1993), p. A-14, Op-Ed article.

[26] Stella Hu et al., "Linkage between Sexual Orientation and Chromosome Xq28 in Males But Not in Females", *Nature Genetics* 11 (1995):248–56.

Ebers reported his findings at a scientific conference, but the study is unpublished as of December 1995. The subjects of the study were forty-one pairs of homosexual brothers. Ebers found "no hint of linkage between sexual orientation and the Xq28 markers. . . ."[27]

In the meantime, the Office of Research Integrity of the Department of Health and Human Services has undertaken an investigation of the allegation by one of Hamer's fellow researchers in the 1993 study that he manipulated data to obtain his results.[28]

H. Meyer-Bahlburg

Another recent study that gained media attention is one by H. Meyer-Bahlburg and his colleagues. Meyer-Bahlburg is a careful and circumspect researcher specializing in hormone studies. The study investigated adult women who had been exposed in utero to diethylstilbestrol (DES), a synthetic estrogen formerly used to prevent miscarriages in high-risk pregnancies. DES was banned in 1971 because of the risk of its causing vaginal cancer.

The study compared DES women with control groups of women not so exposed before birth. DES did not affect basic gonadal sex. It is known from animal research that DES reaches the fetal brain of rodents and nonhuman primates and interacts with estrogen receptors. The hypothesis for the study stated that prenatal DES exposure would correlate with an increased rate of bisexual or homosexual orientation. Such a result would follow from the defeminizing effect of interference with estrogen. Subjects who had been exposed to DES were compared

[27] J. M. Bailey, "Sexual Orientation Revolution", *Nature Genetics* 11 (1995):354.

[28] E. Marshall, "NIH's 'Gay Gene' Study Questioned", *Science* 268 (1995):1841.

with control groups of their unexposed sisters and other groups of unexposed and unrelated women.

Interview data indicated that the DES subjects did have significantly higher rates of homosexuality than did the control groups on such indices as daydreams, night dreams, lifelong sexual attraction, and sexual relations. Though this finding was reported in the general media, the finer distinctions discussed in the report were passed by. For example, though the differences among groups were statistically significant, "the extent to which bisexuality and homosexuality were increased in DES women was rather modest. . . . Most of the differences between DES and control women were limited to degrees of bisexuality, and for many of the women, the bisexuality was confined to imagery and not expressed in actual sex with partners."[29]

The authors conclude that the results in this study are compatible with the prenatal hormone theory of psychosexual differentiation, yet note, "our findings do not constitute a proof of the hypothesis."[30] They again call attention to their working hypothesis "of multiple developmental pathways that may lead to . . . [sexual] orientation, involving the dynamic interplay of both biology and social variables that interact with each other throughout a person's life course."[31]

The foregoing detailed review of some publicized studies leads to at least three conclusions. We should not, as the homespun saying goes, believe everything we read in the newspapers (or hear reported on TV). These reports are almost always oversimplified, often to the point of being inaccurate. Secondly, scientific studies are printed in ink, not etched in stone. Studies

[29] H. Meyer-Bahlburg, A. Ehrhardt, Laura Rosen, and Rhoda S. Gruen, "Prenatal Estrogens and the Development of Homosexual Orientation", *Developmental Psychology* 31 (1995):17.

[30] Ibid., 19.

[31] Ibid., 20.

meet with academic and scientific criticism that rarely gets reported outside the professional journals. Not infrequently, subsequent research fails to support the original study. Finally, our knowledge of the biological and psychodynamic influences in the development of homosexuality generally advances by accruing small bits and pieces of verified information. This is the ordinary process of most advances in scientific knowledge. Small increments are important because, it is hoped, they eventually will provide clarity to the emerging but still hazy synthesis of an interaction between predisposing constitutional factors and activating experiential factors in the development of psychosexual orientation.

Patience is a scientific as well as a moral virtue. Experimental studies require careful scrutiny as they appear. They also require time to mature, so to speak, through replication that confirms and refines their findings.

Psychodynamic Factors in Psychosexual Development

Psychosexuality in the sense of awareness of one's sexuality has its own developmental course. Psychosexuality is at least partially a learned characteristic, though not acquired simply by direct teaching, as one might learn arithmetic. One's sense of being male or female, masculine or feminine, is absorbed more than consciously learned. It is absorbed primarily from parents (or parental figures), with later influences from siblings, relatives, peers, and significant adults. We learn psychosexuality much as we learn other basic personal orientations: trust or mistrust, autonomy or dependency, self-esteem or inferiority. These various orientations develop through emotional interpersonal experiences that are filtered through a child's fantasies and conceptualizations. There are biological bases even for nonsexual orientations, which are formed as typical, characteristic ways of responding. For example, a youth in American culture endowed with an athletic physique is at advantage toward becoming a secure, independent, and confident individual, but his life experience will have the more profound influence on developing assertive and competent character traits than inherited physical agility or attractiveness. Basic convictions about oneself are precipitated out of experience and woven in the warp and woof of personality. The nucleus of these convictions is structured before one can understand or reflect on them, cognitively label them, or verbally express them. We know them intuitively: we sense them, feel them.

At birth the infant is assigned its sex on the basis of its external genitals. The formation of psychosexuality, however, begins with "psychological birth" around the eighteenth month. Psychological birth is the infant's passage from the original symbiotic, blissful fusion with the mother to a sense of being a separate self. Even at one and a half years the child is not convinced of the merits of separateness vis-à-vis oneness, a conflict ordinarily resolved by age three by establishing definite individuality.[32]

With the dawning of consciousness as a separate person and the initial capacity to fantasize and interpret (or misinterpret) experience, the child forms an individual identity and a gender identity. The child forges psychosexual as well as personal identity out of the unending series of messages from parents and others by word, behavior, and attitude. Core gender identity— "I am male/female"—is irreversibly established during the third year. But untoward events in the child's life to this point may leave him with a sense of threat to the integrity of gender identity, as will be discussed later.

Gender identification, which is much deeper than imitation, requires that the same-sex parent be seen as nurturing. Identification can be impaired when the parental model is experienced as hostile or as detached and unresponsive. Closely allied

---

[32] Louise Kaplan, *Oneness and Separateness* (New York: Simon & Schuster, 1978).

is the child's need to see the same-sex parent as competent and respected by other important persons in the child's life. In the traditional family the most significant other person is that parent's spouse. A wholesome parental marriage is one of the better guarantees of normal psychosexual identification.

Gender role identity is the ongoing internalization of the behavior, interests, and attitudes typical of a given sex in a particular culture or, closer to home, in a particular family.

The labeling of behaviors as more typical of one sex may be done rigidly or with wide latitude. Unfortunately, there is no doubt that rigid stereotypic labels, past and present, have fostered caricatures of both masculinity and femininity.

However, a society that completely blurs the differences in sex roles distorts the complementary features of the sexes by which they ultimately become two in one flesh and establish a loving, communal life. A unisex approach that clouds sex differences makes it difficult for both sexes to establish a clear gender role identity.

The cultural denial of sex differences makes it especially hard for boys to confirm their sexual identity through their gender role. Boys first identify with their mothers, the original source of security, and therefore have a greater need of role reinforcement for a sense of manhood. Robert Stoller, a clinician who specialized in gender identity disorders, proposes that in boys the period of marked intimacy between mother and child necessary for healthy development leaves behind "a trace, a touch of uncertainty that their masculinity is intact".[33] While overstated to make the point, boys have to shift identity; girls do not. Cultures intuitively have realized this need, which is one reason why most societies are less tolerant of cross-over of sexual roles by boys than by girls.

The child learns what is judged appropriately masculine or

[33] Robert Stoller, *Presentations of Gender* (New Haven, Conn.: Yale Univ. Press, 1985), p. 8.

feminine from the example of parents (and others) and from the positive or negative reinforcement of manifest interests, attitudes, and activities. The fact that a girl is energetic and competitive, or a boy aesthetically inclined, may help or hinder gender role identity, depending on the affirmation or disapproval shown by parents and to a lesser extent by close relatives and peers. Praise and approbation confirm appropriateness to a child; harsh criticism is likely to spawn self-doubt about one's acceptability as a person and one's adequacy as feminine or masculine.

As a case in point, an adult therapy client whose boyhood interest in music brought crude teasing from his athletic brothers, and a sense that his father was distant and indifferent to him generally, never had his masculinity sufficiently affirmed; rather it was derided. When his mother noticed his social isolation, she suggested kindly that he would do well to be out with other boys. He perceived her stance as one more disaffirmation added to those he sensed from father and brothers. He felt he did not measure up as a boy, and this belief was a contributing factor in developing a homosexual orientation.

Note that athletic and artistic talent may well be inherited, even affected indirectly in uterine development by hormonal influences on the brain. These biologically influenced traits may be valued or disvalued by significant figures in one's environment, whether parents, siblings, or peers. Such responses would boost or undermine one's sense of self as appropriately masculine or feminine. Thus the interaction of genetic and/or prenatal hormonally influenced traits with later social history could affect one's sense of self as a sexual being.

Homosexualities

A vast corpus of clinical literature and child development research points to impairment of core gender identity and/or gender role identity in the development of homosexual orientation.

Pro-homosexual apologists point out, rightly, that many clinical research findings do not apply to all homosexuals but wrongly argue that lack of universal application invalidates these findings. A child may undergo experiences that traumatize psychosexual development at different periods of growth, some more critical than others. These conflicts deflect, in varying degree, the strong cultural and environmental forces promoting heterosexual development. On this account various life experiences may contribute dynamically to homosexual orientation, some more in one person than another. Every person has a unique, rich, and dramatic psychological history.

Bell and Weinberg titled their massive study *Homosexualities* because they found diversity in lifestyle and personality type among the nearly one thousand homosexual men and women interviewed for the study.[34] In similar fashion this current overview would propose three broad categories of homosexualities as a useful framework for those who minister pastorally to homosexual persons or engage them in counseling. The three types are compulsive, symptomatic, and episodic homosexuality.

Compulsive Homosexuality

Charles Socarides, a psychoanalyst who has had a long career in therapy with homosexual persons, maintains that the first category, the obligatory or compulsive homosexual orientation, has origins in the second and third year of life as a result of disturbed mother–child relations at the time of individuation. This disturbance in the resolution of psychic separation from the

---

[34] A. Bell and M. Weinberg, *Homosexualities* (New York: Simon & Schuster, 1978).

mother may resonate into one's core gender identity, the formation of which coincides with initial ego development.[35]

Should the child experience the mother as noticeably ambivalent during the period marking psychological birth, the
child's developing ego becomes ridden with anxiety. The child
may experience a double message—maternal rejection and
close-binding intimacy—and be caught in a bind. The forceful
trend to separate, to be an individual, is hampered by a fear of
abandonment, while the pull to remain united arouses fear of
engulfment. This conflict, with its dread of personal dissolution,
ultimately is repressed, only to be triggered in later life situations
wherein one feels slighted, criticized, humiliated, or weakened.
Because individual identity is so interwoven with gender identity, perceived assaults on one's self as a person are experienced in
deep psychic levels as assaults on one's sexual integrity as well.
The individual later pursues homosexual contact in a driven
manner as a reparative device: the homosexual act provides the
male homosexual with a shot of manhood, the lesbian with an
infusion of womanhood. The compulsive homosexual is protecting ego identity and gender identity by a sexual fusion with
another person of the same sex.

The main motive is not sexual gratification. Rather, it is to
assuage the anxiety arising from a deep-seated threat of isolation,
helplessness, and even disintegration.

This fear may break into consciousness. The person will say
of the homosexual act, "I'll fall apart if I don't have it", and
protest, "It's not an indulgence; it's something I *have* to do."
Homosexual acts discharge this primary anxiety for the time
being, but the person is often suffused with guilt, anguish, self-
hatred, and remorse.

Even when the compelling anxiety remains unconscious due
to effective repression, it is still evident in the driven character

---

[35] C. Socarides, *Homosexuality* (New York: Aronson, 1979).

of the pursuit. A man may be single or married, a father of a family, a professional or blue-collar worker, and find himself driving miles to homosexual haunts, taking what he knows are ridiculous, insane risks, and later he will say that something stronger than himself just seemed to pull him toward it. The confessor who presumes the motivation to be ordinary sexual desire or the sympathetic mentor who advocates a monogamous homosexual relationship as a better lifestyle does not begin to fathom the addictive nature of the problem. Nor does the critic who protests the Church's refusal to sanction the same-sex relationship by claiming that this moral position contributes to promiscuity.

This dynamic explanation of compulsive homosexuality may seem fanciful. We all feel at times that we can not cope with a situation, that we can not make it. For a person afflicted with an unresolved individuation conflict, and consequently a tenuous ego structure, even minor distress activates extraordinary inner tension, a sense of overwhelming helplessness and fear of annihilation. Individuality and psychosexual identity are so enmeshed that homosexual activity serves to stave off the threat of psychic disorganization.

Moreover, it is precisely because the homosexual behavior is so effective in neutralizing anxiety in the short term that it allows the compulsive homosexual person to function with apparent ease occupationally and socially. Many compulsive persons are highly productive and adjusted in many areas of life apart from the compulsive symptom itself.

Following individuation, a child's experiences may strengthen or undermine the sense of maleness or femaleness, the core gender identity. Among the more negative factors is the perception that one's sex is a disappointment to a parent or parents. It is less than affirming for a child to hear, "I (we) wanted a girl (boy) but took you because God sent you."

Elizabeth Moberly sees the developmental roots of the

homosexual condition in a damaged relationship with the same-sex parent. In this scenario, proper identification, already under way, is derailed by perceived rejection and unmet emotional affirmation from the parent of the same sex. The child defensively detaches from this parent and thereby loses the psychosexual and psychosocial growth that ordinarily comes through attachment to the parent of the same sex. The homosexual resolution of this conflict is an attempt to restore and repair attachment to one's own sex and obtain love from a same-sex partner. Yet ambivalence from early hurt and disappointment in relation to the same-sex parent endures in a new relationship by the transference of the need for love and affirmation *and* the hostility for the failure of the primary same-sex figure in one's life to provide it.[36] Psychiatrist Herbert Hendin observes: "The same disastrous early experiences of homosexuals that have led them to a homosexual adaptation operate to insure that pain, rejection and degradation are an integral part of their relationships."[37]

Symptomatic Homosexuality

The second category is symptomatic homosexuality, that is, homosexuality as a symptom of a more general personality problem. This does not imply that there is no impairment of psychosexual identity, only that the stronger impetus toward homosexual activity is to resolve some ancillary conflict that has become sexualized. Symptomatic homosexuality also has a driven quality, but it falls short of the obligatory strength of compulsive homosexuality. Ruth Tiffany Barnhouse summarizes the unresolved issues that may lead to homosexual adaptation under these headings: (1) problems of unsatisfied dependency needs,

[36] Elizabeth Moberly, *Psychogenesis: The Early Development of Gender Identity* (London: Routledge and Kegan Paul, 1983).

[37] H. Hendin, *The Age of Sensation* (New York: Norton, 1975), p. 116.

(2) unresolved power or dominance needs, and (3) fear of heterosexuality.[38]

Some youngsters, feeling unaffirmed and deprived of affection, come to look for acceptance on any terms. They may drift to homosexuality hoping for affirmation and thereby solidify homosexual leanings. Homosexual behavior becomes a constant, obsessive search for affirmation.

For others, homosexuality may be a quest for dominance, a sense of power. A man in his late twenties sought treatment because he feared growing old in a subculture where youth is idolized even more than in society at large. He pitied the forty-year-olds who were hangers-on at gay bars, trying to look twenty, in desperate search for a pickup. As his story unfolded, his anger emerged against a father who had rejected him. His parents had been divorced when he was three. As a teenager he sought out his father in another city and camped on his doorstep all night with the hope of starting a father–son relationship. When his father finally showed up, he gave the boy bus fare for the return trip and told him to get lost.

Upon reaching eighteen, the young man's first act was to change his surname legally, thereby announcing to the world his disidentification from the father he had desired so keenly. He was equally contemptuous of his mother, who had indulged him with whatever he wanted as a child and in his teens had insisted that he should not get a job because it would require mingling with supposedly inferior-class youth. The message he had absorbed was that he was weak, useless, unmanly, and unable to make it on his own. During early therapy he said with disdain, "I could never have a woman lead me by the hand." Later he confronted his own collusion in enjoying the comforts of indolence at the cost of his manhood.

Eventually, he admitted that his homosexuality was a passive-

[38] Ruth Tiffany Barnhouse, *Homosexuality: A Symbolic Confusion* (New York: Seabury Press, 1979), p. 51.

aggressive ploy, a contemptuous declaration to his parents, "Look what you did to me." He acknowledged his motivating hatred; homosexuality was a way to strike back at parents he felt had failed him and whom he resented implacably as well as striking back at a self he demeaned as weak. In a tearful burst of insight he declared, "I've always treated sex as a degradation of the other person. I wanted to tear down the other person, to prove that he's just as bad as I am. When I'm with some man I'm interested in, I want to share life with, I know it's not right; it's not meant to be this way." It is not uncommon that a male homosexual cannot continue having sex with a male partner as genuine affection toward him deepens; he senses that for him sex has been a devious and deviant way to dominate.

Fear of heterosexuality may arise from many sources. Sexual maladjustment may spawn a child's feeling that sex is dirty, that heterosexual relations are gross and coarse. Hearing themes such as "your father thinks of only one thing" can contribute to heterosexual aversion in a child of either sex. Sexual abuse of a child is patently traumatic. A girl abused in childhood, especially by a male family member, may turn from an abiding heterosexual revulsion to homosexuality. Others turn to lesbianism with the unspoken premise "I could never destroy a man as my mother destroyed my father."

Episodic Homosexuality

Finally, a catch-all category of homosexuality is variously called situational, variational, or episodic. It includes those who engage in homosexual activity occasionally or regularly but whose basic orientation is nonetheless heterosexual.

Episodic homosexual behavior may occur in situations where heterosexual activity is not possible, in prison, for example. Adolescents may engage in homosexual activity out of experimental curiosity, not from psychosexual need or conflict. Some persons engage in homosexual acts for money, in search of a new thrill, or from indifferent sexual morality. Homosexual behavior may simply express a countercultural protest against conventional standards and inhibitions, a declaration of liberation by having erotic adventures. For these and other reasons the definitive criterion of sexual orientation is not necessarily sexual behavior. John Money would assign as a criterion the sex of the person with whom an adult has the potential to fall in love or become infatuated.[39]

The notion of *homosexualities*, several types of homosexuality, provides a plausible explanation for some of the puzzling exceptions in experimental studies and variations in clinical theories of etiology. Studies regarding origins of homosexual orientation lack results as neat as a researcher would hope. For example, in the 1993 study of Hamer et al., a number of homosexual twins did not show genetic markers that matched their brothers. Or, switching to a psychodynamic study such as Bieber's landmark research, not all subjects came from the family pattern that correlated strongly with a homosexual son.[40] Studies with subjects limited to specific types of homosexuality might afford more clear-cut results.

The Question of Disorder

Psychiatry developed from medicine as a special field and took notions of health and illness into the psychological realm by analogy. Though most people think they recognize what health is and what illness is, most also find exact definition and delineation difficult. Medicine uses a working definition of health as the absence of painful symptoms, infection, and disability,

[39] J. Money, "Sin, Sickness, or Status?", p. 385.

[40] I. Bieber, H. Dain, R. Dince, et al., *Homosexuality: A Psychoanalytic Study* (New York: Basic Books, 1962).

whereas illness exists when any are present. Definitions of mental health and mental illness have followed the same pattern. However, the term *mental illness* is no longer used professionally; it has been replaced by *mental disorder*.

Actually, modern psychiatry is not all that precise regarding mental disorder. Unfortunately, mental disorder is a term that implies a false split between mental and physical illness, for there are mental elements in some physical disorders and physical elements in some mental disorders. Yet the term *mental disorder* has been kept because psychiatry has "not found an appropriate substitute". Mental disorder is defined as a "psychological syndrome or pattern . . . associated with present distress . . . or disability . . . or an important loss of freedom".[41]

The mental health professions no longer officially include homosexuality under the rather wide umbrella of that definition. In late 1973 the board of trustees of the American Psychiatric Association (APA) voted to drop homosexuality per se as a mental disorder. Homosexuality is now considered a normal variation of sexual expression. This decision, which erased a hundred-year-old professional position, was confirmed by a referendum among the membership, roughly six to four. The American Psychological Association followed suit.

One might think that the poor fit between human sexual anatomy and sexual desire in homosexual orientation would suggest that something went askew in developmental history. But evidently this notion would be considered psychologically naïve and biologically rigid since it calls into question what homophile organizations laud as the wonderful diversity among human persons.

Psychiatrist Ruth Tiffany Barnhouse observed that many APA members felt conflicted because they thought upholding an appraisal of anomaly based on scientific evidence was con-

---

[41] *Diagnostic and Statistical Manual of Disorders*, 4th ed. (American Psychiatric Association, 1994), p. xxi.

tributing to discrimination. It was a dilemma, she says, born of muddy thinking.[42]

The APA explained its decision by stating:

> The crucial issue in determining whether or not homosexuality per se is to be regarded as a mental disorder is not the etiology of the condition, but its consequences and the definition of mental disorder. A significant proportion of homosexuals are apparently satisfied with their sexual orientation, show no significant signs of manifest psychopathology (unless homosexuality, by itself, is considered psychopathology), and are able to function socially and occupationally with no impairment. If one uses the criteria of *distress* or *disability*, homosexuality per se is not a mental disorder. If one uses the criterion of *inherent disadvantage*, it is not at all clear that homosexuality is a disadvantage in all cultures or subcultures.[43]

Psychodynamic psychology takes a somewhat different tack from viewing healthy or disturbed functioning in terms of a symptom approach. It offers a criterion of normality or abnormality distinct from cultural norms or ethics in that it considers not the act itself, its cultural setting, or the subjective comfort of the agent but rather the psychological mechanisms involved.

Lawrence Kubie, a psychiatrist and commentator who proposes an essential criterion of health or dysfunction, points out that every act is influenced by a constellation of motives. Insofar as an act, thought, feeling, or impulse proceeds predominantly from conscious and preconscious motives, that is, forces within oneself *accessible* to consciousness, it is healthy. To the degree an act is determined primarily by anxiety and/or conflict of which an individual is unaware and cannot, unaided, become aware, the act is unhealthy. Thus depth therapy aims at raising unknown motives and conflicts to consciousness, dealing with them and resolving them, thereby restoring an individual's impaired free-

[42] Barnhouse, *Homosexuality*, p. 51.

[43] *Diagnostic and Statistical Manual of Mental Disorders*, 3rd ed. (American Psychiatric Association, 1980), p. 380. Quoted with permission.

dom. It will be recalled that an essential note in the APA definition of mental disorder, given above, was an important loss of
freedom.

An act is unhealthy to the degree it is cut off from possible
conscious control, ranging from minor determination to inflex-
ible repetition.[44] This criterion is proper to psychology itself; it
does not arise from ethics or values except the value that it is
better to know why one does things than to be impelled by
motives of which one is unaware. If this criterion is extended
from single acts to patterns and general trends of behavior, it
then becomes the essential consideration for assessing mental
health or disorder.

By this criterion it is a rare individual indeed without some
disordered functioning. It is a rare person who has not asked
himself "Why do I keep doing that?" when he feels unable to
shift to more constructive behavior. The challenge of life, and the
specific task of depth therapy, is to know oneself, to become
more aware of one's inner workings, to discover the reasons reason does not know, to confront the motivations that we keep
even from ourselves through defensive maneuvers.

It is also true that anyone afflicted with a psychological disorder has reserves of health. Psychological health and illness are
not mutually exclusive terms. Both can coexist in various degrees.

The balance between the alliance of conscious and preconscious forces on one side and unconscious processes on the other
is intricate and complex in every person. For this reason only
God can make the final and certain judgment on a person's freedom or culpability.

The decision to drop homosexuality as disorder ignores the
large body of accumulated literature indicating psychodynamic
connections between unresolved and largely unconscious con-

[44] L. Kubie, "The Fundamental Nature of the Distinction between Normality and Neurosis", *Psychoanalytic Quarterly* 23 (1954):167–204.

flicts and homosexual orientation. This literature, wrought from clinical experience, sees compulsive and symptomatic homosexuality as a sexualized resolution of conflict in which the particular traumatizing experiences of an individual became interwoven with psychosexual development. Episodic homosexuality usually is not psychologically disordered because its motives generally are accessible to consciousness.

Despite the official position of the APA duly confirmed by a membership vote, a significant number of psychiatrists did not agree with it. A survey taken four years after the APA decision by the journal *Medical Aspects of Human Sexuality* found that 69 percent of responding psychiatrists agreed that "homosexuality is usually a pathological adaptation, as opposed to a normal variation."[45] Perhaps the muddy thinking referred to by Dr. Barnhouse had cleared somewhat.

As of 1995, the membership in NARTH, the National Association for Research and Treatment of Homosexuality, numbered 425 mental health professionals. NARTH, founded only in 1992, is composed mostly of accredited therapists who work with homosexual persons distressed by their condition and seeking change toward heterosexual functioning. It is evident that not all professionals subscribe to all the diagnostic or policy positions of their professional organizations.

Postscript

The position one takes regarding homosexual orientation as a normal or abnormal development is a separate issue from one's treatment of persons who are homosexual. To treat anyone as an outcast is certainly not a humane, much less a Christian, response.

[45] Reported in *Time* (Feb. 20, 1978), p. 102.

We too easily dismiss the pain that any person with psycho-sexual problems suffers. This was brought home to me as a fledg-ling psychologist by a young man who helped me more than I helped him.

He was a candidate for a religious community for which I was a consultant. In the course of the psychological evaluation it became clear that he was predominantly homosexual and un-happy about it. At his request I arranged for him to enter a therapy group for homosexual persons conducted by a former teacher, a New York City psychiatrist. At the end of our meet-ing he told me that I was the first person in his Catholic experi-ence who discovered his orientation and "did not treat me like a barrel of shit". The crudity of his remark underscored how bit-terly he felt about the insensitivity of persons in his life from whom he expected compassionate treatment.

He related some rough experiences in the confessional, where he heard condemnatory remarks and even grunts of dis-gust. He described how he cringed inwardly when the nuns on the faculty of the school where he was a teacher would tell de-rogatory jokes about homosexual persons. He was left with little hope for acceptance, empathy, or attempted understanding from Church functionaries. I appreciated his compliment, but I was more grateful for his help toward some affective appreciation of the devastating hurt, isolation, shame, and self-hatred felt by many homosexual persons. Some of them cover these feelings with militant anger or flaunting behavior, but the currents of pain still run deep.

Over the past couple of decades there has been progress in social attitudes toward persons burdened with alcoholism. Alco-holism is now widely viewed as a disease. It is a physically addic-tive disease, and, prior to admitting one's problem, it is a psychological "disease of denial". We need a corresponding shift in attitude toward homosexual persons. Denying that homo-sexuality is a developmental anomaly or a disorder is not the way to accomplish this turnabout. Nor need one compromise personal moral conviction if one holds that homosexual actions are wrong because they lack an intrinsic purpose of human sexuality. Each individual's primary task is to deal with whatever prejudice or visceral fear of homosexuality delimits his practice of the gospel law of love of neighbor. Sadly, many homosexual persons have left the Catholic Church at least partially because some Catholics reacted to them in a less than Christian manner.

4

POSSIBILITY OF CHANGE
OF ORIENTATION

In the previous chapter Father Jeffrey Keefe presents a comprehensive overview of the multiple factors involved in the origins
of the homosexual orientation, while carefully distinguishing
and describing three different kinds of homosexuality: compulsive, symptomatic, and episodic. He also gives careful attention to
the meaning of *disorder* in psychological discourse. It is now my
task to show the correlation between Keefe's survey and my own
on the question of change of orientation. For this purpose I shall
refer to his work, as well as published research, in presenting my
thoughts on this question.[1] From his study it is clear that the
view that homosexuality is primarily an innate tendency is an
assertion without proof; however, those who hold that homosexuality is primarily environmental should be willing to concede that there can be genetic and hormonal factors that may be
understood as predispositive to a homosexual orientation. There
is no evidence, however, that either biological, hormonal, or environmental factors *alone* inevitably produce the homosexual
condition.

Through research and experience we have come to know that
there are no simple explanations for the origins of homosexual

[1] John F. Harvey, "Updating Issues concerning Homosexuality", in *Homosexuality: Challenges for Change and Reorientation, Journal of Pastoral Counseling* 28
(New Rochelle, N.Y.: Iona College, 1993):8–39.

orientation. In my book *The Homosexual Person*, chapters 3 and 4, I presented authors who stressed the psychogenic origins of homosexuality against genetic and hormonal theories. I still believe that psychological elements are predominant in the formation of a homosexual orientation; however, I also believe that in certain instances genetic and hormonal factors can *predispose* certain individuals to move toward homosexuality if these individuals happen to be in a certain psychological atmosphere, such as those described in *Psychogenesis* by Elizabeth Moberly or in *The Broken Image* by Leanne Payne. In one way or another the environment has an influence on the homosexual orientation of the person, and this influence, in my judgment, is more important than genetic or hormonal ones; however, there is no way that we are going to settle the issue of nature versus nurture in the genesis of homosexual orientation. As Steven Goldberg said in his article in *National Review* (Feb. 3, 1992), the same data may be open to conflicting, if not contradictory, interpretations. If the homosexual condition is a mix of genetic, hormonal, and psychological factors, we are still not able to discern how these factors converge in the formation of a homosexual orientation in John Smith or Mary Doe. My purpose in this chapter, however, is to consider whether a person with a homosexual orientation is able to move out of it. I shall draw on the experience and research of many as well as on personal pastoral experience.

Change of Orientation[2]

Most authors are willing to concede that genetic, hormonal, and psychological factors can interact in the development of a homosexual orientation, but they will differ from one another in estimating the *relative* strength of each contributing factor. Per-

---

[2] In going through academic and psychological abstracts under "Homosexuality", one gets no entries under the subtitle "Change of Orientation" but many entries under "Change of Behavior or Attitude".

sonally, from my reading and pastoral experience, I lean toward those theories which regard the psychological as more important than the genetic or the hormonal. At the same time, as I have already said, when working with an individual, male or female, who has homosexual tendencies, I have no way of acquiring certitude concerning the origins of homosexuality in that particular case.

This brief review of the present situation leads to the following questions: (1) Is it possible to change one's sexual orientation? and (2) If this is not possible for a given individual, can he lead a life of sexual abstinence? The first question is hotly debated among social scientists and professional therapists;[3] it is also discussed by theologians and philosophers with a background in psychology.

Some Protestant groups believe firmly that individuals who follow their religious therapy programs can move from a homosexual orientation to heterosexuality and hopefully to marriage. The best example is Exodus International, a national organization of such church-related groups, which has spread throughout the United States and Canada. Every year they sponsor a week-long conference. Over 500 people come annually to this conference to hear Christian therapists, ministers, and psychologists offer suggestions on a variety of ways of moving out of the homosexual condition. Well-known leaders of Exodus, such as Frank Worthen, Andy Comiskey, Bob Davies, Joe Dallas, Lori Rentzel, Alan Medinger, and many others, present papers that are certainly worth our serious attention.[4] With goals similar to

[3] J. Nicolosi is quoted in "Born or Bred", *Newsweek* (Feb. 24, 1992), as holding that there are no cures as such, but "a diminishment of homosexual feelings" to the point where some patients may marry and have families. He is quoted also as believing that treatment is "probably a lifelong process" (p. 53).

[4] Exodus International, P.O. Box 77652, Seattle, WA 98177–0652; tel. 206-784-7799, fax 206-784-7772. Exodus has an efficient referral agency with tapes of their annual meetings. On the east coast, Regeneration, Inc., provides a

those of Exodus, Homosexuals Anonymous (H.A.) also has many local groups.[5] While Exodus groups must be church-affiliated, Homosexuals Anonymous is Christian interdenominational.

However, as Fr. Keefe has pointed out, many psychiatrists and psychologists consider the possibility of change of orientation settled in the negative by the decision of the American Psychiatric Association in 1973 to withdraw homosexuality from the third edition of the *Diagnostic and Statistical Manual* (DSM III).[6] From this political decision that homosexuality is a normal variant of human sexuality there have been few dissenting voices in more recent years; thus, it has become more difficult for a professional therapist to contend that change of orientation is not only possible but has happened in certain instances.

Perhaps the following quotation from John Money sums up the viewpoint of many researchers and therapists in the present age: "Homosexuality, like heterosexuality, is not a matter of preference, choice, or voluntary decision. It is like a status, like being tall, dwarfed, or left handed, and it is not changed by desire, incentive, will power, prayer, punishment, or other motivation to change."[7]

To Money and his associates I reply that we need to make a distinction between having an orientation without deliberate choice and having the capacity to change one's orientation through deliberate choice of the means of change found in the

---

great variety of reading materials on the issue of homosexuality and reorientation: P.O. Box 9830, Baltimore, MD 21284–9830.

[5] Homosexuals Anonymous (H.A.) is an interdenominational group with fifty local chapters throughout the country. Reading materials are available from H. A. Fellowship Services, P.O. Box 7781, Reading, PA 19603. Colin Cook, author of *Homosexuality: An Open Door?*, was the cofounder of H.A.

[6] Washington, D.C.: American Psychological Association, 1980. That form of homosexuality in which the individual is perfectly satisfied with his orientation (ego-syntonic) is no longer classified as a mental disorder (p. 282).

[7] John Money, *Love Maps* (New York: Irvington Publishers, 1986), p. 105.

order of nature and of divine grace. But at this point I wish to make a note about our method.

A Methodological Note on the Debate

In reviewing selected studies claiming that homosexuality is an irreversible condition, as well as studies indicating that some individuals have been able to change their orientation, we must be aware of the limitations of all such research. Those who hold that the condition of homosexuality is irreversible should acknowledge that one case in which a so-called constitutional homosexual has been able to move over to heterosexuality disproves their position.[8] To be sure, the transition to heterosexuality must be well documented, that is to say, there must be evidence that the individual really was homosexual in orientation for a period of time before becoming heterosexual, not only in behavior but also in emotions and sexual attraction to the other sex.

The matter becomes even more complex when we consider that we have no universally accepted definition of homosexuality, researchers tending to lump bisexual behavior with homosexual behavior, as was done in the Pillard-Bailey study of identical twins, with resultant confusion. Critics will assert that an individual involved in both heterosexual and homosexual acts did not really *become* heterosexual; he was already that way, and so there is no question of *cure*.

Then there is the matter of statistics. One wonders whether empirical psychology will learn from the recent research of Judith Reisman and Edward Eichel, *Kinsey, Sex, and Fraud*, about criteria for the selection of subjects, the reliability of testimony,

[8] Richard Green, however, insists that the condition of homosexuality is legally immutable if there is a low rate of reorientation from the homosexual condition. Indeed, in his judgment the condition itself is innate: *Journal of Psychiatry and Law* 16 (Winter 1988):537–75. As we shall see, the rate of reorientation is no longer low for those who make the effort.

the possible bias of given questionnaires, the philosophical assumptions of the authors of the study, and many other factors. Unfortunately, many are unduly impressed by statistical studies called "scientific", while they reject idiographic studies (case histories) and autobiographical materials. Many of the major insights of early psychology, however, came through thorough studies of a single person, a single case history, as one finds in the works of Freud, Jung, and Adler. Such studies can be and often are rich sources of knowledge. At present many researchers make good use of such materials, often combining statistical and biographic studies. Gerald van den Aardweg is one example of a psychological researcher using both kinds of evidence (*On the Origins and Treatment of Homosexuality*). Needless to say, autobiographical materials have contributed to empirical psychology since the *Confessions* of Saint Augustine.

This leads us to one more facet of methodology. It is the question of faith. Is it possible that divine intervention in the person of Jesus Christ can be a factor in the movement away from the homosexual condition toward heterosexual orientation? Of course, strictly empirical science is not able to accept such an intervention, but does this mean that we also reject such a possibility? Can a person under the influence of the Holy Spirit gain insight into his sexual orientation that he has not received in ordinary therapy? Actually, some religious writers (Colin Cook, Andy Comiskey, Mario Bergner, and Frank Worthen) center the entire process of change to heterosexuality on the person of Jesus Christ. With these factors in mind, I shall review briefly some of the psychological literature on change of orientation, summing up the conclusions of these studies.

Review of the Psychological Literature

First I wish to review some of the psychological literature that echoes Money's view that sexual orientation cannot be changed,

then some of the literature that holds that such change is possible, and then I will turn to the religious literature that contends
that individuals who follow programs like Love in Action (Frank
Worthen), Desert Streams (Andrew Comiskey), or Homosexuals
Anonymous (Colin Cook) can change their sexual orientation.[9]

But first I turn to authors who hold that sexual orientation
cannot be changed. C. A. Tripp writes:

> There are no known "cures" for homosexuality, nor are any
> likely, since the phenomena which comprise it are not illnesses
> in the first place. Of course, the issue does not end there. Smok-
> ing and drinking are not illnesses either, but they can be stamped
> out by various means. With these and other considerations in
> mind, the Kinsey Research made a concerted effort over a pe-
> riod of years to find and to elaborate the histories of people
> whose sex lives had changed either during or following therapy
> of any kind. None was ever found.[10]

Unfortunately, Tripp, who wrote in 1975, relied heavily upon
the data from the two Kinsey Reports of 1948 and 1953. In this
respect he was like other researchers who used Kinsey's data
without realizing how unscientific it was. He says, for example,
that he was surprised to find that the "Kinsey Researchers did
not find any instances of people whose sexual responses were
altered during therapy".[11]

Recently, however, Dr. Judith Reisman, Edward Eichel, and
associates have written a documented study pointing out fraud-
ulent aspects of Kinsey's work.[12] Since Tripp's research was based

[9] We shall say more about these Exodus groups and leaders later.

[10] *The Homosexual Matrix* (New York: McGraw-Hill, 1975), p. 251. To get
the full flavor of Tripp, read chap. 11, "The Question of Psychotherapy",
pp. 243–67. Tripp sees homosexuality as a perfectly normal alternative lifestyle.

[11] Ibid., p. 252.

[12] *Kinsey, Sex, and Fraud: The Indoctrination of a People* (Lafayette, La.:
Lochinvar, Huntington, 1990). See esp. "Misleading Data on Homosexuality",
pp. 184–89. Reisman points out that the uncritical acceptance of Kinsey's "science" has "led to the widespread assumption, heard somewhere almost every

in a significant way upon Kinsey's works, it can hardly pass as *scientific*.

In a study of homosexuality among male and female teenagers Robert Bidwell asserts that

> gay teens must know, first of all, that their sexual orientation is not a choice. Nor is it a contagion. Nor is it the product of some developmental interruption or flaw. Rather, their feelings are a completely valid and natural representation of the human experience. They are as likely as their heterosexual peers to lead happy, fulfilling and productive lives once a personal peace has been made with their sexuality.[13]

The author urges parents of teenagers claiming to be homosexual to accept the orientation of their children and to resist any change therapy.[14] This viewpoint, however, needs to be contrasted with that of Dr. Ruth Tiffany Barnhouse, who stressed that one is not able to determine whether an adolescent is really homosexual:

> I use the word *homosexuality* to refer to an *adult* adaptation characterized by *preferential* sex behavior between members of the same sex. The emphasis on *adult* is very important. Much of today's rhetoric does not allow for the fact that adolescence is often accompanied by a period of transitional anxiety or confusion about sexual identity.[15]

Bidwell is asking a teenager who is—by definition—immature to make a life decision that he should not have to make until he is mature.

---

day, that 10 per cent of the male population is gay. These false assumptions remain scientific lore, perpetuated through constant repetition in a so-called skeptical media and through appropriation as givens in medical and psychological journals" (p. 184).

[13] "The Gay and Lesbian Teen: A Case of Denied Adolescence", *Journal of Pediatric Care* 2 (Jan.-Feb. 1988):6.

[14] Ibid., 7–8.

[15] *Homosexuality: A Symbolic Confusion* (New York: Seabury Press, 1977), p. 22.

With the objective of demonstrating that the homosexual condition is an immutable trait and, as such, should be protected from discrimination, Richard Green argues that research evidence points to an innate origin of homosexuality; he bases his position on his review of the literature on monozygotic twins, prenatal hormonal influences, and other biological factors. He also seeks to repudiate the arguments of analysts and of behaviorists who claim success in helping persons make the transition from homosexuality to heterosexuality. Then he sums up his own fifteen-year longitudinal study of sixty-six boys, ages four to twelve, who had displayed extensive cross-gender behavior. He believes his study points "to the very early and essentially irreversible establishment of sexual orientation in the male".[16]

His conclusions go beyond the data he presents to demonstrate such an "irreversible sexual orientation" in the male. It is unscientific to draw a universal conclusion, such as that all homosexual orientation is immutable, from particular premises based upon particular data.

Green, of course, will counter that he has not drawn such a conclusion but only "points" to such, and that such "irreversibility" can admit of some exceptions, what he calls a "low rate of reorientation". Green is playing with words. He says above that sexual orientation is *essentially* irreversible in the male, and then he adds that the irreversibility has exceptions. Furthermore, Green has no way of explaining the data that we shall consider later in this chapter indicating that the rate of reorientation among those who make the effort to change orientation is by no means "low". I think it may be said, however, that the earlier the developmental interference in the child's life, the more difficult it will be to correct it in therapy.[17] It is also clear from the article

[16] "The Immutability of (Homo) Sexual Orientation: Behavioral Science Implications for a Constitutional (Legal) Analysis", *The Journal of Psychiatry and Law* 16 (Winter 1988):567.

[17] Correspondence with Dr. Jeffrey Keefe, the author of chapter three.

that Green assumes that the homosexual lifestyle is as normal and good as marriage.[18] This is a common assumption among authors who regard homosexuality as a normal variant of human sexuality. Diane Richardson challenges this assumption.

A Clinical Practitioner Views Homosexual Behavior

Diane Richardson approaches the problem of homosexuality as a clinical practitioner who desires to help the homosexual to adjust positively to his orientation. Previously, she had seen clinicians accepting uncritically various theories about the origins of homosexuality, but now in the light of more recent studies, she challenges the view that "people have an essential sexuality that is either homosexual or heterosexual and which remains fixed and unchanging throughout their lives."[19] Richardson goes on to make several important distinctions. We need to distinguish between homosexual attraction and activity as "compared with homosexual categorizations and identities."[20] Thus, there is "no necessary relationship between a particular pattern of sexual behavior and a particular sexual identity".[21]

Instead of categorizing the patient, Richardson holds, clinicians should help the individual to interpret the *meaning for himself* of his fantasies and activities. The trouble with such help, however, is that the client will tend to make the same assumptions as the clinician in interpreting his fantasies and behavior. Richardson believes that one may not assume that a homosexual orientation is immutable: "We need to consider the processes whereby, for each individual, either stability or *change* [italics in the original] of sexual identity occurs. We must, in other words,

[18] Green, "Immutability of (Homo) Sexual Orientation", 569.
[19] "Recent Challenges to Traditional Assumptions about Homosexuality: Some Implications for Practice", *Journal of Homosexuality* 13 (Summer 1987):1, abstract.
[20] Ibid., 3.
[21] Ibid., 4.

address ourselves not only to the question of how individuals develop a heterosexual or homosexual identity, but also how they do, or do not, maintain this identity thereafter."[22]

She goes on to point out that a few studies have shown that "individuals may undergo one or more redefinitions of sexual identity during their lifetime".[23] In light of these studies, then, Richardson believes that the ordinary practitioner is faced with a difficulty if he agrees with the position denying that sexual orientation is predetermined by nature. He must treat patients who believe themselves always to have been homosexual and who interpret all the events of their past life in terms of their belief. Patients will do this even if in the past they had identified themselves as heterosexual, lacking homosexual attraction. In short, the patient wants the clinician to label him, thus giving meaning to his fantasies and behavior. Richardson advises caution and prudence in labeling, because it is her conviction from research and practice that some people do change their sexual identities over time.[24] By changing sexual identity Richardson means changing sexual orientation.

She also believes that one may go in either direction, from homosexual to heterosexual, or the other way around. Her belief resonates with Kinsey's presupposition that human sexuality is polymorphous—like putty that can be shaped in different ways. There is, however, little or no evidence that individuals change from heterosexual orientation to homosexual, and much evidence, as we shall see soon, that many individuals have moved from a homosexual orientation to a heterosexual.

[22] Ibid., 5

[23] Ibid.

[24] Ibid., 7. The author adds that more recent research has also indicated that some individuals may undergo a genuine change of sexual identity during their lives. She refers to E. M. Pattison and M. L. Pattison, "Ex-Gays: Religiously Mediated Change in Homosexuals", *American Journal of Psychiatry* 137 (1980):1553–62; and to B. Donse, *Identities in the Lesbian World: The Social Construction of Self* (Westport, Conn.: Greenwood Press, 1978).

Richardson holds that there should be goals for a person desiring to change from homosexuality to heterosexuality. He should be desensitized concerning his guilt about homosexual feelings and desires. (This is obviously a value-free approach, i.e., it allows no consideration of Judeo-Christian morality.) Unfortunately, Richardson shows her own liberal bias when she approvingly quotes Alex Davidson, who believes that we should also have programs to help heterosexuals to become homosexual if they really desire to be such.[25]

Nevertheless, Richardson's view that sexual identity is an ongoing process in which the *reasons* why the person desires to be homosexual change and *can* change to the point where he seeks to be heterosexual is a departure from the prevalent view of clinical psychologists and psychiatrists. While the majority view remains that the homosexual condition is immutable, it is significant that Richardson gives hope to homosexual persons wanting to change. She is on target, moreover, when she adds that change is very difficult, including a "considerable restructuring of their total view of themselves".[26]

Teenagers with Homosexual Inclinations

The possibility of change of orientation, however, does not appear in most of the literature concerning teenagers with homosexual inclinations; it is the thesis of one author, Robert Bidwell, that society has denied adolescence to gay and lesbian teens. A similar view is expressed by Gilbert Herdt: heterosexuality is assumed by the culture to be the norm of sexual activity, and consequently gay and lesbian youth feel guilty because of the discordance between their fantasies and desires and the expectations of their parents and society. He adds that the conflictual problems of adolescent persons over the issue of homosexuality

[25] Richardson, "Recent Challenges", 9.
[26] Ibid., 10.

need the help of counselors and support groups that will affirm a homosexual lifestyle. He laments the fact that in America and in other countries gay and lesbian teenagers have no adequate "coming out" process, because the culture and the family are not supportive of homosexual behavior.[27]

Like Bidwell's, Herdt's views make two unfounded assumptions: (1) that the teenager really knows his sexual orientation and (2) that he has achieved the emotional maturity to make a decision concerning his future sexual lifestyle. Encouraging adolescent persons to pursue the gay lifestyle is really the seduction of the innocent.

Reiter's Conclusions

By making her distinction between sexual orientation and sexual identity, Laura Reiter comes to the conclusion that sexual orientation is immutable. She defines a homosexual as "an adult whose fantasies, attachments, and longings are predominantly for persons of the same gender, who may or may not express those longings in overt behavior and whose orientation may or may not be accompanied by a homosexual identity".[28]

It is not clear what Reiter means by "identity". From her study it seems that "identity" is the present *perception* of the individual as to whether he is homosexual or heterosexual. Again, by stressing the difference between orientation and behavior, Reiter makes behavior less meaningful and orientation basic and essential. In her understanding orientation is the result of inborn predispositions and very early experience and remains unchanged. It is the *predominance* of erotic responses that helps one

---

[27] "Introduction: Gay and Lesbian Youth, Emergent Identities, and Cultural Scenes at Home and Abroad", *Journal of Homosexuality* 17, nos. 1–2 (1989):1–42.

[28] "Sexual Orientation, Sexual Identity, and the Question of Choice", *Clinical Social Work Journal* 17, no. 2 (Summer 1989):140.

to decide whether one is homosexual, heterosexual, or bi-sexual.[29]

Reiter's position is confusing. When one considers the vagueness of the term *bisexuality* and the controversy in psychology whether the term means a fixed state, as Reiter contends, or is merely a term describing patterns of behavior but not of orientation, then one wonders whether Reiter has understood the problem.

According to Reiter, subjective identity is what one considers oneself to be. If someone experiences persistent homosexual feelings, he becomes fearful as he does not want to be identified as homosexual. In this situation Reiter would want the individual to bring his claimed identity into agreement with his fixed sexual orientation. Otherwise, there will be conflict within the person. The effort, however, to "come out" to one's true orientation can be very difficult because of the stigma attached by society to homosexual people. However, she says, therapists should not encourage persons with homosexual orientation to try to shift to heterosexuality. She sees these "cures" as effecting no real change in orientation: "Behavioral changes usually were not accompanied by a fundamental shift in underlying erotic preferences. And so what shifted in most cases was behavior and (claimed) identity. What endured usually was sexual orientation."[30] The therapist then should provide an atmosphere of "uncritical acceptance of the person's sexuality" to help him integrate orientation into his "overall sense of self".[31]

Finally, addressing the question of choice, Reiter holds that the majority of homosexual men and women are "psychologic homosexuals who did not choose their orientations".[32] (I have never met one who did choose his orientation.) Not only did

[29] Ibid.
[30] Ibid., 144.
[31] Ibid.
[32] Ibid., 145.

they not choose their orientation; they cannot change it: "Free will does indeed allow choice in lifestyle and the identities people construct. Sexual orientation, determined very early in life, is an enduring and essential psychological reality, transcending choice."[33]

This is a *gratuitous* assertion that I shall address in responding to Reiter's position. First, I would question the evidence that she adduces to demonstrate that sexual orientation in the sense that she defines it, namely, as a *preponderance* of erotic feelings toward the same or toward the other sex, remains fixed and unchangeable in the individual. Her empirical data, particular by their very nature, do not justify a universal conclusion. If we are able to show that some persons with "predominant" homosexual tendencies have been able to become predominantly heterosexual in their tendencies, then Reiter's contention that orientation cannot be changed is no longer tenable. Actually, the same argument is applicable to all the authors claiming that homosexual orientation is immutable. As we shall see, there are authors who testify from their own experience concerning change in sexual orientatioin.

It is time now to turn from the authors who hold, with few reservations, that one is not able to make the journey over to heterosexuality to those who hold that one can change not only lifestyle but also basic sexual orientation. Already in my book *The Homosexual Person* I have described the theories of Elizabeth Moberly and of Gerald van den Aardweg (chap. 3, "Some Recent Theories Concerning the Origins of Homosexuality", pp. 37-63). Before going on to other authors who believe that change is possible, I should like to review the results that Gerald van den Aardweg reports in his 1986 book, *On the Origins and Treatment of Homosexuality*.

[33] Ibid., 146.

Gerald van den Aardweg

Over a period of twenty years, Van den Aardweg has treated more than two hundred homosexual men and twenty-five lesbians with a highly original approach called anticomplaining therapy, which I describe in my book. He regards a person as moving into heterosexuality, or as cured, when the person has normal heterosexual interests, wishes, and strivings for at least two years, while homosexual interests and fantasies have been absent during the same period of time. Occasional thoughts and feelings that the person easily resists do not take away from the cure. It should be stressed that the therapy is concerned with curing the whole person and not only sexual tendencies, and that improvement often appears in nonsexual aspects of the person before it appears in sexual feelings and fantasies.

The author gives a detailed analysis of his results with anticomplaining therapy. The results are honestly explained. He began with 101 persons in 1968, but 43 discontinued treatment after two to eight months. Of the 58 who remained, 11 experienced radical change, and 26 experienced satisfactory change. *Radical* is described as having no homosexual interests except for occasional weak temptations and normal heterosexual interests during at least a two-year follow-up period. *Satisfactory* is described as (1) heterosexual interests prevailing, but occasional homosexual upsurges in fantasy, which, though temporary, could be fierce and (2) no more homosexual interests, but still weak heterosexuality over a one-year follow-up period. The third category, *improved*, with 11 persons, is described as having few homosexual interests with or without concomitant heterosexual interests. (This is rather vague.) The last category is called *no change*: 9 persons after three years of treatment showed no lasting improvement.[34]

---

[34] *On the Origins and Treatment of Homosexuality*, pp. 250–56. The author holds that those who showed no improvement were more deeply neurotic and lacked motivation to do the exercises prescribed.

Drawing a modest conclusion from his arduous work, the author says it is not true

that a homosexual neurosis is irremediable, but on the other hand, it would be thoughtless to state that a complete cure would be within reach after a few years of (self) treatment for the majority of the people who suffer from this problem. What the great majority can achieve, however, is a very substantial improvement in their emotional stability, inclusive of its sexual aspects, while a minority even comes to a full cure. This fact contradicts the pessimistic and fatalistic ideas often divulged relative to the changeability of homosexuality.[35]

The Pattison Study

E. Mansell Pattison and Myrna Loy Pattison made an important study of eleven white men from a pentecostal church who made the transition from exclusive homosexuality to heterosexuality without the benefit of formal therapy. Pattison sees this change as "religiously mediated".[36]

The men described themselves as *ex-gay*, a term they chose to denote their opposition to the "gay-liberation" movement, which believes that one should accept a condition assumed to be unchangeable. This change took place within the context of the pentecostal church fellowship without any psychotherapy or other professional intervention. The Pattisons obtained permission to review all the crisis program records, interviewing all eleven members according to professional standards and also interviewing the wives of the six men who had married.

The study provided a substantial body of evidence for the possibility of change from exclusive homosexuality to exclusive heterosexuality. The Pattisons' data showed that significant changes had occurred over an average period of four years, that the age range was 21 to 35 with a mean age of 27, that all the men

[35] Ibid., p. 257.
[36] "Ex-Gays: Religously Mediated Change in Homosexuals", 1553–62.

had experienced homosexual proclivities before the age of 15, and that the mean age for the transition to exclusive heterosexuality was 23. The Pattisons compared their data with two previous larger studies: Bell and Weinberg (1978) and Saghir and Robins (1973). They noted that change was not sudden and magical but occurred over a period of years. The subjects who married did not attempt to hide their orientation from their wives. There was in these men another important difference. According to their religious convictions, "sexual intercourse is the consequence of love and an expected part of a marital relationship. Premarital and extramarital sexual experience is considered immoral; heterosexual promiscuity is as immoral as homosexual promiscuity."[37]

It was also noted that their motivation for marriage was different from other homosexuals who marry in an attempt to prove to themselves that they are *not* homosexual. The six men who married first worked to get rid of their homosexual condition, and later they experienced heterosexual attraction, which led them into marriage. From this the Pattisons observe that "beliefs and values appear to play a significant role in changing sexual orientation."[38] Again, the authors noted that the subjects who married did not experience an immediate disappearance of homosexual dreams, fantasies, and impulses, but, as their marital relationships progressed in satisfactory manner, such "dreams, fantasies, and impulses gradually diminished over time."[39]

The Pattisons emphasize that significant change *gradually* took place in these men, and that comparative youth was in their favor. It was also conducive to change that they did not hold that "gay is good", while at the same time they did not root personal

[37] Ibid., 1556.

[38] Ibid., 1558.

[39] Ibid., 1559. Not surprisingly, "all our subjects displayed some effeminate mannerisms. . . . These mannerisms persisted despite their current strong heterosexual orientation" (1558).

identity in their homosexual tendencies.[40] Finally, the authors note the importance of one's definition of homosexuality. If it is defined as fixed and immutable, then the chances for change are slim; if it is defined as changeable, then change can be viewed as possible.[41]

Unfortunately, I could not find any follow-up of this study, or any replication of it in a group similarly motivated. Stanton Jones and Don Workman comment that the only conclusion one can draw from the Pattisons' study is that "some success is possible through these [spiritual] means".[42]

George A. Rekers

George A. Rekers, who has spent many years researching and writing about the formation of the homosexual orientation in childhood, points out that research and clinical experience show that there are a variety of forms of homosexuality and that there is "a certain amount of diversity in the combination of influential variables present for one individual *vs.* another individual".[43]

Rekers acknowledges the fact that there are many variables in the formation of a homosexual orientation—a point not made by authors who begin with the premise that it is an unchangeable condition. In his review of the literature on the formation of both male and female homosexuals during childhood, Rekers singles out "childhood gender nonconformity" as the most important variable—"a very strong predictor of adult sexual preference".[44]

[40] Ibid., 1561.

[41] Ibid., 1562.

[42] "Homosexuality: The Behavioral Sciences and the Church", *Journal of Psychology and Theology* 17, no. 3, Rosemead School of Theology (1989).

[43] "The Formation of a Homosexual Orientation", in *Hope for Homosexuality*, ed. Patrick Fagan (Washington, D.C.: Free Congress Research and Educational Foundation, 1988), p. 1.

[44] Ibid., pp. 9 (males), 14 (females).

Rekers makes copious reference to the Bell, Weinberg, and Hammersmith study of 1981, which held that "prior theories on the development of homosexuality have exaggerated the role of the parents in the development of their sons' sexual orientation. . . . [Also] identification with the parent of the same sex was found to have only a weak connection to the development of the individual's sexual orientation".[45]

So far all the references have been to *retrospective* studies. *Prospective* longitudinal studies also indicate that effeminate behavior in boys is fairly predictive of adult homosexuality.[46] Rekers stresses that

> gender roles then become stereotypic expectations reenforced in individual children by differential parental practices in child rearing. These day to day child-rearing practices differentially received by boys and girls are considered to constitute the major contributions to gender development and sexual identity formation, if we can generalize from all the currently available research.[47]

The Importance of Rekers' Conclusions

From his many years of clinical practice and research, moreover, Rekers draws two conclusions: (1) that the "precise sequence and interaction of variables involved in the etiology of homosexual orientation are not yet completely understood" and (2) that the integration of the data would indicate the need for "the prevention and compassionate early treatment of homosexual orientation".[48] Already Dr. Rekers has experimen-

[45] Ibid., pp. 10–11. The full reference is: A. P. Bell, M. S. Weinberg, and S. K. Hammersmith, *Sexual Preference: Its Development in Men and Women* (Bloomington: Indiana Univ. Press, 1981). This study is in contrast to the findings of Elizabeth Moberly in *Psychogenesis*.

[46] Rekers, "Formation of a Homosexual Orientation", p. 16. Unfortunately, prospective studies on girls with gender disturbances are scanty (p. 17).

[47] Ibid., p. 19.

[48] Ibid., p. 21.

tally demonstrated an affective treatment (treatment of emotions) for "gender identity disorder of childhood", which is meant to hold potential for preventing homosexual orientation in males.[49]

Rekers' work is important for several reasons. First of all, he stresses that the homosexual condition varies from individual to individual in terms of the factors that brought it about; secondly, he places more emphasis upon childhood nonconforming behavior and less on failure to identify in gender with a same-sex parental figure. Thirdly, he has used an affective treatment for gender identity disorder in childhood, which may help to prevent the development of homosexual tendencies.

Ismond Rosen

Ismond Rosen, a British psychoanalyst, sees homosexual orientation as learned, and, if it becomes a part of the individual's sense of identity, "the chances of that person changing to a heterosexual orientation become much more remote".[50]

From his study and clinical practice he understands the deep self-hatred of the homosexual person as coming from the traumas of his childhood and not from society's disapproval of homosexual behavior.[51] Like Irving Bieber, he sees the importance of the father–son relationship: "For males the presence of a good loving father during development is probably the best proof against homosexual development. I can think of no case of homosexuality I have had to deal with where such a father has been present in the childhood years of development."[52]

It is interesting that in Rosen's criteria for change he rates

[49] Ibid.

[50] Ismond Rosen, "Psychoanalysis and Homosexuality: A Critical Appraisal of Helpful Attitudes", in *Hope for Homosexuality*, p. 33.

[51] Ibid., p. 35.

[52] Ibid., p. 40.

three elements in this order: (1) high motivation; (2) youthfulness (late adolescence, young adult); and (3) fantasies, with little genital experience. In his criteria for lack of change he places first "no desire for change", and second "excessive passivity".[53] He stresses that *full* heterosexuality goes beyond sexual behavior, requiring *emotional* detachment from the same-sex object, the ability to become emotionally involved with a person of the opposite sex, and the ability to love such a person. Rosen concludes by reiterating that psychoanalysis can help individuals "to gain understanding of their inner and outer reality and can bring change, alleviation, or acceptance."[54] In other words, some can become heterosexual, some are not able to change orientation but have gotten rid of many negative feelings, and some accept an orientation without the need for destructive acting out.

Rosen does not make any exaggerated claims for his method. He singles out high motivation as the most important element in change of orientation and the lack of motivation, coupled with "excessive passivity", as the most important factors in those who do not change. This correlates well with the positions of counselors and therapists who make the person of Christ the inspiration for wanting either to get rid of homosexual orientation or to reduce its effects upon one's interior life of prayer and external behavior. Rosen also places his finger upon emotional overattachment to a person of the same sex as a *real obstacle* to the development of an emotional attachment to an opposite-sex person. This insight is often lacking in persons who have ceased homosexual behavior but remain in an emotional attachment to a same-sex person. Learning how to remain friends with such a person, while reducing the emotional attachment, is the task that the therapist or counselor should give the individual. In some situations the client needs to break completely with the other person.

[53] Ibid., pp. 40–41.
[54] Ibid., p. 43.

Charles Socarides

At the Free Congress Conference where Rekers and Socarides presented their papers, Charles W. Socarides approached the issue of homosexuality and change from another angle, as the title of his paper indicates: "Sexual Politics and Scientific Logic: The Issue of Homosexuality".[55]

Socarides describes in historical detail the manipulative manner by which a small group of psychiatrists in league with gay organizations succeeded in having the American Psychiatric Association remove the condition of homosexuality from the *Diagnostic and Statistical Manual* (DSM III). Henceforward, homosexuality would be considered a *normal* variant of sexual behavior. Eventually this led to the elimination of the word *homosexual* as a scientific category from the DSM Revised 1987 edition (DSM-III-R).[56]

Among the disastrous effects of making homosexuality a normal variant of sexual behavior is the abandonment of those persons with homosexual tendencies who want help to move toward heterosexuality as the natural and God-given state for men and women. Why should one seek therapy for a lifestyle now considered "normal"? As a result, much research works on the premise that a homosexual lifestyle is a perfectly valid alter-

[55] In *Hope for Homosexuality*, pp. 46–64. In his new book *Homosexuality: A Freedom Too Far* (Phoenix, Ariz.: Adam Margrave Books, 1995), Socarides contends that the homosexual movement had a legitimate purpose in overcoming bias and violence against homosexual persons but that now it has gone too far by attempting to alter the basic male–female design. He views the homosexual movement as an attack on our civilization.

[56] Socarides, *Hope for Homosexuality*, p. 52. The author notes that he received unexpected proof of "the politicization of American Psychiatry" from Ronald Bayer, a fellow of the Hastings Institute of New York, "who leaves no doubt as to his being in sympathy with such action" (p. 54). See Ronald Bayer, *Homosexuality and American Psychiatry*, esp. chap. 4, "Diagnostic Politics and the American Psychiatric Association" (Princeton, N.J.: Princeton Univ. Press, 1987), pp. 101–54.

native to marriage. Pastoral counselors (and indeed some confessors) say to clients or penitents, "What's your problem?" The implication is clear: Go, find your steady lover. It is clear, then, that Socarides holds that homosexuality is a disorder that should be treated.

Lawrence Hatterer

Our next author, Lawrence Hatterer, will agree. His extensive research and clinical practice cannot be ignored. *Changing Homosexuality in the Male* [57] remains an important contribution to the issue of whether one is able to change one's sexual orientation from homosexual to heterosexual. From a study of his data I believe he has made his point that homosexual men can make the transition from homosexual orientation to heterosexual. Indeed, I invite the reader to peruse the more than 450 pages of data Hatterer has gathered. One may object that the individuals were able to change their behavior but not their deep fantasies and desires, and this may be true in some cases, which he designates as "partial" cures; but other persons come across as having made the internal transformation necessary to be really heterosexual in orientation.

Hatterer is rigorously honest in summing up his exhaustive ten-year study: "To confirm my own observations I have used a mass of tape-recorded data collected during the four pilot studies (1959–69) conducted at the Payne Whitney Psychiatric Clinic and in the Department of Psychiatry of the Cornell U. College of Medicine." Adding that he has treated patients for periods ranging from one month to fifteen years, from three to 375 hours, and from ages sixteen to sixty-five, he continues: "I have also collected two- to fifteen-year follow-ups on some patients. Of this group forty-nine patients recovered, nineteen par-

[57] L. Hatterer, *Changing Homosexuality in the Male* (New York: McGraw-Hill, 1970).

tially recovered, seventy-six remained homosexual. Among those who recovered, twenty married, ten remain married, two divorced, and eighteen achieved sexual and social heterosexual adjustments. One- to five-year follow-ups were positive for nineteen patients and five- to fifteen-year follow-ups were positive for eighteen patients. Of those partially recovered patients, all remained single but one, and one- to fourteen-year positive follow-ups exist on seven patients." [58]

Hatterer did not continue with men whom he judged "untreatable" at the time; however, he would ask them to come back when they were ready for treatment. Believing that the attitude of the therapist is all important, he states his own credo: "*No man should be yoked by any stereotyped notion of idealized maleness or a single way of life. Every man has to be the kind of man that he can be within the limitations of his past, his present, and what he can envision as a future for himself*" (italics in original). [59]

While I cannot agree with one part of Hatterer's methodology, namely, the encouragement of masturbation based upon fantasy of a person of the other sex and the acceptance of foreplay and sexual intercourse before marriage, I accept many other dimensions of his treatment program, such as inquiry into self-acceptance, into relationships with parents, into relationships with members of one's own sex, into fear and hostility concerning the other sex, in brief, into all the other aspects of human relationships, going far beyond the sexual-genital. What is lacking in Hatterer's approach is the spiritual and the supernatural, but that is not surprising since his unspoken premises are evolutionary and naturalistic. But one thing he has done well. He has documented the fact that some persons who were truly homosexual at the onset of treatment have been able over the course of time to make the difficult transition not only to heterosexual behavior but also to a heterosexual orientation.

[58] Ibid., pp. vii–viii.
[59] Ibid., p. ix.

Prominent Christian Therapists

It is time now to review several prominent Christian therapists who have helped persons of both sexes to move away from a homosexual orientation. The first will be Leanne Payne, author of *The Broken Image*, *The Healing of the Homosexual*, *Crisis in Masculinity*, and *Restoring the Christian Soul through Healing Prayer*. In *The Broken Image* one finds the core of Payne's thought and method, the integration of prayerful insight, garnered from the great spiritual masters, including C. S. Lewis, with psychological truth. She makes use of healing prayer to help persons with homosexual identity problems to attain spiritual wholeness, since in her view homosexuality is a sexual neurosis.

Leanne Payne

To understand Payne's philosophy, I shall turn to *The Broken Image* and review the case of Lisa.[60] Lisa sought out Payne because she was lonely, estranged from her parents, and besieged with lesbian fantasies as the result of such an experience in childhood. Payne prayed with her for the healing of memories, invoking the presence of Jesus to explore the first years of life. But Lisa's memory was blank for the first five years, and after that she remembered much that was traumatic. Payne then asked Jesus' help so that Lisa could go further back into memory for some clue to explain her estrangement from both parents, and after a time Lisa remembered being sexually abused by her father and her mother coming upon the scene and throwing her daughter across the room. The father shouted that the child would never remember. That is what happened; the child quickly suppressed the memory, but it continued to fester in her, leading over the

[60] Leanne Payne, *The Broken Image* (Westchester, Ill.: Crossway Books, 1981), pp. 15–32.

years to estrangement, not only from her parents but also from others and even from herself.

With the help of Jesus, and with Payne alongside her, Lisa was able to face the horrible memory. She was able to forgive her father and her mother. She became a new person from that day onward. For nineteen years the unhealed memory had lain like a cancer within her heart, and now the process of healing had begun.

Lisa had to take other steps, learning to practice the presence of Jesus even if she did not sense him, hearing the word of the Spirit instead of the negative words of self-hatred, knowing herself as God's child and accepting herself and others, and placing her identity in Christ. She learned to relate to other women her own age. As she reviewed the years of unhealed memories, everything was seen in a new light.

All this points out the power of memory:

> In prayer for the healing of memories the power of the memory to make the past present to us in a very real way is extraordinary. The reason for this, of course, is that Jesus, the Infinite One, who is outside of time and to whom all things are present, enters into what for us is a past occurrence, one known only in retrospect, though we experience its consequences in the present.[61]

Payne is careful to point out the nature of healing of memories: "The *essential* action that differentiates healing of memories from psychological methodologies is the action of the Holy Spirit pointing to the *Presence of our Lord who is there*" (italics in the original).[62] Again, the healing of memories is not magic, as the story of Lisa illustrates. It is a work of prayer done under the careful guidance of a Christian therapist like Leanne Payne, who, in turn, seeks the help of the Holy Spirit and the presence of Christ. It is, then, more than psychological methodology.

[61] Ibid., p. 27.
[62] Ibid.

I shall omit the rest of Lisa's journey to psychological and spiritual wholeness. The point I wish to make is that a deeply spiritual therapist who also understands the dynamics of the human heart can help her client integrate prayer with sound psychological procedures. With regard to Lisa, Payne says that

> she needed to be brought into the Presence of the Lord, there to be healed of this traumatic memory. . . . Coming into union with Him who not only *heals*, but *completes*, she would gain release from self-hatred and fear, and the strength to rise above the limitations the circumstances of her life had placed upon her. Enabled to accept herself, she would then be able to love and accept others.[63]

In Lisa's life this is particularly true with respect to her relationship with her mother, who, she felt, had rejected her at the time of her father's sexual abuse. To be sure, Lisa was not consciously aware of this rejection, but she was aware of her need to be close to another woman. Thus, she fell into the hands of a lesbian school teacher. Commenting on this dynamic, Payne observes that "as a sexual neurosis, lesbian behavior . . . is not nearly so complicated as male homosexual behavior".[64]

Leanne Payne's ministry to thousands of wounded persons, many of them with homosexual problems, has expanded into Pastoral Care Ministries. This is a team of persons who follow her approach.[65]

Her recent work *Restoring the Christian Soul through Healing Prayer* goes beyond the problem of homosexuality to help persons suffering from other emotional problems; nonetheless, her insights in this volume apply to homosexual strugglers, as the reader may discern when she says:

[63] Ibid., p. 31.

[64] Ibid., p. 29.

[65] *Restoring the Christian Soul through Healing Prayer* (Wheaton, Ill.: Crossway Books, 1991), pp. xi–xii.

> We are continually helping Christians to hurdle one or another
> of the three great barriers to personal and spiritual wholeness in
> Christ. They are (1) the failure to gain the great Christian virtue
> of self-acceptance, (2) the failure to forgive others, and (3) the
> failure to receive forgiveness for oneself. [66]

While the data showing change of sexual orientation are
anecdotal and biographical in the works of Leanne Payne (as
well as in some of the other authors I will present), that fact
does not detract from the *credibility* of her data. A careful reading
or review of *The Broken Image* will help the reader to see that
Payne gives at least ten biographies of men and women with
homosexual difficulties, none of which is a carbon copy of the
others. She discerns the many factors operative in the development of a homosexual orientation.

Another Christian woman psychologist has similarly provided
professional therapists with germinal concepts for the healing of
the homosexual person: Elizabeth Moberly, in *Psychogenesis: The
Early Development of Gender Identity*. Since I have already reviewed Moberly's research,[67] I am considering here authors who
have applied her theories in clinical or pastoral practice. In doing
so I credit Moberly with very original and significant insights.

Andy Comiskey

Pursuing Sexual Wholeness: How Jesus Heals the Homosexual, by
Andy Comiskey, follows the gender-specific therapy approach
of Moberly, while also imitating the forms of prayer used by

---

[66] Preface, p. xiii. In my book *The Homosexual Person*, I refer to Payne's
analysis of narcissism in *The Broken Image*: "The flipside of the wrong kind of
self-love will always be some form of self-hatred. Inordinate self-love, which
is, psychologically speaking, an immaturity in the personality, is the reverse
side of a deep insecurity" (p. 94). I also comment on Matthew's story (p. 194).

[67] See *The Homosexual Person*, pp. 38–48, 60–62; see also *Linacre Quarterly*
(May 1984), pp. 185–88, for my review of *Psychogenesis*, and (February 1986),
pp. 87–90, for my review of *Psychology of Self and Other*.

Payne. Comiskey presents a detailed investigation of the interaction of psychological factors and insights gained through prayer. Intellectually he has grasped the theory of Moberly concerning the psychodynamics of the homosexual condition, and he has applied it in his pastoral practice.

Coming out of a biblical understanding of the meaning of human sexual activity as found in Genesis 1:2 and throughout the Old and New Testaments, Comiskey believes that the counselor and the counselee must both center their lives in Jesus Christ, the God-Man, praying constantly for the light of the Holy Spirit to understand the innermost dispositions of one's heart.

He is eloquent in his analysis of modern idolatry:

> What does Israel's spiritual and sexual idolatry have to do with us today? *Plenty*. Whenever anyone, Christian or not, yields his body to another for erotic gratification outside the heterosexual context, he makes a sacrifice to Baal. The principality of perversion is alive and well. We bow down to it whenever we engage in sexual immorality. We may not mouth prayers to Baal or Asteroth, but we worship them with each illicit orgasm, each immoral fantasy, each pornographic watch we keep, each seductive, controlling gesture.[68]

Comiskey shows how Moberly's insights concerning the need for same-sex identification worked their way out in his own life and those of other men and women. He is honest about the difficulties of moving away from homosexuality into a heterosexual way of thinking and feeling, about relapses, about beginning again, and about the gradual nature of change. He stresses the need that each person has for others: "Christ's indwelling presence in no way frees people from needing others; it simply enables them to need others in a normal and appropriate way."[69]

---

[68] A. Comiskey, *Pursuing Sexual Wholeness* (Lake Mary, Fl.: Creation House, 1989), p. 100. Comiskey publishes a companion guidebook that he uses in his instructions at Desert Streams (a ministry to persons with homosexual difficulties).

[69] Ibid., p. 167.

From Comiskey's testimony and that of his counselees, more-over, it is clear to me that he and some of his counselees have been able to overcome homosexual tendencies while developing a lasting physical attraction to members of the other sex. In this "struggle", as he aptly calls it, he has been willing to become part of a support group, sharing his vulnerabilities as well as his strengths. As I have said, Comiskey sees Christ at the center of his work. "And that wholeness won't be completely realized until we see Him face to face in glory "[70]

Comiskey states eloquently two points about the conversion process:

> Two keys can be drawn from this realization. First, since Jesus is the goal, personal wholeness is *not*. Our priorities must be or-dered correctly. When strugglers make perfect heterosexual responsiveness the mark, they subordinate Christ's call to dis-cipleship to a static psychological ideal. They become increas-ingly whole as they will to follow him; sexual reorientation occurs out of spiritual conversion. . . . Second, we cannot ex-pect to experience a complete absence of sexual struggles in this lifetime. . . . That means the homosexual struggler may still ex-perience homosexual temptations. . . . None of that minimizes God's healing power. . . . What the struggler can reasonably ex-pect is to become *whole enough* in this lifetime to sustain ful-filling, heterosexual relationships. By this I mean the capacity to relate intimately, but non-erotically, with the same sex and the freedom to encounter the opposite sex as a desired counter-part—with interest, not fear or distaste. . . . Furthermore, Jesus has granted me enough heterosexual desire and personal matu-rity to love a woman, take her as my wife, and oversee a house-hold and growing family.[71]

This long quotation reveals the realistic goal that Comiskey set for himself. It is refreshingly different from the artificial dis-tinction between heterosexual behavior and homosexual orien-tation, in which without empiricial evidence the orientation is

[70] Ibid., p. 187.
[71] Ibid., pp. 187–88.

considered fixed forever. Comiskey also centers in on the destructive effects of an unaffirmed gender identity, giving examples from his counseling experience, indeed including his own struggle in this regard.[72]

There are, however, views of Comiskey's with which I have some difficulties. There is little discussion of the contribution that a professional therapist can make to the theocentric process used by Comiskey. This is not a criticism of Comiskey's use of prayer. Together with others in Exodus Comiskey gives the impression that one does not really attain sexual wholeness unless one marries. That some persons can be sexually whole and celibate is not adequately discussed. These are questions upon which we could have a fruitful ecumenical dialogue.

Nonetheless, Comiskey demonstrates that some Christians can change their sexual orientation to the point where they are predominantly heterosexual. More importantly, he places the whole question of change of orientation in a theocentric context, making union with Christ the primary objective of his program while demonstrating the overwhelming impact that spiritual motives, rooted in the gospel, have in the process of change.

Dr. Jeffrey Satinover regards the ministry of Desert Streams with its Living Waters Program as one of the largest and most successful groups under the Exodus umbrella. He praises Comiskey's book for its biblical approach to the healing of male and female homosexuality as well as for his own story of movement out of the homosexual lifestyle into marriage with full commitment to his roles as father, husband, and ministry leader. In his Living Waters Program Comiskey takes an average of fifty-five people over a forty-week program, with 50 percent completing it "with substantial progress out of homosexuality and into heterosexuality, while 33 percent make little or no progress, fre-

[72] Ibid., pp. 113–25.

quently regressing back into active homosexual behavior upon leaving the program".[73]

Dr. William Consiglio and "the Overcomer"

Our next author who believes that homosexual orientation and behavior are learned and subject to change is Dr. William Consiglio. With over a decade of counseling homosexual men through an approach called "reorientation therapy", Dr. Consiglio offers practical strategies to those who want not only to overcome homosexual behavior patterns but also to develop a heterosexual orientation. Like Comiskey, he makes good use of biblical insights, and, in my judgment, he develops on the level of individual guidance an effective integration of faith-knowledge and self-understanding and awareness. His book has something for the homosexual person wanting to get out of the condition. It proposes a spiritual plan of action that utilizes transactional analysis techniques and biblical reflections to guide the counselee in daily life, leading to what the author calls "daily self-therapy".[74]

The author gives sound advice to counselors as well, stressing the need for loving patience in guiding their counselees over a period of time while delineating clearly the steps leading unconsciously to a homosexual orientation: low self-esteem, gender emptiness, gender attraction, sexual attraction, homosexual reinforcement, and homosexual identity. Through "Bob's Journal" he illustrates these stages,[75] asking the question "What do I have to do to change?"[76]

[73] Jeffrey Satinover, "Psychotherapy and the Cure of Souls: Faith and Religious Belief in the Treatment of Homosexuality", *New Techniques in the Treatment of Homosexuality* (Encino, Calif.: NARTH, 1994).

[74] *Homosexual No More: Practical Strategies for Christians Overcoming Homosexuality* (Wheaton, Ill.: Victor Books, Scripture Press, 1991).

[75] Ibid., pp. 57–83.

[76] Ibid., pp. 84–99.

The "overcomer", as Cosiglio terms the counselee, needs to seek change in two different areas, the external and the internal. The external refers to habitual ways of behaving and the environment that one frequents—what the moral theologian might call the external occasions of sin. The internal refers to the way in which he thinks and feels about things, the inner life privy to the person. Changes within this inner life are more difficult, because they have to do with rebuilding self-esteem and getting rid of patterns of denial. Internal changes are then more gradual and imperceptible.[77] But at this juncture one may ask whether complete internal change is possible. Consiglio gives a good response.

Alluding to the truth that men and women, with the exception of Mary and Jesus Christ, are subject to unruly concupiscence, Consiglio believes that homosexual temptations are not completely eradicated, although they can be reduced to the point where they are "minimally bothersome".[78]

In other words, overcomers, counseled by Consiglio, can go through long periods of time without homosexual feelings. Of course, God could eliminate all traces of homosexual desire, if he so willed. But, ordinarily, God gives us graces to bring our emotional life into some degree of stability.[79] It is important that the overcomer tries to find means to cope with emotional difficulties; otherwise, emotional pain may cause him to act out homosexually. This effort to change internally must be in conjunction with efforts to change externally. The author suggests several personal changes.[80] These include wearing gender-appropriate clothing, getting rid of all pornographic materials,

[77] Ibid., p. 84.

[78] Ibid., p. 85.

[79] Ibid., pp. 85–87.

[80] Ibid., pp. 87–94. *Acting out* is a technical term meaning a pattern of defense in which unconscious emotional conflicts are expressed (acted out) in behavior that tends to be maladaptive or antisocial; see, for example, *Abnormal Psychology*, ed. Ephraim Rosen (Philadelphia: Saunders, 1965), p. 524.

and learning one's "triggers" and "setups". "A trigger is anything which directly stimulates sexual excitement or arousal. Erotic books, videos, music, TV programs, the use of alcohol or drugs, provocative clothing, . . . and the like, are all triggers."[81] The author refers to vacation times, loss of a friend, and changing jobs as examples of setups, which he describes as "the people, events or circumstances which provoke the deprivation complex, that wounded area of emotions and defenses which is at the root of homosexuality".[82]

When setups and triggers occur together, it is almost "inevitable that you will be severely tempted to seek out some homosexually related avenue of relief and release. . . . Learning how to tolerate and process your wounded emotions and defenses is at the very heart of healing homosexuality."[83]

With regard to temptation, particularly the temptation to masturbation, Consiglio gives detailed and practical directives. Among the relational changes suggested are chaste same-sex friendships, breaking emotionally dependent relationships, and participation in a spiritual support group that deals with homosexual difficulties. In all these matters the counselor should be an alert coach of the overcomer.[84]

Consiglio sees the process of healing as involving pain, as the chapter title "It Begins to Hurt. You Begin to Heal"[85] indicates. He believes that the overcomer must be in touch with his emotions, because homosexuality has very little to do with sex:

> The sexual involvement with another same-sex person is a symptom; a result; a compromise for the need to be accepted and loved. Healing is emotional work. It is to experience anew as an adult the closeness and oneness, which was not given from

[81] Consiglio, *Homosexual No More*, p. 88.
[82] Ibid., pp. 88–89.
[83] Ibid., p. 89.
[84] Ibid., pp. 89–99.
[85] Ibid., pp. 100–117 (chap. 6).

the first father-male in a child's life. It is the healing of that emotional complex of feelings which was left wounded and sensitive from earliest childhood.[86]

Using the theory of conflicts between inner child and inner parent, Consiglio suggests a series of exercises that will bring about healing. He reminds the overcomer that there is another and stronger part of his personality, and this is his inner adult, which is the voice of his personality, and which is meant to take greater control and direction over his personality. "Your inner adult is the mature and Spirit-led voice of Christ in you."[87]

It is through the Holy Spirit working in us that we can be healed of our wounded emotions. Through our inner adult voice God will heal the conflict between the inner parent and the inner child. The homosexual man will begin to accept himself as a person, no longer needing to look to other men for sexual-genital gratification.[88]

Consiglio conceives three conversations taking place in the overcomer's inner life. The first conversation is with the Lord. The second is between himself and the inner parent; and the third is between himself and the inner child. These conversations affect all of our lives. Turning to the first conversation with God, Consiglio explores the ways overcomers (and probably the rest of us) distort their inner conversation with God, thus blocking the healing power of God. The distortion arises from the false attitudes of the critical inner parent and sensitive inner child.

One must counterbalance these false attitudes with spiritual truths that stress the unconditional love of God. He mentions that we should worship God, not work for him. Here Consiglio means that one does not have to prove his acceptability before God by keeping score on the number of good actions per-

[86] Ibid., p. 101.
[87] Ibid., p. 115.
[88] Ibid., pp. 116–17.

formed. To do that is to be like a child thinking that he will be loved by his parents only if he keeps doing good things. As the overcomer comes to know the real God, he will learn to put away "childish things".

The second conversation is between the inner parent and the self, which Consiglio describes, illustrating his theory with examples from his clinical experience. From the overcomer's first significant relationships in childhood (to parents, siblings, and others) he has learned emotional reactions, which he continues in his present situation—repetitively and unconsciously. Unfortunately, many of these relational reactions are negative and inhibiting, keeping his wounded area sensitive, unhealed, and in need of the homosexual compromise. One's emotional reactions to people are major setups for homosexual temptation.[89]

These transferences from significant relationships of the past to the present are for the overcomer usually negative. The spiritual strategy, then, is to make the overcomer aware of the conversations between the inner parent and the inner child so that he may be able to free himself from the homosexual need that often flows out of the conflict between inner parent and inner child.

In Consiglio's experience it is the voice of the *inner adult*, led by the Spirit, that leads to inner healing. This voice prevents the old familiar complex of painful feelings from overwhelming him and opening the door for homosexual acting out. Consiglio goes on to demonstrate how he uses positive transference in his therapy work, allowing, for example, "a close and emotionally positive transference to take place"[90] with his male clients.

When this is openly discussed and worked through, the male client is able to experience a loving relationship with a male

[89] Ibid., p. 136.
[90] Ibid., p. 138.

that is nonsexual and a powerful source of healing. The over-comer begins acting with the therapist as he would with a good and nurturing parent. This is a powerful and therapeutic transference. It gives the overcomer the opportunity to relive his past anxieties in a trusting relationship, with the result that the underlying wounds, such as distrust, dependency, anger, and the like, begin to lose their grip. The overcomer begins to realize that someone really cares for him. "Experiencing love is the heart of this therapy, for God is love (1 Jn 4:8) and this is God-led therapy." [91]

Consiglio has seen this happen in his clients. For this reason he instructs both therapist and client to look for six transference relationships that either hinder or help the client on the road to healing. Without discussing these dynamics in detail, I found interesting Consiglio's connection of feelings of emasculation with homosexual temptations. He has noticed among his clients a preoccupation with preserving a youthful identity well into their forties and fifties and with changing "gestures, postures, voice and behavior which are effeminate for males or masculine for females." [92] It is encouraging to realize that such mannerisms can be at least toned down, if not eliminated.

Consiglio also has stressed the phenomenon of emotional overdependency, which, as we have often noted, is a problem for many homosexual people, even though they may not have been sexually involved with the other person. Since, in helping homosexual persons, we often concentrate on their relationships with persons of the same sex, it is important to realize that the overcomer often has problems concerning closeness and inti-macy with the *opposite* sex. Homosexual women often have such fear of the opposite sex because of painful memories of the opposite-sex parent. [93]

[91] Ibid.
[92] Ibid., p. 142.
[93] Ibid., p. 148.

Consiglio sees the role of the inner adult as reconciling the inner parent with the inner child by emotionally freeing the inner child from the inner parent. Then the healing of the emotions begins to take place, while homosexual needs begin to fade away. It is a gradual process.[94] Now, however, we need to look into the wounded inner child, to which Consiglio devotes a full chapter.

Invoking the light of the Holy Spirit, Consiglio sees the inner adult as the agent that will bring the inner, emotional child out of hiding. In short, the inner child needs reparenting. It is the role of the inner adult to discipline in love the inner child, to help him see things through, and to act responsibly, or as Consiglio terms it, to be "proactive".[95]

The overcomer must get to know himself all over again by going through four steps, which Consiglio explains with examples.[96] Consiglio warns, however, that whenever the client tries to move through these four steps to get in touch with his inner child, he will experience strong resistance within himself. Since the person has become accustomed to protecting these painful feelings, he may find it difficult to touch them now.

It is not surprising, then, that Consiglio has found that homosexual persons resort to three defensive reactions to avoid coming to terms with buried, painful feelings: fight reactions, flight reactions, and fright reactions. Giving examples of these, Consiglio points out that each reaction "interferes with mature and constructive emotional expression and with interpersonal relationships".[97]

They also keep one isolated and deprived of the intimacy one should have with other men and women. To counterbalance

[94] Ibid., p. 151.
[95] Ibid., p. 155.
[96] Ibid., pp. 156–63.
[97] Ibid., p. 143.

these tendencies, Consiglio suggests that the overcomer should "proact", i.e., come to grips with his wounded feelings:

> It means doing what does not come naturally . . . forcing yourself to overcome the tendency to continue protecting yourself and hiding your sensitive emotions. It means engaging in actions and behaviors which counteract what you have always done before.[98]

Again, Consiglio, giving an example of an overcomer who used this approach, concludes that whenever one acts maturely and forcefully, he will change: "He will begin to feel whole and manly. He will start to see the end of the homosexual attraction and desire." [99]

But this will not happen unless the counselor gives constant and positive direction, using all the steps suggested by Consiglio, and, most particularly, providing overcomers with "a model of a mature, reasonable, and rational adult voice in their lives",[100] which they may internalize.

Consiglio concludes his study with advice for both the overcomer and the counselor, suggesting a series of exercises for the overcomer, while he encourages the counselor to stay with the counselees despite the fact that healing may be as slow as a turtle's movement. Setbacks will probably occur, and at these moments the overcomer will need the support of the counselor. Above all, the counselee must do the daily and weekly work necessary for sustained progress. At the top of the list is *daily prayer of the heart.*[101]

This detailed summary of Consiglio's thought proposes a practical program for many persons with a homosexual orienta-

[98] Ibid., pp. 165–66.

[99] Ibid., p. 168.

[100] Ibid.

[101] Ibid., pp. 170–78. See also William E. Consiglio, "Doing Therapy in an Alien Culture with Christians Overcoming Homosexuality", *Journal of Pastoral Counseling* 28 (1993):66–95, esp. 73.

tion who desire to get rid of the orientation with the hope of developing their heterosexual potential. As he points out in a subsequent article in *The Journal of Pastoral Counseling*, research with similar groups reveals varied outcomes of such programs. Consiglio sees three subgroups of "overcomers".

He terms the first group *functional heterosexuals*, the 25 to 35 percent who follow the program and are able to form enduring and stable heterosexual marriages. The second group, *functional resolution* (35 to 45 percent), have not yet achieved sufficient heterosexual orientation to marry, but they are in transition; some will be able to become heterosexual, while some will remain chaste and Christian in a celibate life. The third group, *dysfunctional* (20 to 40 percent), are those who do not achieve positive change in behavior or in internal reorientation.[102]

Recent Literature on Reorientation

Among more recent books on the issue of reorientation are the studies of Bob Davies and Lori Rentzel, *Coming Out of Homosexuality*; Joe Dallas, *Desires in Conflict*; and Joseph Nicolosi, *Healing Homosexuality*.[103] Like Consiglio's work, each of these books provides insights and valuable guidelines to persons struggling with homosexual desires.

With over a decade of experience in counseling men and women with homosexual conflicts at the live-in community of Love in Action, Bob Davies and Lori Rentzel provide not only theoretical knowledge but also practical guidelines for those willing to do the work of reorientation. Davies himself made the journey out of homosexual orientation and has now been

[102] See Consiglio, "Doing Therapy", 150, for full reference to Consiglio's article. The discussion of outcomes is on p. 73 of the article.

[103] *Coming Out of Homosexuality* (Downers Grove, Ill.: InterVarsity Press, 1993); *Desires in Conflict* (Eugene, Ore.: Harvest House, 1991); *Healing Homosexuality* (Northvale, N.J.: Aronson, 1993).

married ten years. It is significant that in his struggle he practiced his religion faithfully, remaining chaste with group support. Although heterosexual, Lori learned much about her
own femininity as she counseled women with homosexual
orientation. As a result, this book is very balanced in that it
gives serious attention to women's struggles. Lori also writes
insightfully on emotional overattachments in both men and
women.[104]

Joe Dallas, president of Exodus International, approaches the
questions concerning homosexuality from the perspective of
conflict. Writing as a Christian to men and women with homosexual tendencies, Dallas shows the conflict between the desire
to love God and the desire to be loved in a way that God forbids.
A person in such a dilemma is also caught in the conflict between the desire to express sexual love in a normal way in marriage and the desire to seek sexual intimacy with another person
of the same sex. Finally, the desire to share with others comes
into conflict with the desire not to be misunderstood. Dallas
takes an integrated approach to the problems of homosexuality,
using Christian principles and sound psychology to help the individual man or woman. He still believes in sin, interpreting the
classical passage from Romans 1:21, 26–27 to mean that the real
problem is sin, of which homosexuality is but a symptom. He
counsels that homosexuality is not one isolated problem but a
complex phenomenon.[105]

I can cite still other psychologists and religious counselors
who have witnessed change of orientation in their counselees. In

---

[104] *Coming Out of Homosexuality*; see esp. pp. 106–21, "Forming Healthy
Friendships", for a classical treatment of emotional attachments. It is noted
that both Bob Davies and Lori Rentzel worked at Love in Action for more
than a decade under the guidance of Frank Worthen, who came out of many
years in the homosexual lifestyle to found Love in Action. In 1984 he published *Steps Out of Homosexuality*, the pioneer guidebook in this field.

[105] *Desires in Conflict*, pp. 7–14. See also Thomas E. Schmidt, *Straight and
Narrow?* (Downers Grove, Ill.: InterVarsity Press, 1995).

my book *The Homosexual Person*, I refer to the work of Colin Cook.[106] From his clinical experience Jeffrey Keefe also testifies to change of orientation.[107]

Among more recent authors speaking about change of orientation is Joseph Nicolosi, with *Reparative Therapy of Male Homosexuality* and *Healing Homosexuality*. Based upon the ground-breaking research of Elizabeth Moberly, *Reparative Therapy* prefers to use not the word *cure* but rather the word *change*: change in the sense of change in self-identification, seeing self not as homosexual but as "a heterosexual man with a homosexual problem".[108] Once one has made this change in how he views himself, he is receptive to new ways of understanding homosexual behavior and its "motivational basis in early unmet love needs".[109]

Nicolosi then explains how his reparative therapy does not focus directly on heterosexual conversion, concentrating rather on "issues of personal power, gender identity and self image".[110] Believing that change is a lifelong process, Nicolosi quotes at length from a letter by a twenty-five-year-old client explaining his process of change. The client says that therapy

> has broken down most of the fantasy world I had built up around other males. My self-esteem and sense of masculinity have improved, and this is reflected in my success at work and my newly

[106] See pp. 136–45. See also Cook's Tape of the Month (TOM, P.O. Box 18522, Denver, CO 80218); these monthly tapes provide interesting insights into the psychological and spiritual dimensions of homosexuality. Recommended with reservations concerning his theology of original sin and grace.

[107] "The fact, reported in the literature, proves the possibility. I have seen some homosexuals in treatment—and have met more former homosexuals (including those who were exclusively so)—who now respond physically and emotionally as heterosexuals in successful marriages": *The Homosexual Person*, p. 76.

[108] *Reparative Therapy of Male Homosexuality*, p. 165.

[109] Ibid.

[110] Ibid., p. 166.

established male relationships. I have even started dating, and now I definitely see marriage and children in my future.[111]

The letter goes on to point out that the attraction to other men has not gone away, but it has certainly diminished. One learns how to form wholesome male friendships through therapy, prayer life, including the sacraments of the Church, and participation in a group support system.

I believe that Nicolosi's position is rooted in reality. His use of the word *change* instead of *cure* makes sense if we consider other psychological conditions. It is held, for example, that the alcoholic is never fully cured of his desire to drink, yet the A.A program and rehabilitation centers offer him an effective way of dealing with his condition. Persons with low self-esteem are seldom fully free of self-doubting. For this reason Nicolosi thinks in terms of growth into "healthy, non-erotic male relationships. Then, for some, celibacy will be the solution; for others, heterosexual marriage is the hoped for goal."[112]

Nicolosi seems to be referring to some individuals who have moved away from homosexual fantasy but have not been able to develop physical attraction to the other sex.[113] In this situation celibacy should be pursued instead of marriage. We must make room, moreover, for the person who, having developed physical attraction to persons of the other sex, chooses celibacy for reasons of faith.

Without attempting to give a full list of authors who have written about change of orientation, I shall mention a few more. Ed Hurst, in *Laying the Axe to the Root of the Trees*,[114] looks at nine sins that are the roots of homosexual temptations. J. A. Conrad's *You Don't Have to Be Gay*[115] is written as a series of letters from

---

[111] Ibid., p. 167.

[112] Ibid., p. 168.

[113] *Healing Homosexuality*. Here the author applies reparative therapy.

[114] Revised ed. (St. Paul, Minn.: Outpost, 1984).

[115] Newport Beach, Calif.: Pacific Publishing House, 1987.

the author, a former homosexual, to a friend who is struggling with whether or not to try to leave the gay life. The books of Frank Worthen, Hurst, Conrad, and others on the subject can be purchased through Regeneration Books (P.O. Box 9830, Baltimore, Md., 21284). From the same address comes *Regeneration News*, published monthly by Alan P. Medinger, with timely articles on heredity, change, and the meaning of "healing".

Conclusions

At the beginning of this section I asked whether it is possible to change from a homosexual orientation to a heterosexual one. After mentioning organizations that believe such a change is possible, I referred to the American Psychiatric Association, which by and large represents the view that such change is not possible. Then I reviewed representative authors of the negative opinion: C. A. Tripp, Robert Bidwell, Richard Green, and Laura Reiter. I added my critical analysis of these views, pointing not only to the limitations of their empirical data but also to the a priori assumptions that guided their research. One of these is that human sexuality is purely evolutionary. Another is that it is value neutral, or that a homosexual lifestyle is a normal variant from marriage.

Next, I turned to clinical psychologists and psychiatrists who believe that one can move from homosexuality to heterosexuality. Among these are Gerald van den Aardweg, E. Mansell and Myrna Loy Pattison, George Rekers, Charles W. Socarides, Ismond Rosen, and Lawrence Hatterer. Among religious counselors who have professional knowledge and experience of this question I singled out Elizabeth Moberly, Leanne Payne,[116] Andy Comiskey, William Consiglio, Joe Dallas, Bob Davies, Lori Rentzel, and Frank Worthen. All these professional men and

---

[116] See Jeffrey Satinover's glowing tribute to the ministry of Leanne Payne, Pastoral Care Ministries, in "Psychotherapy and the Cure of Souls", pp. 87–90.

women present evidence that their counselees have been able to make the journey from homosexuality to heterosexuality. Some of these counselors, moreover, were homosexual in orientation themselves, such as Frank Worthen, Andy Comiskey, Colin Cook, Bob Davies, Starla Allen, and Alan Medinger. They make it clear, however, that they were able to make the transition by the help of God's grace.

Thus, from the combined testimony of secular professionals and religious counselors, one may draw the modest conclusion that some persons with a homosexual orientation can acquire a heterosexual one through a process of prayer, group support, and sound therapy. This is not to say that everyone who seeks such change is able to attain it. It does not mean, moreover, that individuals who have traveled over into heterosexuality and, in many cases, have married will be immune from homosexual attractions. They will be able to handle them if they follow the directives given them by their counselors while continuing to relate to the other sex. Now, however, it is time to consider the related question posed at the beginning of this section: If change of orientation is not possible for a given individual, can he lead a life of sexual abstinence, or celibacy?

5

SEXUAL ABSTINENCE
AND HOMOSEXUAL ORIENTATION

In response to the difficulty found in the situation of an individual who has not been able to get rid of the condition of homosexuality, for whatever reason, and realizes that the only way he can fulfill the divine mandate of chastity is to practice sexual abstinence, I make the following points:

(1) Sexual abstinence means precisely the avoidance of genital acts and all that leads up to orgasm. It does not mean that one may not express physical affection by nongenital acts, such as kissing, embracing, and hugging. (2) Such sexual abstinence becomes a form of love if the motive is the love of Jesus Christ. In this way sexual abstinence becomes consecrated celibacy. It is the only effective motive, because not even the fear of death keeps people from seeking sexual satisfaction. (3) One should not allow the practice of celibacy to become a burden, like the priest who complained to me during a retreat about "this goddamn celibacy". One needs to strengthen his love for Christ through the daily habit of mental prayer, better known as the prayer of the heart, and through the formation of chaste friendships, which often begin at spiritual support meetings, like those of Courage.

(4) One must work out a spiritual strategy for contending with bouts of loneliness, restlessness, and discouragement. It is important to have a spiritual director or friend one can call. Also

one can go before the Blessed Sacrament and talk with Our Lord about the situation. In this way one remains in the *real* world instead of the world of fantasy and isolation. (5) As other writers have pointed out, for example, Father Benedict Groeschel and William Consiglio, one has to be aware of dangerous changes of mood, which in the past have triggered bouts with masturbation or cruising or indulgence in pornography. When these occur, one should immediately take a step back into reality.[1]

While no doubt it is difficult to live a celibate life in our sex-saturated culture, it has been done by the grace of God by many Christians throughout the history of the Church. In the Catholic tradition consecrated celibacy has always been held in high regard. Contrary to widespread opinion, one does not have to be a monk, a nun, or a priest to live this kind of life. For those who sincerely desire to be celibate, God's grace is always present. God always gives to the individual sufficient grace to fulfill the moral law, as Saint Augustine taught: "God does not command impossible things, but, in commanding, He admonishes us both to do what you can do, and to seek His grace to do what you cannot do."[2]

Among gay propagandists celibacy is seen as a form of sexual suicide, a deprivation of the power to love, but this is a myth. The celibate must never renounce the ability to love. His celibacy enlarges his capacity to love God and to love his neighbor. The lives of celibate saints and the lives of many living celibate

[1] John F. Harvey, "The Pastoral Problem of Masturbation", *Linacre Quarterly* 60 (May 1993):24–49, esp. 34–47.

[2] *De natura et gratia*, chap. 43, no. 50 (Migne, PL 44:271). Pius XII referred to the Sixth Session of the Council of Trent and to this passage quoted from St. Augustine in support of the position that at times extended continence may be required of the married: "In confirmation of this argument we have the Council of Trent, which, in its chapter on the observance, necessary and possible, of the commandments, teaches us that, as St. Augustine said, 'God does not command impossible things' ", *Moral Questions concerning Married Life* (Washington, D.C.: NCWC, 1951), chap. 2, no. 40, p. 16. The same principle applies to persons with homosexual tendencies seeking to be chaste.

persons can be understood only in terms of their love of God and of the persons to whom they minister. Like many others, the gay activists confuse human love with sexual-genital satisfaction.[3]

Having affirmed the positive value of celibacy in the lives of many Christians, including individuals with homosexual orientation, I turn now to related questions proposed by members of Courage or Exodus. The first question may be stated in this fashion: If homosexual orientation is an "objective disorder", as the Sacred Congregation for the Doctrine of the Faith holds in its "Letter to the Bishops of the Catholic Church on the Pastoral Care of Homosexual Persons",[4] then are not homosexual Catholics obliged to seek to change their sexual orientation?

I respond that an obligation does not bind in conscience unless the moral law *clearly* demands it and the person is able to carry it out. Thus, the person with homosexual tendencies is bound to sexual abstinence by the gospel precept of chastity and to the means of practicing chastity, but he does not have an obligation to take steps to change his orientation. However desirable this change may be, we can give no guarantee in our present state of knowledge that if one were to follow a certain program and plan of life to change orientation it would always happen; since, therefore, it cannot be proven that such change will inevitably occur if we do certain things, one cannot impose an obligation to take certain steps for such a change. The basic ethical principle applicable to this situation is that one cannot impose an obligation unless one is *certain* it exists.

---

[3] Jordan Aumann and Dr. Conrad Baars, *The Unquiet Heart: Reflections on Love and Celibacy* (New York: Alba House, 1991), pp. 87–95. Fr. Jordan warns celibates not to become involved in a purely emotional relationship that takes away the freedom of celibacy (pp. 87–88).

[4] Section 3: "Although the particular inclination of the homosexual person is not a sin, it is a more or less strong tendency ordered toward an intrinsic moral evil; and thus the inclination itself must be seen as an objective disorder."

Even if a particular program under the direction of a therapist of great reputation worked in the majority of cases and could be considered as a method very probably beneficial to a given individual, it may still be seen as optional and extraordinary for this individual for various reasons, not the least of which is the financial cost. So much, then, for the *obligation* question.

Young people, however, should be encouraged to seek to get rid of the homosexual condition because they are far more likely to be chaste now if they have a vision of hope for the future. In the opinion of Dr. Jeffrey Satinover, who works with Leanne Payne, the hope of change is the main issue for many young people struggling with homosexual desires. Is it not better to struggle to get out of the condition than to resign oneself to the situation as a cross one must bear for the rest of one's life? A young person believing that he cannot get out of the condition is vulnerable to the gay propaganda that states that homosexuality is a natural variant to heterosexuality and that the gay lifestyle is an alternative to marriage.[5]

The person with homosexual orientation lives in the occasion of sin in a special sense; that is to say, the occasion of sin is within his own heart and mind. He may find himself immersed in homosexual ways of thinking and acting. This means getting rid of homosexual literature, tapes, and videos; avoiding homosexual bars, movie theaters, and bathhouses; cutting off emotional overattachments to same-sex persons; and breaking away from homophile groups. This will be painful and difficult, because these persons and places have provided the homosexual person with a little psychological relief from isolation, but it is part of the price one must pay to regain control over one's inner life and to possess interior chastity, or chastity of the heart. Merely removing the occasions of sin, however, is not enough; as Christ says, "It is what comes out of a man that

[5] Audiotape, *Shattered Hearts. . . : Healing in the Work of Leanne Payne* (Boston: Daughters of St. Paul, 1994).

makes him unclean. For it is from within, from men's hearts, that evil intentions emerge: fornication, theft, murder, adultery, avarice, malice, deceit, indecency, envy, slander, pride, folly. All these evil things come from within and make a man unclean" (Mk 7:21–23).

It is time to consider the views of older members of Courage in regard to the possibility of change of orientation. Some who are over thirty seek to change their orientation through professional therapy, prayer, and group support; the majority, however, are satisfied to develop a life of interior chastity. Many view changing their thought and feeling patterns as more difficult, because such habits become more entrenched over the years.

Still others have been brainwashed by the psychological establishment to accept the myth that it is impossible to change one's orientation. Then some become discouraged after years of professional therapy and thousands of dollars spent that they have not become heterosexually capable of marriage, discerning no significant change in their manner of thinking and feeling.

At this juncture in their lives such older persons have to choose either to relapse into their former homosexual lifestyle or to seek to lead a life of sexual abstinence out of love for Christ. Many older Courage members seek to develop an interior life of prayer with Christ. While they rejoice that their younger brothers want to change their orientation, they are intent upon living a life of sexual abstinence. Were one to say to them that they *must* change their orientation, many would not come back the following week .

For this reason Courage does not make change of orientation an obligatory goal. At the same time Courage places greater stress on the need to move away from homosexual ways of thinking and feeling. Persons aspiring to study for the priesthood or religious life should take the means mentioned above to repudiate the homosexual lifestyle and should study the official teaching of the Church on the issue of homosexual behavior.[6]

Another objection to the position that one is not strictly obliged to change one's sexual orientation is that leading a chaste life while remaining in a homosexual condition is to lack complete healing, for one is not spiritually whole until one has acquired a heterosexual orientation. I believe that the best way to answer this objection is to draw a distinction between spiritual and psychological healing. By *psychological healing* from homosexuality I mean that one has now become predominantly heterosexual in patterns of fantasy, thought, and emotions, while there may remain vestiges of homosexual fantasy and desire without serious temptations to homosexual lust. By *spiritual healing* I mean that one can become interiorly chaste, while still occasionally suffering serious temptations to homosexual pleasures despite one's sincere efforts to avoid occasions of sin; or one does not develop any physical attraction to persons of the other sex despite the fact that one is no longer attracted in a carnal way to persons of one's own sex.

In my pastoral ministry I have met many persons who lead an interior life of chastity despite severe temptations. These individuals are daily communicants, leading a life of communion with Christ. They are spiritually but not psychologically healed, although they wish they were. Beyond the question of homosexuality, it is clear that some of the saints suffered severe temptations to impurity, which by God's grace they overcame. They were spiritually but not necessarily psychologically healed, suffering in some cases from neurotic tendencies. Perhaps our friends in Exodus International who hold that one is not completely healed until one has become heterosexually oriented

---

[6] A clinical psychologist of twenty years' experience with seminarians, religious, and priests insists that a seminarian who makes no effort to purge himself of homosexual fantasies and affections has only a minimal chance of remaining chaste (private communication).

should consider this distinction. In our human brokenness, psychological healing does not always follow upon spiritual healing through divine grace.

Another objection to the Courage position that one is not bound to participate in programs designed to change sexual orientation is that one can be healed completely of this orientation if one has deeper faith. This assertion has no proof in Catholic theology. It can lead to cruel judgments about the many men and women I have known who practice their faith assiduously but have not been able to make the journey into a heterosexual orientation despite their desire to do so.

A final objection to our position is that it is practically impossible to practice sexual abstinence for an extended period of time unless one has taken the vows of religion or the promise of priestly celibacy. Celibacy is simply not meant for lay Catholics, because they lack the charism given to religious or priests; hence, in the situation of persons with homosexual tendencies it is reasonable to settle down with one lover rather than be involved in promiscuity with the danger of AIDS. Some members of Dignity, an organization considering itself Catholic though not accepting the teaching of the Church on homosexual behavior, would argue this way.

I have already stated the premise that takes care of this objection. If chastity is an obligation binding upon all persons in every vocation, then it follows that God will give to each person sufficient grace to observe this divine mandate. To say otherwise is to contradict the solemn teaching of the Sixth Session of Trent and Saint Augustine, as already referenced. It is amazing how the false idea that *only* religious and priests are given the charism of complete chastity has spread among the faithful. God gives the gift of celibacy to all who ask for it.

We need to do a better job of teaching the positive meaning of celibacy, not only among the laity but also among seminarians and priests. As we have already seen, the celibate needs to accept this gift interiorly and joyfully live it out, because celibacy is either an act of love for Christ or an empty shell. It is another way of expressing one's sexuality, as John Paul II points out in *Familiaris Consortio*: "Marriage and virginity or celibacy are two ways of expressing and living the one mystery of the covenant of God with his people" (no. 16).

The heart of celibacy is the cultivation of a nuptial relationship with Jesus Christ. The way in which we bring this relationship with Christ into our ministry and into all our other relationships is discussed by many spiritual writers. I should like to recommend three: Benedict Groeschel, C.F.R., *The Courage to Be Chaste*; Christopher Kiesling, O.P., *Celibacy, Prayer, and Friendship*; and Jordan Aumann, O.P., and Dr. Conrad Baars, *The Unquiet Heart: Reflections on Love and Sexuality*.

In chapter seven, "Pastoral Perspectives", I shall consider the difficulties many experience in their effort to lead a chaste life: the seductive influence of the gay milieu, the abundance of gay pornography, the sense of low self-worth, emotional over-attachments, loneliness, the bitter memories of the past, bad friendships, and unresolved anger. I shall call this the human side of celibacy. Such reflections can help us to understand that homosexuality has very little to do with sex.

6

MORALITY OF HOMOSEXUAL ACTIVITY
AND PERSONAL RESPONSIBILITY

Forty years ago, when I first researched the literature on homosexuality, it was taken for granted by Christians and many others
that homosexual acts were immoral, but, as the breakdown of
the moral order progressed, and sexuality was considered *only* in
terms of a relationship between persons, the public began to
accept homosexual behavior as another kind of love—one that
ordinary people who did not understand such behavior would
be willing to tolerate. When, moreover, vast numbers of articulate homosexual persons intimidated the nation with their parades and protests, and when they formulated gay rights bills,
people began to say, "Let them have their rights and their lovers
so long as they don't interfere with my family." After all, it is
conceded, since they are not able to marry, they need some
companionship and sex in life. So let them have their rights.
Soon the media and the culture focused on the *alleged* rights of
homosexual persons while ignoring the nature of homosexual
acts.

There is something radically wrong with a culture that constantly asserts rights without giving the foundations of such
rights in the natural moral law. We talk about abortion rights,
animal rights, and sexual pleasure rights. But few talk about the
foundation (if any) of such rights. In short, there is need to
develop arguments against homosexual activity itself while not

neglecting the personal responsibility of the person involved in such acts.

Argument from the Authority of the Church

In *The Homosexual Person* (pp. 95–117), I have outlined the teaching of the Magisterium on the objective immorality of homosexual activity and the personal *responsibility* of the person. In addition, I have presented arguments based on natural moral law against homosexual acts. Now I see the need to reformulate the argument against homosexual acts by considering what the Church teaches concerning the nature of the marital act and then asking whether homosexual acts can fulfill the purposes of marriage as found in Church documents. I believe this is a better approach than basing one's argument primarily on the classical passages from Leviticus 20:13 and 18:21–22, Romans 1:26–27, 1 Corinthians 6:9, or 1 Timothy 1:9–10.

While I believe these specific passages have probative force, they should be presented only after one has demonstrated that the Church's teaching on marriage in *Gaudium et Spes* (*The Church in the Modern World*) nos. 48–51; in *Humanae Vitae*, nos. 8–12; and in the *Catechism of the Catholic Church*, 1603, 1643 et passim is that there are two *inseparable* purposes in the marital act, the permanent union of man and woman and the procreation of children.[1] Then one compares this teaching on the nature of the marital act with the homosexual act, and it is clear that the latter act in no way fulfills the purposes of the marital act, but sexual-

---

[1] *Humanae Vitae*, no. 12: "There is an unbreakable connection between the unitive meaning and the procreative meaning [of the conjugal act], and both are inherent in the conjugal act. This connection was established by God, and man is not permitted to break it through his own volition." It is noteworthy that Dietrich von Hildebrand in 1929 expressed a similar view, saying, "Love is the primary *meaning* of marriage, just as the birth of new human beings is its primary *end*": *Marriage: The Mystery of Faithful Love* (1929; repr. Manchester, N.H.: Sophia Institute, 1991), p. 7.

genital acts must fulfill the purposes of marriage to be considered moral.

It will be helpful to put this argument in the form of a syllogism: from sacred Scripture and sacred tradition, as understood by the universal Magisterium through the centuries, it is clear that the two purposes of the marital act are the permanent union of man and woman and the procreation and rearing of children, and intentionally to exclude one of these purposes is immoral. But homosexual acts do not fulfill either purpose. Therefore, all such acts are immoral.

For those who believe in rational argument, the use of a syllogism helps them to see that the Church's position on the immorality of all homosexual activity is a necessary corollary of the Church's position on matrimony and marital acts; thus, one can show the immorality of homosexual acts without quoting a specific biblical passage condemning them. In this way one can bypass the arguments of reductionist theologians who try to explain away the obvious meaning of the texts of Leviticus or Romans.[2]

In *The Homosexual Person* (pp. 95–98), I have presented briefly the arguments against homosexual acts from the nature of marriage as found in Church teaching, but now I intend to expand the argument by quoting and commenting upon the sections in *Gaudium et Spes* (GS) dealing with marriage (48–51) and in *Humanae Vitae* (8–12) dealing with the conjugal act. In my opinion, the argument from the nature of human sexuality and marriage is more persuasive for demonstrating the immorality of homosexual activity than the use of scriptural passages condemning homosexual activity. Of course, this presupposes that the magisterial teaching on the purposes of human sexual intercourse is at least theologically certain, if not a matter of faith. (I

---

[2] In *The Homosexual Person*, pp. 88–89, 98–99, I respond to some reductionist theologians, but I believe that arguments based upon the nature of the marital act are more effective.

refer the reader to the *Catechism of the Catholic Church*,[3] which presents the sources of Catholic teaching on human sexuality.) Now I turn to *Gaudium et Spes*.

> The intimate partnership of married life and the love which constitutes the married state has been established by the creator and endowed by him with its own proper laws. . . . For God himself is the author of marriage and has endowed it with various benefits and with various ends in view (GS 48).

Gaudium et Spes (48, n.) gives the sources of this teaching on the divine institution of marriage, namely, the writings of Saint Augustine, the teaching of Saint Thomas, and the Councils of Florence and Trent.

> By its very nature the institution of marriage and married love is ordered to the procreation and education of the offspring and it is in them that it finds its crowning glory. Thus the man and woman, who "are no longer two but one" (Mt. 19:6), help and serve each other by their marriage partnership; they become conscious of their unity and experience it more deeply from day to day. The intimate union of marriage, as a mutual giving of two persons, and the good of the children demand total fidelity from the spouses and require an unbreakable unity between them (GS 48).

Here the footnote refers to the classical letter "On Chaste Marriage" of Pius XI (1930). The above passage gives the two purposes of the conjugal act as well as the unbreakable bond between the two spouses. On conjugal love: "On several occasions the Word of God invites the betrothed to nourish and foster their betrothal with chaste love, and likewise spouses their marriage" (GS 49).

The footnote to paragraph 49 cites Genesis, Proverbs, Tobias, the Song of Songs, and Ephesians, while the text of paragraph 49

---

[3] See sections 1612–17 (marriage as covenant), 1638–42 (marriage as bond and sacrament), 1643–51 (unity and indissolubility of marriage), and 1652–53 (fertility in marriage).

extols the beauty of marital love, describing it as "eminently human" because it involves the good of the whole person. "It can enrich the sentiments of the spirit and their physical expression with a unique dignity and ennoble them as the special elements and signs of the friendship proper to marriage."

Dietrich von Hildebrand in 1929 said that "conjugal love in itself constitutes a completely new kind of love. It involves a unique mutual giving of one's self, which is the outstanding characteristic of this kind of love." [4] The Fathers of the Second Vatican Council desired to show the world the goodness of the marital state: it perfects both spouses; it is a unique friendship; it merges the human with the divine, pervading the whole lives of the spouses. "This is a far cry from mere erotic attraction, which is pursued in selfishness and soon fades away in wretchedness" (GS 49). This is another way of saying that there is no comparison between heterosexual marriages and sex outside of marriage, including same-sex unions, about which more will be said later.

As von Hildebrand had said, marital love is unique. *Gaudium et Spes* expresses it thus: "Married love is uniquely expressed and perfected by the exercise of the acts proper to marriage" (49). The key word in this sentence is *uniquely*. The friendship of husband and wife is unique; it is the only friendship that has the right to be expressed in a bodily union; all other friendships ought to be celibate. The text goes on to praise "the act in marriage by which the intimate and chaste union of the spouses takes place." The "performance of these acts fosters the self-giving they signify and enriches the spouses in joy and gratitude."

In this paragraph one finds no negative note concerning the meaning of marital intercourse; on the contrary, it shows its God-given value. Again, observe that the Council Fathers do not

[4] Von Hildebrand, *Marriage*, p. 7.

praise any other kind of sexual activity. In speaking of the fidelity of the marital relationship (something missing from steady lover sexual relationships between males; see chapter nine, below), they say, "It will never be profaned by adultery or divorce."

Knowing that marital fidelity will not be easy, the Fathers stress that husband and wife will need "notable virtue". They are exhorted to make use of the sacramental graces of marriage, while praying for fidelity, generosity, and the spirit of sacrifice. Thus, the marital act is placed within the larger context of marriage as a communion of life in which two loving persons rear children, going beyond this mission to share their life together as long as God allows them.

By way of contrast you will not find any magisterial teaching extolling same-sex unions as a vocation in which notable virtue, including fidelity, must be practiced. Given the Church's understanding of marriage, there is no way that she can justify homosexual unions. To this I shall come back. Now, however, we need to look at number 50.

The central theme is the fruitfulness of marriage. "Marriage and married love are by nature ordered to the procreation and education of children. Indeed children are the supreme gift of marriage and greatly contribute to the good of the parents themselves" (GS 50). God wanted man and woman to share in his creative power through the marital act: "Wishing to associate them in a special way with his own creative work, God blessed man and woman with the words, 'Be fruitful and multiply' (Gen 1:28)" (GS 50).

Relying on divine revelation, as it has come down to us through sacred tradition as well as sacred Scripture, the Fathers affirm the *procreative* meaning of marriage and the marital act. Married couples are called upon to cooperate with God in the formation of their own family and the family of the Church. In the rest of this section the duties of parents to take full responsibility for their children is stressed. The procreative purpose of the marital act, however, is possible only in the union of *man and woman*, and not in a *same-sex* union.

The Fathers go on to respond to an objection to the teaching concerning the two purposes of marriage, and that is couples who have not been able to have children: "Marriage is not merely for the procreation of children: its nature as an indissoluble compact between two people and the good of the children demand that the mutual love of the partners be properly shown, that it should grow and mature. Even in cases where despite the intense desire of the spouses there are no children, marriage still retains its character of being a whole manner and communion of life and preserves its value and indissolubility" (GS 50).

Notice in this response that the Fathers see both the union of the man and woman and the procreation of children as two parts of a larger whole: marriage persists as "a whole manner and communion of life". But it always presupposes a *man* and a *woman*, something not possible in same-sex unions. This brings us to section 51, which is concerned with harmonizing conjugal life with respect for human life.

It should be remembered that section 51 came out clearly against abortion but did not settle the issue of contraception. Yet it does make a contribution to the relationship between Church teaching and the morality of contraceptive acts. Facing the problem of harmonizing conjugal love with the responsible transmission of life, the Fathers insist that "it is not enough to take only the good intention and the evaluation of motives into account; the *objective criteria* must be used, criteria drawn from the nature of the human person and human action, criteria which respect the total meaning of mutual self-giving and human procreation in the context of true love" (GS 50, emphasis added).

So often in arguments favoring homosexual unions it is said that these individuals love each other so much that there is no other way in which they can express their affection. It is regarded as all a matter of motivation. There is no need to look at the homosexual act itself, because the morality of the act is determined *only* by intentions and motives. It is said, for example, that a strong mutual attraction between two members of the same sex is sufficient justification for a same-sex union.[5] Here the Fathers anticipate the false argument that the morality of homosexual activity can be reduced to motivation alone.

I turn now to *Humanae Vitae* (HV), section 8, where Pope Paul VI teaches that marriage comes from God and not from the forces of nature. Spouses seek a communion of persons through which they might share the task of cooperating with the Creator in procreating and educating new human beings. This repeats the teaching of *Gaudium et Spes*, section 51.

In *Humanae Vitae*, section 9, the special characteristics of conjugal love are stated: it is (1) *human*, of the senses and of the spirit; (2) *total*, a very special kind of friendship; (3) *faithful* and *exclusive* until the end of life; and (4) *fruitful*: "since the whole of the love is not contained in the communion of the spouses; it also seeks to look beyond itself and seeks to raise up new lives." Again, this section repeats the teaching of *Gaudium et Spes*, section 50. As already mentioned, love between two people of the same sex cannot be fruitful, or procreative.

Humanae Vitae, section 10, raises the question of conscience in the *objective* moral order: "Responsible parenthood is rooted in the objective moral order established by God, and only an upright conscience can be a true interpreter of that order."

Already we have heard the Fathers of Vatican II say that moral norms ought to be rooted in the "objective moral order", and not in one's own arbitrary judgments (GS 51). Here that truth is applied to the matter of contraception. One's con-

[5] For example, Thomas H. Stahel, S.J., " 'I'm Here': An Interview with Andrew Sullivan", *America* (May 8, 1993), pp. 5–11; referring to homosexual love, Sullivan says, "I know in my heart of hearts that cannot be wrong" (p. 6).

science ought to be formed according to "objective moral principles". This may be difficult, but the moral law requires that we accommodate our "behavior to the plan of God our Creator". This plan is manifested to us "by the very nature of marriage and its acts" and by the constant teaching of the Church (GS 50–51).

The reason I raise the issue of conscience and the objective moral order is that I find a striking parallel between the arguments used in *Humanae Vitae*, section 10, against contraception and those used against homosexual acts in the "Declaration on Certain Problems concerning Sexual Ethics" (no. 8.4) and in the "Letter to the Bishops of the Catholic Church on the Pastoral Care of Homosexual Persons" (PCHP 7).

First let us look at section 8.4 of the Declaration: "It is not permissible to employ any pastoral method or theory to provide moral justification for their actions, on the grounds that they are in keeping with their condition. Sexual relations between persons of the same sex are necessarily and essentially disordered according to the objective moral order."

PCHP, number 7, states that "it is only in the marital relationship that the use of the sexual faculty can be morally good. A person engaging in homosexual behavior, therefore, acts immorally. To choose someone of the same sex for one's sexual activity is to annul the rich symbolism and meaning, not to mention the goals, of the Creator's sexual design."

Both sets of arguments are based upon the objective moral order, which includes the teaching of divine revelation in its oral and written form and the natural moral law. In both situations an appeal to arbitrary judgments of conscience is rejected. Yet for over twenty-five years many lay Catholics have been told by some priests, "Follow your own conscience." One observes the same kind of advice given to many persons struggling with homosexual temptations: "You feel that you must have some affection in your life. Follow your own conscience."

Section 12 of *Humanae Vitae* states: "The doctrine that the Magisterium has often explained is this: there is an unbreakable connection between the unitive meaning and the procreative meaning, and both are inherent in the conjugal act. This connection was established by God, and Man is not permitted to break it through his own volition" (trans. Janet Smith in *Humanae Vitae: A Generation Later*, p. 281).

Section 12 of *Humanae Vitae* may be used to repudiate homosexual activity, because it repeats the perennial teaching of the Magisterium concerning the two *inseparable* meanings of marriage, meanings inherent in the marital act. But homosexual acts cannot fulfill either meaning and so in no way are in accord with the design of the Creator of human sexuality. Obviously, homosexual apologists have to justify contraception in order to separate the procreative meaning from the unitive. We shall see, moreover, in considering the nature of the homosexual act, that their arguments do not prove that in homosexual activity a true union is achieved.

The Argument from Natural Moral Law

The above arguments are basically drawn from the authority of the Church interpreting the Holy Scriptures and sacred tradition. But many do not accept such an argument, and so it is necessary to present an argument against homosexual activity from human reason or from natural moral law. In *The Homosexual Person* (pp. 100-104), I have outlined arguments against homosexual activity based upon the lack of complementarity between two people of the same sex and the inability to take part in the procreative act. I also developed some persuasive psychological arguments against the homosexual lifestyle. Now I should like to present a philosophical argument by Michael Pakaluk.

Michael Pakaluk

Michael Pakaluk argues that sexual intercourse between a man and a woman has a special status that makes it different from other human activities. If it did not have a special status, then rape would be no different from mere assault and battery. We say sex is special because it is the sign of the union of the *persons* who engage in sex. The sign is the union of bodies, and the sign signifies the union of persons. Thus, it is correct to say that "when a man and a woman engage in sex, the union of their bodies signifies the union of their selves".[6]

Sexual intercourse has a certain meaning independent of our human choices; it signifies a union of selves. Again, one cannot take away this meaning from the act of sexual intercourse. One cannot minimize its meaning, as many unmarried persons do. Now

> a natural sign signifies something by resembling what it signifies. What is it in heterosexual intercourse which resembles a union of selves. There are two elements: First, there is the reciprocal containment of the woman and the man. The man is inside the woman; his penis is inside her vagina, and the woman is inside the man; she is held in his embrace. This signifies the reciprocal containment in affection of the lover and the beloved. When two persons are united in love, each is within the heart of the other.[7]

Since sexual intercourse between man and woman has a re-productive character, the act tends to produce offspring, who combine the characteristics of husband and wife and in so doing promote the unity of the spouses. As we know, homosexual intercourse has no such power.

[6] Michael Pakaluk, "Why Is Homosexual Activity Morally Wrong?" in *Homosexuality: Challenges for Change and Reorientation, Journal of Pastoral Counseling* 28 (New Rochelle, N.Y.: Iona College, 1993):53.

[7] Ibid., 54.

A man and a woman become united in their persons by loving each other. This means that each gives himself to the other. Giving yourself to the other means giving your possessions, time, and control over your life. But this is possible only in marriage, and, therefore, sexual intercourse can be *truthfully* engaged in only within a marriage.

After showing that sexual intercourse between a man and a woman is a natural sign, Pakaluk points out that homosexual intercourse is not a natural sign at all. It lacks the two components that make sexual intercourse a natural sign. It lacks the sign of reciprocal containment. No one gets inside another in homosexual intercourse. Neither the rectum nor the mouth is inside a human being, for the human body has the shape of a donut: "The gastrointestinal tract is a hole running through the body."[8] Hence, oral or anal intercourse remains on the surface of the body, whereas the man's penis penetrating the woman's vagina brings about a real physical union.

Again, as already noted, the homosexual act cannot tend toward procreation, and therefore it cannot unify those engaged in it by tending toward a child who will have characteristics of both parents. For these reasons homosexual activity "lacks those very elements which could make it a natural sign of the union of persons. That is why the most that can be achieved in a homosexual act is mutual masturbation."[9] In chapter eight, below, "A Response to the Gay Rights Movement", John Finnis provides strong additional argument against homosexual activity.[10]

Since, then, homosexual activity cannot signify union, it does not tend to unite those who engage in it. This is a contributing factor to the instability of homosexual relationships. In any case,

[8] Ibid., 56
[9] Ibid.
[10] "Law, Morality, and 'Sexual Orientation' ", *Notre Dame Law Review* 69 (1994):1049–76, esp. 1066–67.

Pakaluk's argument counters effectively the position that homosexual activity can be justified.

In summary, there are two kinds of arguments against homosexual activity: (1) the argument from authority, as found in sacred Scripture, tradition, and magisterial documents. In this chapter I have argued from the data of revelation concerning marriage to the immorality of homosexual acts; and (2) the argument from reason as developed by Michael Pakaluk.

Gregory Baum

It is worthwhile to compare the natural moral law argument of Michael Pakaluk with that of Gregory Baum, who is representative of many contemporary writers. Baum holds that the meaning of sexuality "cannot be defined apart from culture and people's historical experiences".[11]

Baum feels that one can hold on to the natural moral tradition in the Church while developing a reinterpretation of it that would view homosexual experience in a more positive way. He believes that the Church has opened herself up to new insights in her understanding of slavery, religious liberty, and "the essential equality of men and women".[12]

It was through the leadership of courageous individuals that the public began to realize that the institution of slavery was against the dignity of every man. A similar phenomenon, according to Baum, came about after World War II, when the Church modified her opposition to religious liberty, recognizing human rights as part of the natural law. Through prophetic voices the Church came to recognize the right to follow conscience in pursuit of religious liberty. The third example given by Baum is that the Church has recognized the "essential equal-

[11] "Homosexuality and the Natural Law", *The Ecumenist* 1:34.
[12] Ibid., 35.

ity between man and woman", while in previous centuries she taught that women were by nature inferior to men.

Baum goes on to point out that in all three examples "deeper insight into the natural law or the inner structure of human beings was not obtained by abstract reasoning, but by people's new ethical experiences and their historical struggle to transform the public consciousness. . . . In each case, the new insight was tested by the Scriptures and found acceptable."[13] Baum draws inferences from these examples to justify the homosexual lifestyle, following the arguments of John Coleman in "The Homosexual Revolution and Hermeneutics".[14]

Coleman and Baum argue from the personal experience of men and women concerning their sexual orientation, in which these men and women formed their own moral evaluation from their experiences. The literature of personal witness and the experiences of such men and women constitute the basis for their collective judgment that active homosexual relationships, preferably in an exclusive union, are morally acceptable.

Baum calls upon the Church to accept such homosexual relationships. If the Church has changed her theory and practice with regard to slavery, human rights, and the equality of men and women, why can she not change her teaching and moral guidance with regard to homosexual behavior?

Baum does not explicitly draw the conclusion that homosexual acts can be moral in certain circumstances. But in approving the literature in favor of the homosexual lifestyle, he implicitly approves them. He suggests the Christian churches take a "second look at their teaching" and "ask themselves whether the dignity of homosexuals as human beings does not demand that their sexual orientation be respected".[15]

I have given this summary of Baum's thought so that the

[13] Ibid.
[14] *The Sexual Revolution: Concilium*, no. 173 (March 1984):55–64.
[15] "Homosexuality and the Natural Law", p. 36.

reader will understand why I find it so misleading. What is completely lacking from his argument is any analysis of homosexual acts (such as is found in Pakaluk) and the moral justification for them. The first analogy concerning slavery fails to bring out that throughout the centuries from the time of Saint Paul the Church's official teaching has merely *tolerated* the institution of slavery, not approved of it. In Paul's letter to Philemon he exhorts him to take back his slave Onesimus. Paul calls Onesimus his brother in the Lord: "I am appealing to you for a child of mine, whose father I became while wearing these chains: I mean Onesimus. . . . know that you have been deprived of Onesimus for a time, but it was only so that you could have him back forever, not as a slave anymore, but something much better than a slave, a dear brother; especially dear to me, but how much more to you, as a blood brother, as well as a brother in the Lord" (Philemon 10–16, JB).

It seems that Saint Paul had as clear a concept of the dignity of man as any modern. With regard to the second analogy, concerning religious liberty, the Church did come to a deeper realization of religious liberty during Vatican Council II. But the question of the Church's position on religious liberty in the nineteenth century is far more complex than the way Baum describes it. It is difficult to make a comparison between the Church's position on religious liberty in the nineteenth century and our understanding of the morality of homosexual behavior in the twentieth. In one case we are concerned with the error of indifferentism, and in the other, with the analysis of a type of behavior.

The third analogy, which holds that a deeper grasp of the principles of natural moral law has led to the recognition of the equal dignity of man and woman, suffers from the same defect as the analogy concerning religious freedom. True, the dignity of woman was recognized in Holy Scripture and in the Church's documents, and over the centuries this concept has been developed. But in the case of homosexual activity it would mean *not* the development of the original intuition that homosexual activity was immoral but a *contradiction* of this teaching. This is hardly a *development* of natural moral law teaching.

Again, Baum holds that the three "insights" were tested by the Scriptures and found acceptable. But the Scriptures must be understood as firmly condemning homosexual activity, not only in the classical texts but also implicitly in their teaching on marriage.

In summary: Baum makes a valid point. The experience of people does contribute to our understanding of natural moral law. But such experience must be taken in conjunction with the authentic teaching of the Church, rooted as it is in the Scriptures, tradition, and natural moral law. To build a moral norm on the collective experience of many homosexual men and women and their literature, while ignoring the above sources of wisdom, is grossly inadequate. Experience alone is not an adequate determinant of moral norms. In the case of homosexuality one can refer to the experience of many other persons with homosexual tendencies who desire not only to control their behavior but also to be rid of the condition itself. Thus, Baum's argument from experience is inadequate.

The Value of Argument from Specific Biblical Texts

In developing arguments from marriage against homosexual activity, one does not reduce the probative value of the specific biblical condemnations, as I have outlined them in *The Homosexual Person* (pp. 98–99); on the contrary, their probative value is enhanced, because these texts are seen in the larger context of the biblical teaching on human sexuality and marriage. In the classical texts homosexual activity is always condemned: Genesis 19:4–11; Leviticus 18:22 and 20:13; Romans 1:26–27; 1 Corinthians 6:9–11; 1 Timothy 1:8–11; and Jude 7. Nowhere in the

Bible are homosexual acts approved. If, however, these texts are used apart from the marriage argument, they are subject to reductionist manipulation, as in the writings of the late John Boswell and John J. McNeill.[16] Although their arguments are repudiated by other scholars and the "Letter to the Bishops of the Catholic Church on the Pastoral Care of Homosexual Persons" (1986), still their articulation in an oral debate, particularly on TV, can create doubt in the minds of listeners concerning the truth of the Church's teaching.

The specific biblical condemnations of homosexual behavior are made to appear irrelevant to the situation of homosexual persons in contemporary culture. Genesis, for example, is concerned with inhospitality and homosexual rape; Leviticus is interpreted as seeing homosexual acts as evil when they are part of a pagan cult; and Romans is understood as a condemnation of heterosexual men performing homosexual acts. Saint Paul, of course, knew nothing about the condition of homosexuality, but he knew enough that he could distinguish between homosexual men having homosexual acts and heterosexual men having homosexual acts, a skill usually found only in professional therapists.

In a more recent work, Gerald Coleman, S.S.,[17] comments on the position of Robin Scroggs.[18] Coleman believes that Scroggs makes a good case for the position that the New Testament was reacting against pederasty, but he disagrees with Scroggs in drawing further conclusions about the New Testament position on homosexuality: "In other words [says Scroggs], one can say

[16] John Boswell, *Christianity, Social Tolerance, and Homosexuality* (Chicago: University of Chicago Press, 1980), pp. 93–98; John J. McNeill, *The Church and the Homosexual* (Kansas City, Ks.: Sheed, Andrews and McMeel, 1976), pp. 37–66

[17] Gerald Coleman, *Human Sexuality: An All-Embracing Gift* (New York: Alba House, 1992), pp. 254–55.

[18] Robin Scroggs, *The New Testament and Homosexuality* (Philadelphia: Fortress Press, 1983).

nothing based on the New Testament about whether it condemns any other form of homosexual behavior. This argument is flawed."[19]

In Coleman's opinion, Scroggs makes a good point in holding that pederasty was most probably the particular form of homosexuality to which Paul was reacting , but one may not draw the further conclusion that pederasty was the only kind of homosexual behavior condemned, while other forms of homosexual behavior were permissible. I agree with Coleman that it was not the only kind of homosexual action condemned. This leads to the question: "Did/would Paul see a homosexual relationship by mutual consent as against God's will or not?"[20]

Coleman points out that Paul was using the "natural" versus "unnatural" distinction in a way similar to our usage when we designate homosexual behavior as deviant, while Scroggs holds that this has nothing to do with "natural law". Paul also speaks of males with males, not men with boys, as in pederasty. The reference to female homosexuality, moreover, makes it even more likely that Paul was referring to more than pederasty in Romans 1:26–27.[21]

From my reading of Scroggs I do not think that he makes a good case for the argument that Romans was referring *principally* to pederasty. Why, then, would Paul draw a parallel between the "unnatural" behavior of males and females?

Coleman goes on to point out that nowhere in the New Testament can one find any reference to any sexual vice specifically referring to "boys". The Greek term used in 1 Corinthians 6:9 and 1 Timothy 1:10, *arsenokoitai*, is not restricted to pederasty. It is based upon Leviticus 18:22 and 20:13, which is a generic condemnation of homosexual behavior. In both Old and New Testament passages, then, one finds a *general* condem-

[19] Coleman, *Human Sexuality*, p. 254.
[20] Ibid., p. 255.
[21] Ibid.

nation of homosexual acts, which, of course, would include pederasty.[22]

Coleman's analysis of Scroggs and others is on target in that it argues in favor of the biblical texts as relevant to a moral evaluation of homosexual behavior today. He agrees with my view that the New Testament's "clear pro-marriage statements (heterosexual) are of vital importance in expressing its view about homosexuality."[23]

Personal Responsibility

In moral theology texts the term *subjective morality* refers to the degree of responsibility the agent has for his actions. Since it is well known that many persons perform actions in a state of ignorance or under the influence of compulsive tendencies, it follows that responsibility for their actions is diminished in consideration of their lack of full freedom. But the pejorative connotations of the term *subjective* have caused me to use the term *personal responsibility* as a way of supporting the truth that even those who have acted without due freedom in the past have a responsibility to use the means of recovering their moral freedom in the present and in the future.

It seems that in this question of personal responsibility for homosexual acts one should avoid two extreme attitudes: first, that a person cannot help acting out his homosexual tendencies—it is impossible for such persons to be sexually abstinent; and second, that a person has full freedom to get rid of homosexual fantasies, feelings, and actions. My experience in counseling men and women with homosexual tendencies leads me to believe that many persons have suffered a loss of full freedom because of family background, childhood sexual abuse, igno-

[22] Ibid., p. 256.
[23] Ibid.

rance of the moral law, lack of education concerning chastity during the formative years, and various other factors.

This is not to mention the all-pervading erotic culture proclaiming that one must have physical sex to be normal. While a person with homosexual tendencies may not be compulsive, he may still have greater difficulty in remaining chaste than the ordinary heterosexual person. As I said in *The Homosexual Person*, the noncompulsive individual is generally not able to share his feelings and desires with those around him for fear of rejection, and that kind of secrecy makes temptations all the stronger. It also creates an interior loneliness and a strong desire to be with other homosexual people.

Again, while his heterosexual brother can look forward to marriage, the homosexual is not able to do so, unless he can become heterosexual, and he may not have the financial resources to undergo a therapy program that aims to restore him to the heterosexual orientation.[24] With little or no understanding of celibacy, he may feel "condemned" to sexual abstinence. Add to this feeling a sense that one is "different" in a negative way.[25] Despite all these difficulties, such a person remains responsible for his actions. The point is that it is generally more difficult for such a person to remain chaste than it is for the ordinary heterosexual man or woman.

Sexual Compulsions

To understand the responsibility of the compulsive homosexual person, however, it is first necessary to study sexual compulsions

[24] *The Homosexual Person*, pp. 105–6.

[25] Gerald van den Aardweg, in *Homosexuality and Hope* (Ann Arbor, Mich.: Servant Books, 1985), says, "The young person does not think, 'It is true that I have occasional or regular homosexual feelings, but basically I must have been born the same as anyone else.' No, he feels that he is a different and inferior creature who carries a doom: he views himself as tragic" (p. 21).

in general and then apply our perception to individuals. There is a vast literature on the subject, from which I shall extract a few working definitions that I have found pastorally beneficial. I understand compulsion or addiction as a mode of behavior found within the thought and feeling patterns of an individual or in his relationships with others that clearly show that the individual is out of control, and this despite the fact that he has consciously tried to rid himself of this behavior, with little or no success. Step one of A.A. refers to addiction when it says, "I am an alcoholic, and I am powerless over this condition." [26]

Step One can be adapted to those persons with homosexual tendencies now involved in masturbation, pornography, or both. Their number is legion. The least common denominator in such situations is that the person has consciously tried to overcome his behavior over a considerable period, and, having failed to do so, he falls into a mood of despair. Serious elements in his life are threatened with destruction. He is truly powerless, but, if he admits it, he is ready for therapy.

In understanding the homosexual person, it is important to realize that often he has more than one addiction: alcoholism, drugs, overeating, and chain smoking are frequently additional addictions in his life. Ann Wilson Schaef points out that addictions do not exist in isolation, commenting that

> since we live in an addictive society we have all been exposed to and trained into an addictive *process*. . . . It is of the utmost importance to be aware that this underlying addictive *process* is culturally based and learned. It functions under rules of its own, rules that could be compared to flowing water finding its own course. We all know that when a stream is blocked, it will find its own way. It is not that the water goes away; it just finds

[26] I have discussed addiction as it applies to pedophilia in "The Moral Aspects of Addiction", in *The Twenty-Fifth Anniversary of Vatican II: A Look Back and a Look Ahead*, Proceedings of the Ninth Bishops' Workshop, Dallas, Texas, ed. Russell Smith (The Pope John Center, 1990), pp. 180–202.

another way to express itself. The addictive *process* is much the same. If one path for its expression is cut off, it finds another [emphasis added].[27]

Schaef holds that it is inadequate to treat the specific addiction in isolation, because this leads to switching from one addiction to another. It is necessary to face "each of the addictions and the underlying addictive process together and separately for recovery to succeed."[28]

Schaef also points out that *chemical* addictions (alcohol, drugs) are distinct from *process* addictions, which include addictions to work, sex, and romance.[29] Certain kinds of homosexuality are process addictions, as many have experienced. AIDS may be the result of both kinds.[30]

But there is still another aspect of addiction, which is developed by Gerald E. May. He views an addiction as a

> state of compulsion, obsession or preoccupation that enslaves a person's will or desire. Addiction sidetracks and eclipses the energy of our deepest, truest desire for love and goodness. We succumb because the energy of our desire becomes attached, nailed to specific behaviors, objects or people. *Attachment* . . . is the process that enslaves desire and creates the state of addiction [emphasis in original].[31]

[27] *Escape from Intimacy* (San Francisco: Harper and Row, 1989), p. 1.

[28] Ibid., pp. 1–2; see also Patrick Carnes, *Out of the Shadows* (Minneapolis: Compcare Publications, 1984), p. 19.

[29] *Escape from Intimacy*, p. 2.

[30] Gina Kolata, "New Picture of Who Will Get AIDS Is Crammed with Addicts", *New York Times* (Feb. 28, 1995), p. C3, Medical Science section. Three-fourths of the 40,000 new cases of HIV each year involve intravenous drug users, crack addicts, and other drug abusers, many of whom are women. This is 1994 data. The population is mainly the inner-city poor minorities, black and Hispanic. Recently published statistics indicate that AIDS is now the leading killer of young adults and that the largest percentage increases in new infections are among women. "As many as half of these women are crack addicts" (Kolata). Obviously, the treatment of addictions becomes a matter of life or death and should be high on our pastoral agenda.

[31] *Addiction and Grace* (New York: Harper and Row, 1988), p. 14.

Addiction and Moral Freedom

Later, in considering pastoral programs for subjects of sexual addiction, I shall return to the phenomenon of addiction. My sole purpose in presenting definitions of addiction at this juncture is to highlight the way in which addictions *significantly* reduce the freedom of the human will, thereby reducing imputability for addictive acts. In practice, one must be lenient in forming judgments concerning the formal guilt found in such acts, including one's own behavior. Very often the sexual addict will condemn himself as beyond the saving grace of Christ.

While it may be true that an individual allowed himself to get deep into sexually addictive practices when he had the opportunity to nip addiction in the bud and therefore is theoretically responsible for the development of the addiction, still most individuals are not really aware of what is happening to them in the early stages of addiction. It is recommended, then, that one simply express sorrow to Christ for whatever negligence he may have been responsible for in the past, turning to the future with the resolve that he will use all the means at his disposal to overcome addictive tendencies within himself.

In my judgment, this will usually mean that the addictive person becomes involved in a Twelve Step program designed to help him to overcome his addiction. He should be strongly discouraged by his confessor from going over the past repeatedly to assess his exact culpability. This is futile and even spiritually dangerous, because it may lead the penitent to become mired in the quicksand of *shame*, winding up in despair.

The reader may have noticed that I refer to shame, because there is a vast difference between guilt and shame. A person may accept himself as made in the image of God and feel guilty for an act that he has done, because he perceives that he has offended the God of love. He repents his sin, ridding himself of the guilt.

That is healthy. In contrast, when he believes that he is no good because he has not been able to overcome his promiscuous homosexual acts, he is filled with shame, losing his sense of being a child of God. As we shall see later, he will continue to be involved in such behavior, despairing that he can do anything about it.[32]

I do not want to give the impression that most persons with homosexual tendencies are sexual addicts. That is not so. There are, however, many who are sexually addicted, and that should come as no surprise when one considers the heterosexual population, many of whom are addicted to masturbation, pornography, voyeurism (particularly the fans of late-night cable TV shows), fornication, adultery, incest, and sexual child abuse. Finally, at the other extreme, we should be critical of the view, so prevalent in the culture, that individuals cannot help acting out their sexual desires, that sooner or later our sexual drives will overcome us. True, we suffer the wounds of lust, as a result of Original Sin, but we can be open to the grace of Christ, and we can learn to live chastely by his power. That may also mean that we use the natural means at our disposal to achieve sexual wholeness.

In this chapter I have focused on the objective and subjective morality of homosexual acts; however, I am aware that there are other moral questions in need of study. In *The Homosexual Person* (pp. 116–17), I treated briefly the question of *homophobia,* which I described as unreasonable fear, and sometimes hatred, of homosexual persons, as well as the fears within persons with such tendencies about self-disclosure. These fears are still with us. Nonetheless, the solution of this problem will not be found by declaring same-sex unions to be just as morally acceptable as

---

[32] Monsignor Andrew Cusack, tape 2 of the series "Rekindling the Priesthood", Alba House Casettes, 1994. Cusack uses examples from his rich pastoral ministry to highlight the difference between guilt and shame.

heterosexual marriages.[33] It is unfortunate, moreover, that theologians who hold that homosexual activity is always immoral, or that the inclination to homosexual acts is an "objective disorder"—the official teaching of the Church—are called "homophobic".

Having considered the objective morality of homosexual acts and having reviewed basic questions of personal responsibility for such acts, I turn now to pastoral approaches to persons with homosexual tendencies. As I move through the complex maze of questions, I will attempt in chapter seven to integrate specific moral principles with pastoral programs.

[33] In *Heterosexism: An Ethical Challenge* (State Univ. of New York, 1993), Patricia Jung and Ralph Smith present the view that the homosexual lifestyle in which one has a faithful and loving union should be regarded on the same level as heterosexual marriage. There is nothing imperfect or defective in being homosexual. See also my review of J. P. Hanigan's *Homosexuality: The Test Case for Christian Social Ethics* in *Fellowship of Catholic Scholars Newsletter* (December 1988), pp. 20–22.

7

PASTORAL PERSPECTIVES

It is one thing to determine from divine revelation and natural moral law that homosexual activity is always a serious deviation from the moral order; it is quite another to work out a spiritual plan of life for persons of homosexual orientation so that they may be able to live in union with God by a chaste way of life. The latter task becomes increasingly difficult when our culture remains blind to the objective evil of homosexual activity. In so many instances young people are taught that the best way to cope with homosexual desires is to find a steady lover and live with him. This is called a "pastoral" solution; in this chapter, however, I use the term *pastoral* to mean a spiritual plan of life that will enable the counselee/penitent to live in accord with the divine law of chastity.

From counseling persons with homosexual tendencies over four decades, I have concluded that, besides individual counseling and spiritual direction, some form of group spiritual support is necessary. I shall present some insights on both one-on-one counseling and group spiritual direction. Since many priests and counselors have no spiritual support groups in their area, I shall discuss one on one first, suggesting ways of finding some form of social support, and then discuss Courage as a form of group spiritual support. Before evaluating the various forms of counseling, however, I find it useful to state what I believe the *different* roles of the priest-counselor should be.

Three scenarios can illustrate three different roles of a priest-counselor, and I have been involved in all three. The first scenario is found in large urban centers where priests involved in Courage work have access to clinical psychologists and psychiatrists who agree with Catholic teaching on homosexuality. The Courage member has access to Courage meetings as well as to professional help. The priest can concentrate on spiritual direction, knowing that the professional with whom he is working will take care of the psychological dynamics. In the ideal situation, the person involved gives *explicit* permission to the spiritual director and the therapist to discuss his situation. This approach works very well.

The second scenario is different from the first in that the counselee is not able at present to pay the cost of professional therapy. In this situation, the priest-counselor should help the individual person by what is best described as supportive counseling. Negatively, that means the priest avoids any form of depth counseling for which he is not professionally trained. Positively, this means that he makes use of approaches that are concerned with conscious motivation; if in either a group or one-on-one situation an individual is able to reach elements of the unconscious as he freely shares, he is to be encouraged to try to understand them with the help of the counselor and the group.

In some instances, however, the individual must be referred to a professional therapist, particularly if the insight that emerged spontaneously could lead to depression and the temptation to suicide. To avoid getting in "too deep", the priest-counselor should have ready access to professional advice. This is exactly what I have been doing in Washington, New York, and Philadelphia for over thirty-five years with the help of Catholic professionals, and I have reason to believe that other priests have also been in close contact with such experienced practitioners. The truth is that some of our priestly counseling overlaps with theirs, as the late Dr. John Cavanagh pointed out to me many years ago when we worked together in Washington, D.C. Psychological professionals and priests truly do work together to help not only persons with homosexual tendencies but also persons with many other emotional difficulties.

The third scenario is different from the first two in that the homosexual person involved lives in a part of the country where professional help and group support systems are not available, and the priest is the only one available to help. In Courage work this is not a rare occurrence. What I have done in these situations is to listen regularly, helping the individual to acquire a few close friends with whom he can share his struggles. I ask him to follow a spiritual plan of life,[1] to go to confession regularly, and to keep in contact through phone calls or writing. Other priests and I have done this for years. Priests should be encouraged to undertake this difficult work, because many persons with homosexual orientation urgently need spiritual direction and emotional support. The Holy Spirit does guide priests in such situations.[2]

One-on-One Counseling

The attitude one has toward the counselee depends very much on one's recognition that the counselee is a human person made in the image and likeness of God, baptized by water and the Holy Spirit, the recipient of the Holy Eucharist and the other

---

[1] John F. Harvey, *How to Redirect Your Spiritual Life* (Boston: Daughters of St. Paul, 1979). I wrote this pamphlet before I was involved with Courage.

[2] One Courage priest-counselor has made good use of charismatic prayer in group sessions, pointing out that elements of the unconscious do emerge with positive insight for the individual and the group, an experience similar to that of persons who have been guided by Leanne Payne in her method for the healing of memories. The same priest points out that his group sessions turn out to be for some of the members a preparation for professional therapy. In the process, members point out, they are able to get in touch with their deeper feelings within a prayerful milieu. Similar phenomena are observed by some members at meetings of S.A.

sacraments, still struggling to overcome the effects of Original Sin by means of God's grace, destined and desirous of heaven, always emotional, sometimes rational, not as reasonable as the philosopher would have him be, but not as irrational as the psychiatrist thinks he is.

The counselee searches for God, although perhaps unaware that he is doing so. He is painfully aware that he needs help, and the counselor's task is to give him spiritual guidance. We begin with knowledge. In our current culture people are confused about norms of behavior. Young persons, particularly, have little understanding of moral principles. All morality is perceived as a matter of opinion. What is good for you may not be good for me, and what is evil for you may be good for me. The counselor needs to explain the *objectivity* of moral norms in a general way, and the norms of sexual behavior in a specific way, together with the objective immorality of homosexual activity.

It is important that the counselor recognize the unique nature of the person who claims to be "gay", realizing that there are different degrees of homosexuality and that some individuals are not really homosexual but only imagine themselves to be so. A professional diagnosis is often in order. The counselor, however, should stress that we are all meant to be heterosexual, and that homosexual orientation should be seen as an "objective disorder", which the counselee did *not* will to have and may be able to overcome through prayer, professional therapy, and spiritual support groups. In no way is his orientation the most important part of him. He is an adopted child of God capable of transcending this difficulty and leading a full Christian life. The counselor needs to enlarge the vision and strengthen the hope of the person who comes for help.

As one counsels, one notices that many counselees have an intense dislike of themselves, something not unique to them, but definitely connected with their own bad image of homosexuality. It is a species of *homophobia*, an unreasonable fear of homosexuality and of homosexual persons. It will take time and prayer for the counselee to accept himself as loved unconditionally by God.[3]

Homosexual Orientation: Objective Disorder

Because professed homosexuals have deliberately distorted the message of the "Letter to the Bishops of the Catholic Church on the Pastoral Care of Homosexual Persons" (1986), many homosexual Catholics believe that the Church said they were "essentially evil". It is crucial that such persons understand that the term *objective disorder* has nothing to do with moral worth or with the free will of a person. It is the *tendency* to homosexual desires and acts, since such desires or acts are objectively immoral, that the Letter calls an *objective disorder*.

Unfortunately, the term *objective disorder* continues to be distorted or misunderstood. In a commentary on a speech by Andrew Sullivan, editor of *The New Republic* and gay rights advocate, Peter Steinfels agrees with Sullivan's criticism of the Church's position that homosexual activity is immoral even when the two persons are in a kind of marriage. Sullivan contends that the Church says that the condition of homosexuality is not sinful but the expression of the condition is sinful. What both Sullivan and Steinfels overlook, or ignore, is that the Church states that the tendency toward homosexual acts is not sinful in itself, but *disordered*, because, if expressed, it is a sin.

Steinfels portrays Sullivan as struggling "with the Church's teaching that his emotional and sexual longings must never manifest themselves in physical intimacy and a lasting companionship. Ultimately, he had found that impasse spiritually de-

---

[3] See *Catechism of the Catholic Church*: homosexual persons "must be accepted with respect, compassion, and sensitivity. Every sign of unjust discrimination in their regard should be avoided" (no. 2358).

structive, choking off his ability to love either himself or others."[4] Steinfels does not criticize this view, obviously agreeing with it. But chastity has never kept anyone from loving himself or others!

Another misunderstanding of the meaning of *objective disorder* is found in the recent pastoral letter of Cardinal Basil Hume of London.[5] In attempting to clarify a statement he had made two years previously, Hume added two new sections—on friendship (section 8) and human love (sections 9–10)—but, ironically, these brought about a round of criticism from both the secular and Catholic press. In fairness to Hume, we need to look at the context of this pastoral letter. In section 7 he defends the term *objective disorder*, saying that it is not demeaning to the person. Still, in the same section he adds that when the Church speaks of the inclination toward a homosexual act as an "objective disorder", "the Church can be thinking only of the inclination toward homosexual genital acts". From studies of homosexuality it is clear that the homosexual orientation includes far more than the inclination to sexual-genital acts. One English homosexual writer, using a pseudonym, says:

> Gayness covers much more than mere sexual orientation. It is a whole culture. From my, admittedly limited, experience of this culture, it is like another world, where different values, politics and aspirations operate. There, ideas of normal life, with its ordinary pleasures and trials, are shunned in favor of the cult of sex. There where there is no chance of sex fulfilling its natural purpose of propagating the human race, it becomes an end in itself.[6]

A clinical psychologist summed up the views of many of his colleagues when he said that "homosexuality has very little to do with sex". There is a whole way of thinking and feeling that

[4] "Beliefs", *New York Times* (Feb. 18, 1995), National section.

[5] "Note on Church Teaching concerning Homosexual People", *Origins* 24 (April 27, 1995):765–69.

[6] Ben Manser, "My Life Is My Own", *London Sunday Telegraph* (March 19, 1995).

occurs long before the inclination to genital acts with persons of the same sex arises in the heart. While it is true that the "Church does not consider the whole personality and character of the individual to be thereby disordered",[7] nonetheless, the disorder itself is rooted in unhealthy emotions.[8]

Turning now to section 8 of the Hume letter, one finds a troubling passage: "To equate friendship and *full* sexual involvement with another is to distort the very concept of friendship. Sexual loving presupposes friendship, but friendship does not involve *full* sexual involvement" (emphasis added). I am troubled by the connotations of the word *full*, as were many who wrote letters to the *Catholic Times* of London. Does friendship, with the exception of marriage, have to involve *any* sexual-genital involvement? Should it involve "partial" sexual involvement? Is it licit, for example, for two persons of the same sex to nourish erotic feelings toward one another? If one has these feelings, should he try to transcend them in favor of a friendship with the other person on a spiritual level? Many times heterosexual persons learn how to transcend such erotic feelings in the interests of friendship.

It may be presumed that Cardinal Hume did not want his statement to be understood as approval of deliberate nourishing of erotic feelings between two persons of the same sex. But that needs to be clarified, as a letter to the *Catholic Times* of London (March 24, 1995) by Christine Hudson says:

> When teaching on such a sensitive issue, though, it really is necessary to avoid any ambiguities which can be seized by the Press to distort the original meaning. On Friendship the Cardinal states "sexual loving presupposes friendship, but friendship does

---

[7] Hume, "Note on Church Teaching", no. 7.

[8] See Elizabeth Moberly's *Homosexuality: A New Christian Ethic*, Leanne Payne's *The Broken Image*, William Consiglio's *Homosexuality No More*, and Gerald van den Aardweg's *Homosexuality and Hope* for an analysis of such emotions.

not involve full sexual involvement". This particular statement needs to be further developed to state that friendship does not require any sexual involvement, and that there is a complete difference between pure caring love (as between parents and children or best friends) and sexual love. Because this vital difference was not highlighted, I was horrified to hear the radio news transmitting an unfortunate illustration, given by Nicholas Coote, of Jesus loving Mary Magdalene, and St. Francis loving St. Clare, implying sexual attraction, albeit they had chosen to live celibately.

Hudson adds that in a society that equates lust with love such an analogy is wrong.

Another writer in the same issue makes the same point concerning how a statement from a bishop will be received by the general public. For most persons with homosexual orientation "any special relationship based on physical attraction is going to be a most serious occasion of sin, and in this respect it seems to me it needs pointing out that the Church's requirements that the unmarried observe chastity demand far more than that we abstain from genital acts".

A Presbyterian marriage counselor pointed out that the only friendship that should involve erotic feelings, eventually leading to the desire for sexual-genital intercourse, would be that between a man and a woman freely intending to marry. All other friendships should not involve this erotic-genital component, and, if it were to arise, one must rise above it. From this perspective, then, these sections of the pastoral letter fail to make proper distinctions concerning friendship, sex, and love.

In observing friendships among men with homosexual inclinations, I have noted that they use ascetical means to purify their erotic feelings; those, however, who have *fostered* erotic feelings toward others wind up in promiscuity, masturbation, or liaisons. This leads me to section 10 of the letter, on "human love".

The first sentence fails to distinguish between homosexual love, as such, and heterosexual love: "to love another, whether of the same sex or of a different sex, is to enter an area of the richest human experience".

In a context other than the pastoral care of homosexual persons, this sentence can have a perfectly acceptable meaning. In its present context, however, it was interpreted by the press as placing marriage and homosexual friendship on the same level, despite the fact that in section 5 Hume had repudiated such an equation. If Saint Aelred had a chaste friendship with one of his fellow monks, it would not have been due to an allegedly homosexual inclination because he would have transcended this erotic component, this objective disorder or psychic defect, within himself.

In friendships among people of the same sex, however, persons with homosexual inclinations have a more difficult challenge if they discover erotic inclinations toward their friend, particularly if the friend also is homosexual. For this reason Christian therapists recommend that the homosexual person seek to form a same-sex friendship with a heterosexual person. It can be a step out of the homosexual subculture. Today there is a whole body of literature recommending that persons with homosexual inclinations seek out heterosexual models of masculinity and femininity in order to free themselves from the homosexual subculture.[9]

In sections 11 and 17 of the letter, the word *ideal*, as applied to marriage and friendship, may lead to misinterpretations. One may fail to fulfill the "ideal" of a perfect friendship without sinning, but one who does not fulfill the obligations of marriage does sin. Again, in section 17, "law" and "ideal" are interchangeable when one distinguishes between the obligation of observing the law of chastity and fulfilling the ideal of voluntary poverty. The latter is optional, whereas chastity is an obligation, or obligatory ideal.

[9] See the discussion of this issue in chapter four.

Section 15 speaks of "homophobia" and "homophobic attitudes" without defining them. Definition is necessary, because advocates of the gay lifestyle and the secular media frequently label as "homophobic" theologians who explain Roman Catholic teaching and lawyers who oppose gay rights bills. At public meetings I have been called homophobic, and I am not, because I do not fear, hate, or dislike persons of this orientation.

Section 16 speaks of the need for "enlightened and effective pastoral care with pastoral ministers who are properly trained to meet these pastoral needs". The section, however, does not elaborate on the specific content of such care. No program is proposed to challenge the homosexual person to a life of virtue. Nothing is said concerning the content of pastoral training or by whom it is given. How is it integrated into Catholic moral teaching? While it is true that we need a "demanding understanding", we also encourage the homosexual person to a life of prayer and virtue.

Homosexuality and Bisexuality

It is also important, particularly with teenagers and young adults, to have a working definition of homosexuality. Many counselees have a *subordinate* desire toward persons of the other sex or seem equally drawn to both sexes. For the purpose of guidance I submit this definition of homosexuality: a *predominant* physical attraction toward members of one's own sex that persists into adulthood. The term *predominant* needs no further explanation; but the phrase "persists into adulthood" helps the counselee to understand that one is not certain one has the tendency until it lasts into adulthood. Many teenagers who think they are "gay" realize in early adulthood that they are heterosexual.

In homosexual literature, moreover, one notes that the term *bisexuality* is used to describe individuals who find themselves attracted to persons of both sexes. Without going into the complexities of this condition, I suggest that in trying to understand such persons one distinguish between the emotional life of the person and his behavior. The bisexual person is capable of sexual-genital relations with either sex but, generally speaking, is emotionally involved with persons of his own sex and not so involved with a person of the other sex.

One finds bisexual people struggling in a marriage with children. What kind of counsel can a priest give? What I have found is that such individuals are capable of chastity with regard to members of their own sex and of relating well enough with their marital spouses to maintain the marriage. Usually the individual's love for his spouse, coupled with some degree of erotic attraction, enables him to fulfill his duty to the spouse. I recommend professional therapy in some cases. Sometimes, however, the person may have been incapable of marriage, and an annulment should be sought.[10]

Although I have treated the arguments against homosexual activity in chapter six, I think it prudent to make sure the person counseled understands the reasoning behind the arguments. So often the faithful are confused by the manner in which reductionist theologians explain away both Old and New Testament texts concerning the condemnation of homosexual acts. But there is no way the same theologians can repudiate the argument against homosexual acts that is based upon the biblical understanding of human sexuality and marriage. If one accepts the biblical perspective, one must hold that homosexual activity is necessarily immoral. The ordinary counselee, moreover, can understand the immorality of reducing the human body to a mere instrument of pleasure, which is the way many homosexual advocates perceive it.

[10] In these cases the "bisexual" person is actually homosexual and determined to live the homosexual lifestyle, or the person is sexually addictive and unwilling to be faithful to his spouse.

Masturbation

In the previous chapter, I treated briefly the phenomenon of sexual compulsions and the need for support groups to help one regain what such groups call "sexual sobriety".[11] Since in my counseling experience among Courage members everywhere I have found either the habit or compulsion of masturbation a serious problem, I shall develop some insights that I hope will be helpful.

Members of Courage, as well as members of S.A., regard masturbation as a definite obstacle on the road to sexual sobriety. They consider erroneous the opinion of some counselors and professional therapists that the habit of masturbation is a "safe" form of relief from sexual urges, only a very minor matter not worthy of further consideration. In the light of their own experiences, shared at Courage meetings, members become very honest with themselves in avoiding the kinds of triggering events that lead to daily or very frequent masturbation. They realize that growth in the practice of chastity is a gradual process, sometimes marked by painful relapses. "It demands regular consultation with a spiritual director, heartfelt admission of personal powerlessness, faithful attendance at meetings, utter honesty in talking about self, and the daily practice of meditation or the prayer of the heart."[12]

At meetings dealing with chronic masturbation I have read the following verses entitled "Autobiography in Five Short Chapters":[13]

> 1. I walk down the street. There is a deep hole in the sidewalk. I fall in. I'm lost. . . . I am helpless. It isn't my fault. . . . It takes forever to find a way out.

[11] See chapter six, above.

[12] John F. Harvey, "The Pastoral Problem of Masturbation", *Linacre Quarterly* 60 (May 1993):32.

[13] Portia Nelson, quoted in ibid., p. 34.

2. I walk down the same street. There is a deep hole in the sidewalk. I pretend I don't see it. I fall in again. I can't believe that I am in the same place. But it isn't my fault. It still takes a long time to get out.

3. I walk down the same street. There is a deep hole in the sidewalk. I still fall in. It's a habit. . . . My eyes are open. I know where I am. It is my fault. I get out immediately.

4. I walk down the same street. There is a deep hole in the sidewalk. I walk around it.

5. I walk down another street.

These verses resonate with the members, as they do with anyone struggling to overcome a bad habit or compulsion. There are also other elements worth noting in masturbation by persons with homosexual tendencies. The kinds of fantasy involved in masturbation reveal the inner nature of the person's problem. If the fantasy by the adult is concerned with children or teenagers, it is strongly suggested that he seek professional therapy; likewise, if the fantasy is filled with sadomasochistic images, therapy is in order.

If the person, moreover, considers himself bisexual because he has had sexual experience with both sexes, and his fantasy is primarily of a heterosexual nature, the chances are that he is heterosexual in orientation; in contrast, if his fantasy is predominantly homosexual in nature, then it is likely that at this stage in his development he has become fixated toward homosexuality. I qualify my opinion because teenagers who fantasize about persons of the same sex may move out of this kind of fantasy in the course of maturation, particularly with the help of therapy.[14]

Again, on the basis of pastoral experience I believe that homosexual persons have more difficulty with masturbation than do heterosexual:

The homosexual person often does not want to admit even to himself that he has this orientation, sometimes withdrawing

[14] Harvey, "The Pastoral Problem", p. 41; also Leanne Payne, *The Broken Image* (Westchester, Ill.: Crossway Books, 1982), pp. 46–47.

into an intense fantasy life with compulsory masturbation. Again, he fears admitting this orientation to others, considering masturbation a safe alternative, particularly now with the AIDS crisis. Since, moreover, such a person has more difficulty finding intimacy and friendship than the ordinary heterosexual person, it is not surprising that he tends to masturbation. The habit of masturbation, however, renders many homosexual persons vulnerable to promiscuity. First, fantasy and masturbation, then cruising the haunts, and later, finding someone for a one-night stand.[15]

While Courage members have become aware that mutual masturbation has become the principal form of "safe" sex, they also know that it destroys the relationship of the person with God while preventing the person from becoming sexually integrated in relationship to self.[16]

In the literature on masturbation, moreover, it is rare to find any discussion on the spiritual effects of masturbation. Two authors who can enlighten the homosexual person on this aspect are Dr. William Kraft and Father Bernard Tyrrell. Kraft holds that the habit of masturbation carries the message that the person has not yet integrated his social, spiritual, emotional, and physical life.[17] Father Tyrrell's position appears in a critique of Father Donald Goergen's *Sexual Celibate*. He does not agree with Goergen's hypothesis about the guilt-free masturbating of the vowed religious. Masturbation must be seen as contrary to the vowed life of celibacy.[18]

[15] Harvey, "The Pastoral Problem", 41.

[16] William F. Kraft, "A Psychospiritual View of Masturbation", *Human Development* (Summer 1982):39–45. E. Michael Jones, in "The Solitary Vice Goes Public" (editorial), *Fidelity* 4 (March 1985):5, calls masturbation "the introductory and most accessible vice. . . . Masturbation is, in a sense, the root sexual evil first of all from a developmental point of view—it is the child's introduction to sexual sinning—but also because all other sexual sinning is at its root masturbatory."

[17] Kraft, "A Psychospiritual View", 39–45.

[18] "The Catholic Celibate and Masturbation", *Review for Religious* 35, no. 3 (1976):399–408.

In overcoming the habit of masturbation, one of the most important elements in the spiritual armor of the person with homosexual tendencies is the support of the other members of the group. Members of S.A. who suffer from the same weakness will reaffirm their need of their support group. This is not a denial of the help each person receives from his spiritual director, from good reading, and from prayer, but it is an affirmation of the power of the group to help each individual to be himself in his relationships to God and to his neighbor. The young people, for example, who are striving to get out of the condition itself find renewed motivation in the company of others with the same goal. Older members of the group encourage them as well.

Again, when individuals present their life story, they see the roots of homosexual tendencies and masturbation in their family and school background. As I point out in chapter four concerning the possibility of change of orientation, the factors discussed are overwhelmingly psychological. In forty years of counseling I have heard time and again in the life accounts of my directees stories of lack of close relationships to parental figures combined with isolation from peers, beginning very early in grade school and still present in their twenties. These and other psychological influences are discussed more fully in chapter four.

The point I make is that the attraction to the same sex was present very early, making them wonder whether they were born that way. As counselors and spiritual directors, we need to listen carefully to the person's own perception of his interior life, so that we may help him to rebuild his spiritual life.

Hope for Change

I believe that counselors and spiritual directors should acquaint themselves with the claims of the American Psychiatric Association and the American Psychological Association that once a person realizes that he has a homosexual orientation, he should resign himself to the condition, embracing an active homosexual lifestyle, preferably with a steady lover. Vigorously opposing this view on the basis of empirical evidence, a relatively small group of psychotherapists have formed a new organization to provide counsel and therapy to Christians struggling with this difficulty. They propose programs to help individuals to grow out of the condition itself. The younger the counselee, the greater the chance he can move out of his present condition. It will take time for Catholics to discover the existence of NARTH (National Association for Research and Therapy of Homosexuality).[19]

Until very recently, Catholic clergy and counselors have not given the person with homosexual orientation any hope of change. In my early research and writings I had assumed that such persons should commit themselves to a life of consecrated celibacy, but over the last fifteen years I have changed my mind, as the result of the research of Elizabeth Moberly, Gerald van den Aardweg, Leanne Payne, and others. I now see such a change as a live option, adding that it takes prayer, self-discipline, group support, patience, and professional therapy.[20]

I insist, however, on two things: (1) This is an option, not an obligation; and (2) individuals who pursue a change of orientation should not allow themselves to be discouraged if after several years of therapy they personally are not able to develop a

[19] For information write to NARTH, 16542 Ventura Boulevard, Suite 416, Encino, CA 91436 (tel. 818-789-4440). NARTH published a collection of papers given at their annual spring conference, May 22, 1994, *New Techniques in the Treatment of Homosexuality*.

[20] The *Catechism of the Catholic Church* seems to assume that one has no real hope of getting out of this condition: "They do not choose their homosexual condition; for most of them it is a trial. . . . These people are called to fulfill God's will in their lives and . . . to unite to the sacrifice of the Lord's Cross the difficulties they may encounter from their condition" (no. 2358). I believe, as do other theologians, that a future edition of this work will address the hope of change.

genuine attraction toward the opposite sex; they should then resign themselves to a life of chaste service to Christ in the world.

From listening to Courage members over the last fourteen years, I believe that in general they have received minimal help from psychiatrists and psychologists in overcoming homosexual desires. This is not surprising, in light of the pro-gay movement within the American Psychiatric Association, with its attempt to make homosexual activity a normal variant of human sexuality.[21] Its 1973 decision to withdraw homosexuality from the *Diagnostic and Statistical Manual*, third edition (DSM III), has had an impact upon thousands of counselors as well as professional therapists, social case workers, and clergy of all faiths; moreover, it has been accepted *uncritically* by the media that the homosexual lifestyle is merely a diverse way of expressing one's sexual nature.

Under these circumstances it is difficult for a therapist, convinced that his client has a good chance to come out of homosexuality, to practice his profession. I know several therapists who, despite the hostility of professional peers, continue to work with persons desiring such change. That is why NARTH is necessary.

At the May 1994 meeting of NARTH, psychiatrist Jeffrey Satinover analyzed the current relationships between psychiatrists and religious counselors vis-à-vis homosexuality, offering some hope that the level of hostility on the part of psychiatrists toward religious counselors will diminish. He goes on to say that

> as physicians and healers we ought not to allow our philosophical assumptions to stand in the way of our patients' well being.

[21] The American Psychological Association holds (1980) that the form of homosexuality in which the individual is perfectly satisfied with his orientation (ego-syntonic) is no longer classified as a mental disorder. See Ronald Bayer, *Homosexuality and American Psychiatry* (Princeton, N.J.: Princeton Univ. Press, 1987), esp. chap. 4, "Diagnostic Politics and the American Psychiatric Association". Bayer openly admits the politicization of the issue of the normalization of homosexuality, a process he supports.

And it is no stretch of the Hippocratic Oath to insist that knowingly to withhold treatment that works would be to do harm just as certainly as to apply treatment that certainly harms (an ethical point assiduously avoided by the pro-Gay lobby within, and the current leadership of, the American Psychiatric Association). The potential conundrum in our field, the treatment of homosexuality, is that there is a considerable amount of evidence that at least some of the religious approaches to the healing of homosexuality are, indeed, quite effective in healing, or at least helping to heal, this very difficult problem, and, while not always perfect in its results, in restoring people to full, effective heterosexual functioning.[22]

Satinover describes and distinguishes the diverse spiritual support groups working with persons who desire to become heterosexual under the umbrella organization Exodus. In chapter four I have already given Satinover's positive evaluation of Comiskey's Living Waters program, with its high rate of success in helping persons out of homosexual orientation and into heterosexuality. Here I add his thorough analysis of the pastoral care ministries of Leanne Payne.

Payne uses the "inner healing" movement, which in Satinover's judgment provides "the clearest understanding of the relationship between faith and psychological process, hence it is the most scientific—and yet it is firmly rooted in the Charismatic Renewal movement within the Church, embodying a distinctly ecstatic form of worship".[23]

As I have already commented on Leanne Payne's method of "inner healing" from the perspective of moral theology,[24] I shall add here the viewpoint of Dr. Satinover, who also is seeking to integrate the findings of science with the insights of faith. He

[22] "Psychotherapy and the Cure of Souls: Faith and Religious Belief in the Treatment of Homosexuality", in *New Techniques in the Treatment of Homosexuality*, pp. 82–83.

[23] Ibid., p. 87.

[24] See chapter four.

points out that the counselee "need no longer fear and therefore deny the pangs of conscience; indeed, he learns instead—in a way which, to an extent, parallels psychoanalytic insight, but in other ways is quite different—that acknowledgement of sin leads directly to a deep sense of being thoroughly loved".[25]

In short, having studied the work of Leanne Payne, Dr. Satinover concludes that her method not only satisfies the highest standards of professional therapy but also leads to real cure of the condition of homosexuality through an interaction of factors, one of which is the power of the Holy Spirit—an element one accepts on faith or not at all.

Courage and Other Support Groups

Having considered the fact that Courage is open to helping people who desire to move out of homosexuality and having described some of the methods used by various Exodus groups to facilitate the process of change of orientation, I turn now to a pastoral situation of Catholics who want the help of Courage but have no Courage unit in their diocese. I would ask them to check in their vicinity for another spiritual support group that holds firmly to the belief that all homosexual activity is immoral, such as Homosexuals Anonymous (H.A.), Regeneration, Harvest, Metanoia, Desert Stream, and Sexaholics Anonymous (S.A.; but not the "reformed" version of S.A., which allows sexual activity between steady partners). For some years now I have recommended such organizations. I usually send a copy of the pamphlet *How to Redirect One's Spiritual Life*, suggesting that the person seek out a spiritual director or regular confessor. I have sent persons to H.A., Regeneration, and S.A. with good results, while hoping that in the future a Courage unit would be established in their diocese. I believe that Courage gives the person a

---

[25] "Psychotherapy and the Cure of Souls", p. 89.

Catholic identity not attainable in the other groups, however good they are in themselves.

I would not recommend a Catholic group that compromises on the issue of the immorality of all homogenital activity, and I would ask the person seeking counsel to make sure the group he joins is in accord with the authentic teaching of the Church. It is indeed a tragedy that Catholics seeking the support of their Church have not been able to find it in some dioceses. Many letters in our Courage files express the desire to know where one can find a Courage group, or at least a regular confessor; sometimes the plea is for a therapist who believes in the Church's teaching on homosexuality.

Insights into One-on-One Counseling

In stressing the great value of spiritual support groups for the practice of chastity, I may have given the impression that individual counseling and spiritual direction are no longer necessary, and I want to correct that by describing typical cases of individual counseling and spiritual guidance.

Adolescent Men and Women

While I cannot discuss every kind of situation, I can comment on a few. A teenage boy or girl confesses homosexual activity or (rarely) masturbation with homosexual fantasies. One does not assume that the young person is set in a homosexual orientation. One needs to know more about the motivation. Is this already a pattern? Or an isolated act done under the influence of alcohol or drugs? If possible, have the teenager visit a competent clinical psychologist to determine the depth of the orientation. This is very important, because late teenagers on the college level can easily be seduced by gay propaganda. The combination of gender identity confusion, peer pressure, gay and lesbian social clubs on campus, and the media acceptance of the gay lifestyle probably will have undue influence on their thinking and behavior.

Since I have treated the situation of the apparent adolescent homosexual at some length elsewhere,[26] I shall only repeat here a few pertinent insights. The counselor should ponder Ruth Tiffany Barnhouse's definition of homosexuality: "I use the word *homosexuality* to refer to an *adult* adaptation characterized by preferential sex behavior between members of the same sex" (emphasis in original).[27] From her many years of clinical experience, Barnhouse concludes that guidance of such teenagers is crucial for the future direction of their lives. In no way does she accept the theory that one's sexual identity is sealed during the first six years of life. She treats the impact of an extremely competitive and power-oriented culture on the adolescent. If he is already torn in different directions, he may succumb to a lifestyle that seems to have the approval of his peers. He needs education in the basic meaning of human sexual-genital activity and in the truth that homosexual groups are *not* a minority in the proper use of that term. He needs to be made aware of his own ambivalence together with youthful propensities to narcissistic behavior and emotional overattachments.[28]

Another factor of which the adolescent person or the adult may not be aware is the close connection between mood swings and sexual acting out—a phenomenon I call the *internal* occasion of sin. From listening to individuals who have acted out frequently in the past one notes how the down mood of self-pity or the up mood of triumph seeking a reward affects the imagination, moving swiftly to the porno shops, the gay bars, theaters,

[26] *The Homosexual Person* (San Francisco: Ignatius Press, 1987), pp. 189–200.
[27] *Homosexuality: A Symbolic Confusion* (New York: Seabury Press, 1977), p. 22.
[28] Particularly useful is Lori Rentzel's pamphlet *Emotional Dependency* (InterVarsity Press; obtainable from Regeneration, Inc.).

and bathhouses.[29] The need, then, is to control dangerous moods.[30]

Finally, among the practical directives found in *The Homosexual Person,* I suggest that the adolescent develop an attitude of *interdependence*, the very rationale of group support systems. Interdependence is sharing love through good friendships, such as often occur among those who regularly attend Courage meetings. Two years ago a young man of twenty, a college sophomore, joined Courage after recognizing his homosexual tendencies. Stephen wanted to get rid of his homosexual tendencies because he hoped some day to marry and have a family. He was dating a young lady who encouraged him to seek professional help. Later, a Catholic psychiatrist sent him to Courage, where he has been for several years. Within the group he has grown in the art of prayer and in his ability to articulate his feelings at meetings when one or another member is presenting one of the Twelve Steps. He continues his therapy with a Catholic clinical psychologist, who—with Stephen's permission— keeps in touch with his spiritual director. Through regular attendance at Courage meetings, Stephen has come to a deeper understanding of himself and an ability to relate with the other members present. He has support from his family as well as the members of Courage. Our hope is that more young adults will seek the help of Courage. With the exception of the Courage units near the universities of San Francisco and Steubenville, Courage has not succeeded in establishing groups at other Catholic colleges. The only Newman center with a Courage unit is the one at the University of Maryland in College Park; meanwhile, on many campuses, gay and lesbian groups flourish.

[29] *The Homosexual Person*, p. 199. See also chapter four, n. 80.

[30] *The Homosexual Person*, pp. 199–200. Patrick Carnes, *The Sexual Addiction* (Minneapolis, Minn.: Compcare, 1988), pp. 134–39, analyzes the belief systems of Theresa in *Looking for Mr. Goodbar*. He shows the interconnection among her romantic beliefs, moods, and behavior.

It is a human given that we all desire acceptance by others and friendships with a few. This is an intense yearning in the teenagers and young adults who have a homosexual orientation. They treasure friends but at the same time are terribly afraid to reveal their innermost feelings to peers for fear of rejection. Often this fear leads them to the homosexual subculture, where they hope they will be accepted, and then they may be confirmed in the homosexual lifestyle, usually beginning with promiscuous activity (male) and sometimes ending in a steady-lover, homogenital relationship. In many instances women tend to a series of steady relationships. In all these situations the individuals are seeking human affection more than they are seeking orgasm, although they may not recognize the deep desires of their heart. Dr. Gerald van den Aardweg addresses this when he writes:

> If you behave normally toward others, you shall find good friendships now and then, but don't *deliberately seek them*, either, for the sake of a "cure". It is infinitely better to try really to love other people, men and women alike, and to search yourself and see how little you in fact do love and give (emphasis in original; correspondence, Oct. 1, 1986).

Adults

Adult homosexual persons frequently complain of loneliness, particularly during the period after they have resolved to stay away from their former homosexual environment. They have not yet formed any solid friendships either at Courage meetings or in the places where they work, and they are tempted to return to their old haunts, where they believe they had some real friends. Perhaps they did; they realize, however, returning can be very risky. Equally problematic is the question whether one should reveal his inner struggles to a heterosexual friend. Will he reject me? It is not an easy question to answer, and prudence demands that one proceed with caution. Friendships with heterosexual persons of the same sex help one with homosexual desires very much. On balance, it seems better to take the risk of possible rejection in order to identify with heterosexual persons of one's own sex.

At the same time, in striving to overcome homosexual desires and behavior, one should continue to cultivate the support of other members of Courage. Courage meetings, however, should not become a kind of refuge from the real world, in which people with homosexual tendencies form their own subculture. That is another reason why heterosexual persons should be invited to Courage meetings to discuss pertinent topics, including fear of the opposite sex. After all, one of the goals of Courage is to form chaste friendships with persons of the other sex as well as with persons of one's own sex. Since, however, persons breaking out of homosexuality need first to cultivate friendships with persons of their own sex in order to strengthen their sense of masculinity or femininity, one should be willing to wait until one has acquired a sense of masculinity or femininity before taking the next step of cultivating serious relationships with persons of the other sex.

What keeps some from coming to Courage meetings is a fear that they will have to give up a relationship upon which they have become very dependent. Such a fear is often rooted in the early environment. The person had been attached to another person; the relationship disintegrated; a new friend has been found, and the person is afraid he will lose this new friend. Such a person may be able to keep the friendship if it is not an occasion of serious sin. Proceeding with caution and with the help of a spiritual director, he can have healthy friendships.

Detachment and Overattachment

There are two handicaps found in persons with homosexual tendencies that need to be considered. The first is the tendency to be afraid of human intimacy, because one feels that he has been burned in the past in a relationship, and he is not about to take a chance on being let down again. As a result, he does not reveal himself completely to others, always holding back the trauma of the past. This is a form of *hostile detachment*, described by Elizabeth Moberly in *Psychogenesis*. The second handicap, which, by the way, is shared with many heterosexual men and women, is *emotional overattachment*, defined by Lori Rentzel as the condition resulting "when the ongoing presence and nurturing of another is believed to be necessary for personal security."[31] When your worth, security, and peace of mind are rooted in another person and that person's response to you, then you are emotionally dependent.

It is crucial that the counselor understand these phenomena.[32] A person who is suffering from hostile detachment—from a parental figure of the same sex, for example—is often afraid to share with others because he is afraid to trust anyone. He has been so hurt by the trauma of the past, some of which he consciously recalls and some of which he is unaware of, that he will not open up completely even to those he wants to be his friends. He does not want to be hurt again.

Sometimes he will move into sexual promiscuity, like Johnny Rio in *The City of Night*.[33] On the occasion of a sexual encounter, the other man says to Johnny, "Let's have lunch tomorrow so we can know each other better and be friends." Johnny agrees, but he does not show up the next day because he is afraid of a personal relationship.

Sometimes, however, a person will take a chance, confiding completely in another after a period of sharing because he believes he has found the ideal friend. He takes great delight in

---

[31] Rentzel, *Emotional Dependency*, p. 7. See also Bob Davies and Lori Rentzel, "Healthy Friendships", in *Coming Out of Homosexuality* (Downers Grove, Ill.: InterVarsity Press, 1993), pp. 106–21. The authors give examples of both hostile detachment and emotional overattachment.

[32] See *The Homosexual Person*, pp. 193–95; also 196–98 (on narcissism and infatuation; crushes).

[33] John Rechy (New York: Grove Press, 1965).

spending time with his newfound friend, but after a while his new friend begins to resist his possessiveness, making it clear that he needs time to be with other friends. The first person becomes angry, and very often the newfound friend breaks away from the entanglement. I have seen this happen many times, and I refer the reader to Lori Rentzel's monograph "Emotional Dependency".

Courage and AIDS

In our spiritual guidance of men and women with homosexual attractions, we directors of Courage groups must confront the AIDS epidemic.[34] Readers of *The Homosexual Person* will find a section devoted to the issue of AIDS (pp. 201-14). While I still hold to the pastoral principles explained in my 1987 work, I feel the need to consider more recent developments, with the hope that we may dispel some of the distorted views on the issue, helping some individuals to avoid the HIV virus and reaching out to those with the HIV virus to help them to achieve reconciliation with Christ and his Church. Several authors have written that our government at both national and state levels has failed to alert the general public on the gravity of the AIDS epidemic. They have also pointed out various myths about AIDS that have been spread by the media under the influence of gay newspapers.[35]

[34] Father Robert Vitillo, head of Caritas Internationalis programs, has pointed out that 90 percent of the world's HIV/AIDS cases are found in the developing world. He thinks that as many as 40 million people will become infected by the year 2000. There has been a great increase of HIV infection among women. Again, there has been inequity in the targeting of HIV/AIDS prevention and care funds, with the largest part of funding going to the industrialized world. Lastly, he has stressed the need for "effective prevention and behavior change programs, especially for youth": see *Origins* 24, no. 37 (March 2, 1995):622–24.

[35] Gene Antonio, *AIDS, Rage, and Reality* (Dallas: Anchor Books, 1992); Lorraine Day, *AIDS: What the Government Isn't Telling You* (Palm Desert, Calif.: Rockford Press, 1991); Stanley Monteith, *AIDS: The Unnecessary Epidemic* (Sevierville, Tenn.: Covenant House Books, 1991).

It will be worth our while to consider some of these myths.

(1) Myth: *One can be HIV positive and never get AIDS*; in other words, that there is such a thing as a "healthy HIV carrier". It is now commonly assumed by experts that those who are HIV positive will eventually get AIDS. As French researchers state, "Asymptomatic HIV-seropositive individuals are *not* healthy carriers" (emphasis in original.)[36] Eventually, they will get AIDS.

(2) Myth: *AIDS cannot be caught by casual contact.* "There are a number of documented instances where AIDS has been spread by non-intimate contact, such as where a dentist spread the virus through casual contact with his patients."[37]

(3) Myth: *AIDS does not directly cause death; it simply destroys the immune system, rendering the person vulnerable to opportunistic diseases.* Gene Antonio, however, shows that the HIV virus can directly destroy the brain, leading to dementia.[38]

(4) Myth: *Nurses and doctors are safe from the AIDS virus provided they use universal precautions.* This formulation is meant to protect HIV positive patients from discrimination by doctors and nurses who may fear that they are endangered by treating those infected

[36] Antonio, *AIDS, Rage, and Reality*, p. 7. Antonio quotes French AIDS researchers.

[37] Joseph Feldschuh, an endocrinologist and cardiologist, quoted in Antonio, *AIDS, Rage, and Reality*, p. ix. He also points out that no attempts are presently being made to limit the activity of those affected with AIDS. See also Lorraine Day, *AIDS: What the Government Isn't Telling You*, pp. 5–14, where she shows that she, as an orthopedic surgeon, had been deceived by the theory that AIDS could not be contracted by casual contact.

[38] Antonio, *AIDS, Rage, and Reality*, chap. 2, "The Devastating Impact of HIV Brain Deterioration." Antonio draws upon a major report in the *New England Journal of Medicine* concerned with the abnormalities found in the "asymptomatic" stage of HIV disease: "Destruction of the brain is one of the most fearsome consequences of infection with human immunodeficiency virus (HIV). Many patients with acquired immunodeficiency syndrome become demented." This report is by I. J. Koralnik and A. Beaumanoir, "A Controlled Study of Early Neurologic Abnormalities in Men with Asymptomatic Human Immunodeficiency Virus Infection", *New England Journal of Medicine* 323, no. 13 (1990):864–70.

with the HIV virus. It has been shown, however, that the policy
of universal precautions has not given adequate protection to
health care workers. The orthopedic surgeon Lorraine Day gives
examples in her book of the failure of the policy of universal
precautions.[39]

Antonio also documents the failure of top health care officials
to acknowledge the infectious character of the HIV virus and to
make sure that both doctors and nurses who work with HIV
patients are aware that their patients are so infected. Only with
such safeguards in place will doctors and nurses have the opportunity to use adequate precautions in their practice.[40] Antonio
gives numerous examples of doctors and nurses who have become infected while at work. Orthopedic surgeons are most
vulnerable, as Lorraine Day points out in her book.

Antonio adds that the use of universal precautions has been
proven "woefully inadequate in preventing hepatitis B transmission to oral surgeons and other health care workers". He cites a
specific medical report from the *Journal of the American Medical
Association* that the use of gloves, face masks, and other protective devices does not appear to offer any substantial protection
against hepatitis B exposure. These findings have "chilling implications" for oral surgeons, dentists, and other medical professionals, because hepatitis B and AIDS have similar modes of
transmission.[41]

The other side of this issue is that the patient also has a right
to know whether his doctor or health care worker is HIV posi-

[39] *AIDS: What the Government Isn't Telling You*, pp. 1–28. Dr. Day resigned as
chief of orthopedic surgery at San Francisco General Hospital because she
believed that many health care workers are at risk under the present policy. She
holds that the medical establishment is underplaying the threat because of
pressure from professional homosexual groups. She adds: "I personally know
of 17 surgeons who are infected with the AIDS virus from occupational exposure, eight of whom are orthopedic surgeons" (p. 291).

[40] Ibid., chap. 4, "Health Care Workers under Siege", pp. 171–92.

[41] Ibid., pp. 195–96.

tive whenever some kind of invasive procedure may be necessary. Martin S. Lewin, M.D., writes that "medical ethics demands that a physician, more particularly a surgeon, infected with HIV either so inform patients or cease to have contact with them. It is of equal importance that physicians know the HIV status of their patients."[42]

Because the privacy of those who test HIV positive is protected, it is unavoidable that the rights of the uninfected, for the legitimate purposes of self-protection, are denied. For the first time in medical history the law discriminates against the uninfected. In September 1985, Dr. Richard Restak summed up the issue: "The threat of AIDS demands from us a discrimination based on our instinct for survival against a peril, that if not somehow controlled, can destroy this society. This is a discrimination that caution is in order when knowledge is incomplete so that the public interest is protected. . . . This is not a civil rights issue; this is a medical issue."[43] Obviously, both government and public health officials have chosen to ignore Dr. Restak's warning.

Refusal to acknowledge the infectious nature of AIDS, spread mainly by promiscuous sexual behavior, both heterosexual and homosexual, has another dimension of deceit, and that is the promotion of condoms as a form of "safer" sex. The very use of the term *safer sex*, instead of *safe sex*, is a tacit admission that the use of condoms in homosexual relations or promiscuous heterosexual relations is not medically safe. The most that can be said for this usage is that it is *seemingly* safer than unprotected sexual activity.[44]

[42] *American Medical News* (March 18, 1991), p. 21, quoted in Antonio, *AIDS, Rage, and Reality*, p. 192.

[43] "Worry about Survival of Society First, Then AIDS Victims' Rights", *Washington Post* (Sept. 8, 1985), quoted in Antonio, *The AIDS Coverup?* (San Francisco: Ignatius Press, 1987), pp. 172–73.

[44] Antonio sums up many articles in newspapers and periodicals concerning the unreliability of the condom in preventing the HIV virus from entering the body of another person during sexual intercourse when he observes,

In my judgment, the use of condoms is actually *not* safer, because it induces the person who reads the condom ads in the subways of New York to believe that he is "safe" from the virus through the use of the condom. He does not have the fine-print warning on cartons of cigarettes, and he is dealing not with danger to his health but with the high risk of receiving into his body a deadly virus. Then, feeling that he is "safe", he indulges many more times in condom usage until he becomes addictive or out of control. In contrast, the person who on one occasion indulges in unprotected sex may be more willing in the future to face up to the dangers of HIV infection, because after a screening test he appreciates how lucky he is to have tested negative.[45]

In any case, from a pastoral point of view, there are only two truly safe modes of conduct to be taught to our young people: (1) abstinence before marriage and (2) fidelity in marriage with the understanding that both parties to the marriage are free of HIV infection. Catholic men with homosexual attractions who believe that they cannot practice sexual abstinence alone will find both God's help and human support in following the Goals of Courage and the Twelve Steps at Courage meetings. Meetings of Sexaholics Anonymous are also strongly recommended.

It is truly pastoral, then, to help individuals avoid AIDS through pastoral programs like Courage. At the same time, Courage and the Church must also be deeply concerned to give guidance and support to those infected with the HIV virus.

"Handing out condoms is a pathetic, counterproductive substitute for tough, aggressive HIV reportability and contact tracing. If there is to be an earnest effort to prevent the spread of AIDS in the adult and adolescent population, it is essential to stop conducting disease control 'in the blind' " (*AIDS, Rage, and Reality*, p. 235).

[45] A person who is habitually aware of the danger of HIV infection may periodically become careless, engaging in "unsafe sex". MichelangeloSignorile goes on to say, "Now I find myself in total uncertainty about my H.I.V. status, yet fearful of being tested": Signorile, "H.I.V. Positive and Careless", *New York Times* (Feb. 26, 1995), p. E15, Op-Ed article.

Over the last decade we Courage leaders in New York City have ministered to members who have died of AIDS. The first one to die, in 1984, gave us our name. These men were ready for death. They spoke of it openly and prayerfully. Not excusing themselves, they prayed for God's mercy. For some months they came to Courage meetings, and in their last days they were visited by Courage members. It was God's mysterious Providence that they would find Christ in Courage and in the sacraments of the Church.[46]

Confessors, Spiritual Directors, and Psychiatrists

The confessor or spiritual director will wonder at times whether the person with homosexual tendencies should see a clinical psychologist or a psychiatrist. I believe he should do so if the different kinds of neurosis found in heterosexual persons are observed in the directee, or if the person is desirous of changing orientation. Some individuals are primarily intent on getting out of compulsive behavior, and they find all they need in going to spiritual support groups like Courage and Sexaholics Anonymous.

If, however, the confessor or spiritual director recommends that the individual seek professional therapy, he should also seek to keep in touch with the therapist with the explicit permission of the directee, who should also give the same explicit permission to the therapist. In this way the directee will be helped considerably, instead of feeling that the spiritual director turned him over, so to speak, to a professional.

Sometimes two persons have had a chaste relationship, but then on a particular occasion they have fallen into serious sin(s) of impurity. What should the confessor say? I believe he should examine all the circumstances of the fall to determine whether

[46] See "Called to Compassion and Responsibility: A Response to the HIV/AIDS Crisis", U.S. Bishops, *Origins* 19, no. 26 (Nov. 30, 1989):421–34.

these two individuals are able to render what has now become a proximate (probable) occasion of sin a *remote* one. The confessor must consider what good has come in their past from their friendship, whether each is willing to avoid the factors that led to their fall, and whether at least one of them continues to receive spiritual direction from the confessor.

I have also seen an actual case where two women had been in a steady lover relationship involving sexual interaction and later, as a result of prayer and study of the Scriptures, came to the decision that they would lead lives of sexual abstinence, and they continue to do so. Each situation needs careful consideration and prudent direction, keeping in mind the factor of emotional dependency, which appears so frequently in these relationships.

Marriage

Persons with homosexual or bisexual tendencies present spiritual directors with a very complex series of problems. I carefully reread what I said about the matter in *The Homosexual Person*, finding only a few areas where I would refine the position I took there.[47] Since then I have become more convinced of the need for caution in arriving at the conclusion that a given marriage between a heterosexual and a homosexual is invalid. Granted, some of these marriages *seem* to be invalid, but one must carefully investigate the history of the union before advising a couple to seek an annulment. If in doubt, one must presume that a given marriage is valid; indeed, there may be instances where after many years of marriage the couple could be left in good faith concerning its validity.

Beyond the canonical aspects, one should set up a program of spiritual direction for the person in this kind of difficulty; if the situation is complex for the counselor, it is often bewildering

[47] See pp. 175–88.

for the marital partners themselves, who need both individual and group guidance. In the following suggestions, which are really a refinement of my 1987 perspective, I have in mind not only those already married but also those seriously thinking of marriage.

(1) Before marriage: Carefully investigate evidence of homosexual or bisexual tendencies in either of the parties. Is the person *predominantly* homosexual or simply bisexual in behavior? In some cases it may be necessary to consult with a clinical psychologist to ascertain gender identity. The spiritual director should avoid making a diagnosis. If the diagnosis is that the person is predominantly homosexual or that he has no real control over his sexual behavior, then the marriage should be at least delayed, if not canceled. No further plans for marriage should be made until a professional therapist gives a good prognosis concerning the ability of both parties to make a lifelong commitment.

(2) When a married person reveals to us in the forum of conscience that he is homosexual or bisexual, we must get the full picture before making any suggestions. If the confessor discerns that the penitent is willing and able to overcome homosexual or bisexual tendencies, then he should insist that he follow a strict spiritual program, such as that of Courage, Sexaholics Anonymous, or Regeneration in Baltimore—to name only a few—and that he return to his spiritual guide regularly.

If, however, the confessor believes that the penitent is either unwilling to reform his way of living or really incapable of doing so, then he should urge the penitent to take measures for separation, while retaining responsibility for his spouse and children. The penitent should also inform his spouse of the grave reasons for his decision so that in due time an annulment of the marriage may be sought. Although I use the masculine pronoun, the above suggestions apply to women as well. In my pastoral experience of marital breakdowns because of homosexual behavior,

I have met only two women with homosexual tendencies who did not make the effort to continue their marriages. Other women with both psychological and spiritual guidance continue to be faithful to their husbands while rearing families. On the whole, it seems that married women with homosexual or bi-sexual tendencies are more willing and able to make reforms in their lives than are men struggling with similar difficulties. This is only a tentative observation, made by one who is aware that our society knows comparatively little about female homosexuality or bisexuality, for which there is no approved definition.

(3) Since these situations involve at least one other person, the question arises whether the person with these tendencies is bound to tell the fiancée or the spouse. There is no easy answer. Sometimes the individual undergoes what is called "homosexual panic". A person is convinced that he is homosexual because he committed a homosexual act or because as a teenager he was seduced into such an act. This does not prove that he is homosexual. He need not reveal this to his future spouse; however, he may decide to do so because he believes she will not reject him for what happened in the past.

In other situations before marriage, however, where the confessor discerns that there should be no marriage, or at least a delay of marriage, he should advise the penitent to tell his future spouse. One must give the freedom to withdraw from the engagement. Sometimes when the woman is informed of the serious reasons for delay of marriage, she feels that her love for him will "heal" his homosexuality. This is a dangerous missionary instinct that must buckle down to the demands of reason.

After marriage, however, the duty of revelation becomes more complex. I shall illustrate my position with examples. A married man who has been faithful to his wife suffers from a compulsion for homosexual pornography (gay porn), which, in turn, leads to masturbation. He is willing to go to S.A. meetings during his lunch hour to overcome this tendency. He does not wish to tell his wife about it, because he believes that, with God's help and with a spiritual plan of life and S.A., he can regain control in this part of his life. As long as he continues his spiritual therapy, he is not bound to tell his spouse.

Another man in midlife who has been faithful to his wife for over twenty-five years gradually finds himself involved in impersonal homosexual sexual encounters on his way home from work. Although this happens only once a month, taking the form of mutual masturbation, he realizes that he should take steps to overcome this tendency. He can learn to do so with the help of his confessor, prayer, and a support group like Courage. He may believe that it would only harm his relationship with his wife to tell her about his weakness, and, as long as he is willing to take the proper steps to regain self-control, he is not bound to tell her his sins.

In contrast, if the husband has engaged in homosexual sodomistic intercourse or oral sex, he must refrain from intercourse with his wife until he has been tested for the HIV virus and been *proven* negative; in practice, this really means that he should tell his wife what has happened and how he is seeking both psychological and spiritual help. In one situation the husband had been urged by his therapist to tell his wife that he was being tested for the HIV virus. He was reluctant to do so, because he was afraid she would divorce him, after over twenty years of marriage. The therapist then suggested that he bring his wife with him for the next therapy session, so that the doctor could help her to understand the struggle her husband was going through. It turned out well. The wife did not desert her husband; instead she encouraged him to continue therapy and to go to S.A. meetings.

The Christian therapist held that intercourse while there was doubt about the husband's HIV status would place the wife in danger of becoming infected with the AIDS virus. An additional consideration in this case is the positive value of revealing a secret about yourself to someone you trust. The power of compulsion is weakened by humble revelation to someone you trust. In this case, things have worked out well.

Another example involves a wife who did not reveal her homosexual inclinations to her husband until twelve years into their marriage. By this time there were two children, six and three and a half years old. The wife came to me because she had formed an emotional attachment to another woman with whom there was occasional sexual-genital expression. She said that the physical activity was minimal with the other woman, adding that sexual relations with her husband were also minimal. She claimed to have a "low sex drive".

She described the first years of marriage as satisfactory, except she had a very difficult time becoming pregnant. In her view, communications with her husband were very poor. He was always working overtime. She was not able to respond sexually to him, and he eventually sought intercourse with her only occasionally. Meanwhile, she formed an emotional relationship with another woman, and three years ago she told her husband that she was "gay". When he came with his wife on the next visit, he told me that he had great difficulty with the thought of physical intimacy with his wife, knowing that she had a female lover.

As a result of meeting with husband and wife together, I was able to make some suggestions with the hope of saving the marriage. It is not clear at this point whether the wife is willing to take the steps necessary for the healing of her relationship with her husband. She seems willing to give up a physical relationship with the other woman and to seek therapy to restore her relationship with her husband. She sees herself as the source of all the trouble in the marital relationship. Both her husband and I have encouraged her not to give up. I will continue to work with both husband and wife.

There are many other possible situations, some of which are detailed in *The Homosexual Person*. I should like to comment on one more question: If separation is going to take place because of homosexual activity, should the children be told? The answer depends upon the age of the children and the extent to which the spouse's behavior was known. Certainly by the age of twelve children should be told that homosexual behavior was a decisive factor in the separation and possible annulment. But only as much knowledge as is necessary for explaining the separation or divorce should be revealed, and only to those who have a right to know, such as children beyond the age of twelve. The wounded spouse should do all that she can to protect the good name of her estranged husband, and the wounded husband should act likewise.

Aspirants to the Priesthood and Religious Life

Among American bishops and provincials of religious congregations of men there are divergent views on whether or not to admit to the diocesan seminary or religious order any candidate with homosexual tendencies, prescinding from his previous chaste behavior. The existence of the orientation itself is regarded as sufficient reason for excluding such persons from the seminary or religious order. So far as I know, there is no document from the Roman congregations that explicitly forbids a man who has led a chaste life despite a homosexual orientation from entering a seminary or religious congregation; nevertheless, ordinaries of dioceses and provincials of religious orders have the authority to set up such a policy, and some do so.

However, some bishops of dioceses and religious provincials are willing to accept such candidates after careful screening by professional therapists and vocation directors. All this is background for confessors giving direction to a young man who aspires to priesthood or religious life. A few scenarios may be helpful.

The first is the individual who has led a chaste life despite homosexual orientation. If the psychologists conducting entrance tests believe that the person is emotionally stable, it seems that he should be given the opportunity to enter the seminary or religious order. But he will need the help of a spiritual director in order to make progress in prayer and in the practice of virtue, like any other seminarian or religious. He needs to understand the nature of the homosexual condition and the possibilities of getting rid of the condition, which is really an "objective disorder". In no way should he parade his orientation. He should have a few friends in whom he confides together with his spiritual director—people with whom he can talk in times of stress and depression.

Another scenario is that of a youngster who comes to the spiritual director with a habit of masturbation involving homosexual fantasy. From my pastoral experience I believe that such a young man has deep-seated problems and that he should not enter the seminary until he has attended to the emotional problems that give rise to masturbation. Needless to add, he should also achieve control over the habit of masturbation. In this situation professional therapy is often necessary, and the individual should give both spiritual director and therapist *explicit* permission to discuss his situation.

There is another aspect in this question. Will the seminarian have such great difficulties in the practice of chastity that he will be constantly unhappy in the priesthood or religious life? If the answer is "probably yes", then he should be advised to leave. Doubts are to be resolved in favor of the Church, and really of the individual himself. Very probably his departure will help him avoid subsequent spiritual harm to himself and scandal to those who would be affected by his behavior if he had remained in religious life or the clerical state. In this regard Dr. Maria Valdes' probing article, based upon two decades of experience in counseling seminarians and priests, both diocesan and religious, throws additional light on this kind of problem, advocating a careful screening process before admission, with reappraisals at midpoint in formation and one year before ordination.[48]

Reception of the Eucharist

Some will say that the sexually active homosexual person should not receive the Eucharist unless, after receiving the sacrament of penance, he sincerely resolves to avoid such activity in the future. He would be required to tell the confessor the means he intends to use to avoid homosexual acts. Were he to fail after using such means, he could come back to confession, continuing to strive to overcome his weakness, and under these conditions he would be free to receive the Holy Eucharist.

But many other priests say that they would allow certain persons who are actively involved in the homosexual lifestyle to receive the Eucharist, because these individuals are not convinced that the teaching of the Church on this issue is true. After all, they say, prominent Catholic moral theologians teach that under certain circumstances homogenital activity between faithful lovers can be justified.[49] Such faithful relationships are regarded as the lesser of two evils. Some say, "What else can you expect thousands of Catholics to do? Surely, no one is recommending sexual abstinence, and one knows there is no way one can get rid of this condition."

As a result of this rationalization, many priests do not discuss the issue from the pulpit, in the classroom, in private conferences, or in the confessional. Gradually, the same sort of "good faith" mentality that has prevailed in the American and Western

[48] Maria Valdes, "Seminary Policy on Sexuality", in *Homosexuality: Challenges for Change and Reorientation, Journal of Pastoral Counseling* 28 (New Rochelle: Iona College, 1993).

[49] *The Homosexual Person*, chap. 5, "Major Dissenting Theological Views".

European Church on the morality of contraception since 1968 is spreading into the area of homosexual activity.

The priest who follows the teaching of the universal Magisterium, however, should continue to help individuals in the ways discussed in other chapters of this book. However difficult, he should try to persuade persons active in the lifestyle to give it up; at times he may have to refuse absolution, but this may not happen often. Some will listen to his counsel; others will simply not come back to a priest who insists upon true repentance as a condition for sacramental absolution. The priest finds strength in the thought that Jesus allowed some to walk away from him as he taught the people about the Holy Eucharist in John 6.

One may ask, however, whether faithful homogenital relationships, when compared with promiscuous sexual activity, are the *lesser* of two evils. Is this a valid application of the principle of the lesser of two evils? No, it is not, because one may not apply this principle to an action that is already evil in itself, such as the homosexual act.[50] While one may *tolerate* a lesser evil, no one may lawfully engage in an act that is intrinsically evil.[51]

Despite the clarity of Church teaching, however, many persons with homosexual difficulties will not accept it, and this should not disturb the priest. Keeping them in prayer, he should continue to relate to these members of the faithful with the hope that they will come to the sacrifice of the Mass even though they are not receiving Holy Communion. The situation is analogous to that of persons who, knowing that they are in an invalid marriage, may not receive the Eucharist.

But what if persons known to be living together approach the

[50] Germain Grisez, *The Way of the Lord Jesus*, vol. 1: *Christian Moral Principles* (Chicago: Franciscan Herald Press, 1983), pp. 217–20.

[51] Congregation for the Doctrine of the Faith, "Declaration on Certain Questions concerning Sexual Ethics" (Dec. 29, 1975), sec. 8, no. 4, and "Letter to the Bishops of the Catholic Church on the Pastoral Care of Homosexual Persons", no. 3. In the declaration, homosexual acts are described as "intrinsically disordered" and "able in no case to be approved of".

Eucharist? On that occasion the priest should give them Communion, because he has no way of knowing whether they have given up homosexual activity. He should seek, however, to contact one or both of the partners to express his concern and, if they are still active in the relationship, request that they not come to Communion until they have given up the genital activity and received absolution in the Rite of Penance. If in anger an individual refuses, the priest must learn not to take this reaction personally.

To be sure, this is a very painful situation, and the priest may be tempted to compromise his position as a pastor of souls by saying something like this: "Well, I do not approve of your coming to Communion, but if in your heart you really believe that your union is morally good, then follow your conscience." Then the priest will say to himself and to other priests too, "I think it is best that I leave such persons in good faith." In practice, I have met many priests in America who accept uncritically the above "lesser of two evils" and "good faith" arguments. As I said in chapter one, in many parishes where there are hundreds of persons active in the homosexual lifestyle one hears little or nothing from the pulpit or in catechism classes about the serious moral evil of homosexual activity. It is time that we reform our pastoral approaches to this issue.

8

A RESPONSE TO
THE GAY RIGHTS MOVEMENT

In the spring 1994 issue of *First Things*, the Ramsey Colloquium, a group of scholars from Protestant, Catholic, and Jewish institutions, presented its response to the homosexual
movement. As the colloquium describes it, and I agree with their
description, this movement is a collection of claims that groups
of homosexual men and women (in their language, gays and
lesbians) make against the current policies of local, state, and federal governments. This is the voice not of all homosexually
oriented persons, but of a disproportionately small, but very articulate, group who, however, have very great influence on the
decisions of legislators, judges, and presidents. The colloquium
appraised the following claims:

Many homosexual persons believe that they had no choice in
regard to their orientation and that they are not able to change it.
Prescinding from the question of the origin of the orientation,
the colloquium asks whether this predisposition should be acted
upon or resisted. It asks pastors and therapists to help individuals
to recognize the value of chaste living, resisting the impulse for
homogenital gratification. "What is in accord with human nature is behavior which is appropriate to what we are meant to
be—appropriate to what God created and calls us to be."[1] It is
true that we as individuals are subject to serious temptations to

[1] "The Homosexual Movement", A Response by the Ramsey Colloquium,
First Things (March 1994), p. 18; hereafter cited as Ramsey Colloquium.

sin as the result of our fallen condition, but we retain our freedom to resist actions or a way of life contrary to God's purpose. While helping people in their temptations, religious groups should consider as sinful homosexual intercourse or extramarital heterosexual behavior.

It is noteworthy that the above argument is from natural moral law. The colloquium continues with another natural moral law argument against the position, held by heterosexual as well as homosexual persons, that sexual actions are entirely private—no one else's business. But these so-called private acts are very often highly publicized. The real reason for this position is not the right to privacy but the right to absolute personal autonomy.[2] If, however, everyone embraces that attitude, the common good is undercut. There are still other reasons for concern, such as the alarming rates of promiscuity, depression, suicide, and the spread of AIDS in the homosexual community.

Not to be overlooked, moreover, is that public policies that encourage a homosexual lifestyle (such as those of San Francisco and New York) lead to a weakening of normal family life, while the homosexual lifestyle in that locality increases. One cannot be indifferent to the harm that the proliferation of this lifestyle does to family life and the common good.

Thus, there is need for society to support social norms by which sexual behavior is controlled according to right order. In contrast:

> the advocates of the gay and lesbian movement have the responsibility to set forth publicly their alternative proposals. . . . They

[2] In our culture there is a one-sided emphasis on personal rights with little or no consideration of the divine natural moral law as the source of all human rights. Little effort is made, moreover, to correlate rights with duties. In *Pacem in Terris*, John XXIII states the principle that every human being is a person, i.e., his nature is endowed with intelligence and free will. "Indeed, precisely because he is a person, he has rights and obligations which flow directly and immediately from his human nature" (no. 259). In this way human rights are given an objective basis, becoming more than a feeling.

must clarify for all of us how sexual mores are to be inculcated in the young, who are particularly vulnerable to seduction and solicitation. Public anxiety about homosexuality is preeminently a concern about the vulnerabilities of the young. This, we are persuaded, is a legitimate and urgent public concern.[3]

It is important to understand that the Ramsey Colloquium is a Judeo-Christian body using arguments from our shared humanity and concern for the common good. Its response also dissects the argument used so often by gays that they are a minority, like oppressed African Americans at the time of the civil rights movement, seeking justice. But the analogy does not hold: blacks are a minority because of race and the color of their skin but not because of their behavior, while *homosexuals make themselves a minority by their behavior.*

The colloquium argues against the notion that all discrimination against the homosexual lifestyle is wrong. In real life we all need to discriminate in forming social relationships. "Gay and lesbian 'domestic partnerships', for example, should not be socially recognized as the moral equivalent of marriage."[4] In our present permissive society, the institution of marriage is in need of social support. The colloquium concludes on the hopeful note that through reflection on this declaration damage to our society and to families can be prevented.

Review of Recent Studies

Having presented the colloquium's ecumenical arguments against the gay lifestyle, I think it will be useful to review arguments concerning homosexual rights and then to present Christian and Catholic arguments against so-called gay rights. Already in *The Homosexual Person* I examined the question at some length, and I refer the reader to that discussion. The work of

[3] Ramsey Colloquium, p. 19.
[4] Ibid.

Enrique Rueda in *The Homosexual Network* and of Edward Malloy in *Homosexuality and the Christian Way of Life* furnish a rich background for this chapter.[5] Rueda documents carefully and insightfully the beginnings of the homosexual movement and its impact upon religion in general and Catholicism in particular, while Malloy develops the various theological views of homosexual behavior, coming to the conclusion that the active homosexual lifestyle is incompatible with a Christian way of life.

When one checks data on psychological, sociological, and theological studies on the issue of gay rights, one notes immediately that most of the studies are overwhelmingly in favor of the position that the homosexual lifestyle should be regarded as an equal alternative to marriage, and that the political agenda of gay and lesbians must move in this direction. (I deliberately use the terms *gay* and *lesbian* to designate persons who are not only homosexual in orientation but also have adopted the active lifestyle.)

One of the arguments used by professed gays and lesbians is that they are an oppressed minority and that their situation is similar to that of African Americans before the civil rights movement of the 1960s. David Neff, however, denies that there is a valid analogy between African Americans and homosexual people in America,[6] and he is joined in this dissent by Lena Williams, who discusses gays in the black community. A distinction must be made between racism and antigay sentiment. Williams believes that black homosexuals are misappropriating the spirit and legacy of the black civil rights movement.[7] There is

[5] See my *The Homosexual Person*, pp. 107–15; also Reuda's *The Homosexual Network* (West Greenwich, Conn.: Devin Adair, 1982), pp. 299–382, and Malloy's *Homosexuality and the Christian Way of Life* (Washington, D.C.: University Press of America, 1981), pp. 145–62.

[6] David Neff, "Two Men Don't Make a Right", *Christianity Today* (July 19, 1993), pp. 11–15.

[7] Lena Williams, "Blacks Reject Gay Rights Fight as Equal to Theirs", *New York Times* (June 28, 1993), p. A1.

such a phenomenon as a "former homosexual", but there is no "former black American". This, of course, is the result of the fact that homosexuals are identified by behavior and blacks, as Martin Luther King often said, are identified by race and the color of their skin.

Neff goes on to point out that, at the present time, visible gays, in general, are not oppressed; and Andrew Sullivan, gay editor of *The New Republic*, agrees with him: "The Civil rights approach is bound to perpetuate a sense of homosexual identity as the Vulnerable Victim, setting up, in Sullivan's words, a psychological dynamic of supplication that too often only perpetuates cycles of inadequacy and self-doubt."[8] Neff also objects that the civil rights approach locks a person into a homosexual identity as something one must have permanently.[9]

Another gay author, Jonathan Rauch, in *The New Republic*, agrees that the gay community should abandon the oppressed minority argument. Granting that in specific instances there has been violence against homosexual persons, for the most part the oppression diagnosis is wrong. The standard political model is that gays are oppressed and that they must fight for liberation through political action, just like other minorities. But Rauch says that objective evidence indicates that, on the whole, the homosexual community is not oppressed. He provides five signposts of oppression to support his position: (1) Are homosexual persons subject to direct legal discrimination? Yes, in some states that have antisodomy laws and prohibition of domestic partnerships. (2) Are they denied the right to vote and to lobby for their cause? No. (3) Are they denied opportunities for education? No. Various studies indicate that, on the whole, they are more highly educated. (4) Are they in impoverished economic conditions? No. Indeed, they are very well off economically. (5) Are they

[8] Neff, "Two Men Don't Make a Right", p. 14
[9] Ibid.

subject to human rights violations without recourse? Here they are no worse off than the general population.[10]

Rauch proposes a different strategy. Instead of presenting gays and lesbians as oppressed, present them as "an ostracized people seeking redemption through personal action".[11] In the same issue of *The New Republic*, Urvashi Vaid argues that the victories of the gay rights movement are limited in many places by local and state laws and that it is time for all gays to come out of the closet and organize into a political power into which they contribute their wealth. After all, no movement can be built by a people invisible to each other and to society. Obviously, a new agenda is in the process of development in the gay community, aiming to have their lifestyle accepted by the rest of the population. In his book *Virtually Normal*,[12] Andrew Sullivan presents arguments for the full acceptance of homosexual marriages. In his conception of natural moral law, he considers homosexuality as a natural variant from the heterosexuality that is the destiny of the vast majority of the human race.

While it is extremely doubtful that the majority of Americans will approve a homosexual lifestyle, it is more likely that so-called homosexual rights will be imposed upon the public by decisions of federal judges. In Colorado almost a million people opposed affirmative action for persons with homosexual orientation (and in many cases behavior), but the will of the people was thwarted by judiciary decision. According to an editorial in *National Review*, this foreshadows how important decisions on homosexual rights "increasingly will be made": Such decisions will be made by federal judges operating on the premise that the

[10] Jonathan Rauch, "Beyond Oppression", *The New Republic* (May 10, 1993), pp. 18–23. See also Andrew Sullivan, "The Politics of Homosexuality", *The New Republic* (May 10, 1993), pp. 24–26, 32–37, where the author proposes abandoning the oppression argument in favor of a strategy that may win acceptance and equality from the American public.

[11] Rauch, "Beyond Oppression", p. 23.

[12] Andrew Sullivan, *Virtually Normal* (New York: Knopf, 1995).

"equal protection" clause of the Fourteenth Amendment prohibits disparate treatment of gays and lesbians. A federal judge in
New York State ruled that the state adoption laws were unconstitutional because they distinguished between married couples
and homosexual couples. A federal judge in the Midwest overturned an insurance policy because it did not provide for the
"spouse" of the deceased homosexual individual.[13]

In Minneapolis, a Minnesota civil rights panel voted 2 to 1 to
require the city and the public library to pay a total of $90,516 in
compensation and punitive damages to three lesbian library employees because the municipal authorities had refused to pay
health benefits to the "spouses" of the employees.[14] The trend in
these court decisions makes one wonder how both society and
the Church can protect their lawful interests against what seem
to be arbitrary judicial decisions.

I turn now to a theological opinion in favor of homosexual
unions under difficult circumstances. Previously, in *The Homosexual Person*, I had presented major dissenting theological views
within the Roman Catholic Church,[15] while not surveying the
varied views of Protestant and Jewish theologians.[16] Continuing
the same policy, I shall critique one other Catholic view, that of
Father John Yockey.

Father Yockey proposes to go beyond the restatement of the
Congregation for the Doctrine of the Faith concerning the immorality of homosexual activity by outlining a procedure for
applying the ancient theological principle of *oikonomia* (econ-
omy) in cases in which the well disposed cannot meet the standards of Catholic sexual morality. He does not see this procedure

---

[13] "Courting Injustice", *National Review* (March 1, 1993), pp. 16–18.

[14] "Lesbians Win Bias Case in Minneapolis", *American Libraries* 24 (January 1993):18.

[15] Harvey, *The Homosexual Person*, pp. 79–83.

[16] I regret that I cannot cover the Protestant and Jewish views; however, I recommend *Christianity Today*, *Christian Century*, *The Anglican Theological Review*, and *Christianity and Crisis* for presentations of Protestant views.

as a dispensation from moral law held with certitude; it is rather Christ reaching out to the person in a difficult set of circumstances through a prudential decision dictated by pastoral wisdom. This procedure suspends the existing norm of faith and morals in favor of an alternative approach that can better help the individual, severely oppressed by the existing norm, to achieve ultimate union with God.[17]

While I commend Father Yockey for his genuine pastoral concern, I see no essential difference between his view and that of Father Charles E. Curran, which I have critiqued elsewhere.[18] Both theories assume that the given individual is usually not *able* to meet the standard moral norm. This assumption is directly contrary to the teaching of the Sixth Session of the Council of Trent, to which I advert in chapter five, above, on sexual abstinence. In essence, that teaching states that it is a matter of divine faith that each person receives sufficient grace to fulfill the commandments of God. In Yockey's theory, however, the divine law of chastity, which the Church holds as binding on everyone, is seen as an oppressive burden on a particular individual with homosexual orientation. By what criterion do we know that Christ is directly exempting a given individual, or class of individuals, and not others from the divine law of chastity?[19] There is no such criterion. Once again, regarding sexual abstinence as oppressive or burdensome runs contrary to the faith experience of many chaste homosexual persons.

[17] John Yockey, "Economic Mercy for All: A Dialogical Model for the Pastoral Care of Homosexual Persons", *New Theological Review* 3, no. 3 (1990):71–87.

[18] *The Homosexual Person*, pp. 81–84.

[19] See the *Catechism of the Catholic Church*, no. 2348: "All the Baptized are called to chastity. The Christian has 'put on Christ,' the model for all chastity. All Christ's faithful are called to lead a chaste life in keeping with their particular states of life. At the moment of Baptism, the Christian is pledged to lead his affective life in chastity." See also nos. 2357–59, Chastity and Homosexuality. In no. 2357: "tradition has always declared that homosexual acts are intrinsically disordered." In no. 2359: "Homosexual persons are called to chastity."

Arguments against "Gay Rights"

It is necessary now to examine the civil rights claims of gay organizations, because, if accepted by our federal and state governments through legal statutes or through Supreme Court interpretations, they will come into conflict with the free exercise of religion by all those who regard homosexual activity as immoral.

Michael Pakaluk, Richard F. Duncan, and John Finnis help us to see the ensuing conflict between the application of gay rights laws and the free exercise of religious beliefs.[20] First, I shall consider Pakaluk's thought.

Michael Pakaluk

One wonders why gay leaders seek from the law kinds of protection that go beyond the fundamental rights that all Americans enjoy under our Constitution, such as freedom of conscience and religion, freedom of speech, freedom of association, and so on. When injustice is done to us, we have recourse to legal remedies. What claims does the homosexual movement make upon us? Pakaluk sees this group making claims in three distinct but related areas: (1) antisodomy laws should be repealed because they are unconstitutional, (2) discrimination against gays in housing and employment should be forbidden, and (3) same-sex unions should be given all the privileges that states have traditionally given to heterosexual marriage.

(1) The homosexual movement argues that antisodomy laws should be repealed because they penalize persons for their pri-

[20] Michael Pakaluk, audiotape, *Civil Rights Claims of Homosexual People* (Boston: Daughters of St. Paul, 1994), talks presented at Courage National Conference 1994. Richard F. Duncan, "Who Wants to Stop the Church: Homosexual Rights Legislation, Public Policy, and Religious Freedom", *Notre Dame Law Review* 69, no. 3 (1994):393–445. John Finnis, "Law, Morality, and 'Sexual Orientation' ", *Notre Dame Law Review* 69, no. 5 (1994):1049–76.

vate behavior, violating their putative right to privacy. They are an undue restriction upon one's right to the kind of sexual activity in which he chooses to engage. In addition, such laws are unenforceable, creating more problems than they solve, such as blackmail and entrapment.[21] Thus, they should be overturned. Repealing these laws would not necessarily be an approval of homosexual acts, but simply a decriminalization of them.

(2) To justify proposals to prohibit discrimination in employment practices and in public housing, the homosexual lobby claims that homosexual persons are an oppressed minority. Like African Americans, homosexuals should receive equal treatment by reason of the equal protection clause of the Fourteenth Amendment. Therefore, employers and owners of public housing may not refuse employment or housing to someone in the homosexual lifestyle, which in itself should be regarded as morally neutral.

(3) Just as heterosexual persons in their marriage are granted special privileges by the state, so also should same-sex unions have the same benefits, says the gay rights movement, because gays regard their unions as equal to the state of marriage. They give no sound argument for this position or for their insistence on the right to adopt children or to care for foster children.

Pakaluk points out that in the prevailing political climate, where the act of heterosexual intercourse has been divorced from its procreative meaning and where it is claimed that all morality is culturally determined and constantly in flux, like the culture itself, it is not surprising that the civil law is blind to fundamental moral truths. That disordered homosexual desires lead to sodomy, and that we are moving toward a condition of moral anarchy, not only in this issue but also in others, like the "right" to abortion, is overlooked as legal authorities have resort to the so-called right to privacy—something not in the Constitution.

---

[21] These examples are my own—from past discussions of the issue.

Although the "right to privacy" was invoked in *Griswold v. State of Connecticut* (1965) with reference to the "right" to use contraceptives and in *Roe v. Wade* (1973) with reference to abortion, the meaning of this "right" remains ill defined. It has become a kind of absolute value with no reference to the good of family or nation, or to the ultimate source of all rights, the Creator.

In 1961 Justice Harlan referred to certain basic moral principles that form the basis of our civil law regarding the welfare of the family and ultimately of the country. He said, for example, that adultery strikes at the heart of marriage. But, in the court decisions mentioned above and in gay rights legislation, the right of privacy of the individual has been expanded, and the impact of this legislation upon the soundness of family life ignored. The law has become blind to the morality of sexual acts, which, in their judgment, harm no one. Once sexual intercourse of husband and wife lost its procreative meaning in the minds of millions of Americans, any kind of sexual act done in private could be justified. The implicit assumption is that everyone has a right to some form of sexual intercourse, so long as it harms no one and does not offend public decency, and that sexual acts in themselves are neutral, having nothing to do with personal character. This assumption has led to anarchic subjectivism in judicial decisions concerning "private" sexual acts that presumably harm no one.

This view of sexual morality supports gay propaganda in the contention that homosexual orientation and behavior have nothing to do with character.[22] Pakaluk shows the absurdity of saying that sexual behavior has nothing to do with character, asking how society regards the habitual philanderer, the adulterer who wrecks a marriage, or the person who sexually harasses

---

[22] Gay rights bills speak of orientation as including some sort of sexual behavior, often using the term *practices*.

another. Why, then, should homosexual behavior be exempt from the moral norms of society?

Certainly, society does not approve of prostitution, because it symbolizes contempt for the human person whose body is bought; likewise, for thousands of years society has disapproved of sodomy as an act that in no way fulfills the purposes of human sexuality. But now it is regarded as a natural action for persons with homosexual desires. To be sure, the repeal of antisodomy laws does not constitute a legal right to sodomistic intercourse; nonetheless, it is the first step to the equalization of same-sex unions with heterosexual marriage, ultimately leading to the destruction of the traditional family.

Even if antisodomy laws are unenforceable, they have educational value, like the laws against prostitution, expressing society's disapproval of activity contrary to family values. They make a statement that control over one's sexual desires and consequent chaste behavior are intimately related to one's moral character, just as lack of control gives another message.

Pakaluk distinguishes carefully between homosexual orientation and acts, seeing the orientation itself as a handicap, because such desires can lead to the moral disorder of sin. Many persons with this inclination, however, do not disclose it to the public, struggling with the help of support groups like Courage to lead a life of sexual abstinence out of love for God. There is no reason for the person with such an orientation to feel that he is a second-class citizen. As I have pointed out previously, the analogy between homosexuals as oppressed persons and African Americans before the civil rights marches is false. As a group, *known* homosexuals (gays) are economically better off than the average person—they are *not* an economically oppressed minority. [23]

[23] Duncan, "Who Wants to Stop the Church", 407–8: "Have gay rights proponents proven their case that homosexuals have been economically impoverished by discrimination in employment, housing, and public accommodations and are therefore in desperate need of the protection of antidiscrimination laws in these areas? No. . . . the data support the opposite

Agreeing with the argument of Richard Duncan, Pakaluk points out that gay rights laws that fail to distinguish between homosexual orientation and practice and that assume that a person has a "right" to homosexual acts set up an unavoidable conflict between the civil law and the conscience of a landlord of an apartment house who believes that homosexual acts are gravely immoral. Duncan presents a hypothetical case similar to the facts of a recent one in California:

> Margaret McCabe is a seventy-five-year old woman who was recently widowed and is supporting herself on Social Security and a little income generated by a five-plex apartment building she owns and manages. As a devout Roman Catholic, Mrs. McCabe believes that fornication and homosexual behavior are serious sins and that it is sinful for her to facilitate others who wish to commit these sins. . . . Therefore, although Mrs. McCabe is willing to rent to married heterosexual couples and to single men or women, she is unwilling to rent to unmarried homosexual or heterosexual cohabiting couples.[24]

Duncan points out that implementation of the gay rights law on housing leads to an unavoidable conflict with Mrs. McCabe's free exercise of religion. In essence, the government is legislating its view on sexual morality and imposing it on Mrs. McCabe, thereby interfering with her right to follow her conscience in the exercise of religious freedom. Obviously, such laws restrict the exercise of religious freedom by institutions as well as by individuals. There is no middle ground. This leads Duncan to ask the question: "If this regulatory scheme is enacted, are religious objectors entitled to a free exercise exemption?"[25]

---

conclusion: homosexuals are an economically advantaged group in our society. . . . Market surveys support these findings. For example, a 1991 study conducted by Overlooked Opinions, a marketing and consulting firm that specializes in the homosexual market, reported the following" average household incomes: Gay Men, $51,325; Lesbians, $45,927; National Average, $36,520.

[24] Ibid., 395, n. 7.

[25] Ibid., 396. Read nn. 9–10 for further elaboration of the issue.

Turning now to the rights of parents whose children are in public schools, Pakaluk sees the same conflict between the public immorality implicit in promoting the homosexual lifestyle and the parents' concerns that their children are taught that this lifestyle is perfectly acceptable. If parents oppose this teaching at PTA meetings, they are characterized as bigoted by the professional educators and the media.[26]

Moreover, Pakaluk believes that the widespread attitude, fostered by professed gays and the media, that one may not discriminate in any way against the homosexual lifestyle will harm the mission of Courage. Its members who refuse to "come out of the closet" will be regarded as "Uncle Toms" (again the invidious comparison with the truly oppressed blacks of the past) for refusing to fight for "gay rights". From my years of experience with Courage, I may add that our members are already the subject of contempt and derision from many Catholic homosexual persons actively involved in the homosexual lifestyle. We have our hate mail.

Speculating about why the public has been deceived by the false teaching that sexual behavior is independent of character, Pakaluk concludes that, in general, people do not examine the issue critically, listening instead to the slogan "don't discriminate" and accepting uncritically the notion that various legal decisions in favor of gay rights are in accord with the Constitution, when, on the contrary, there is a *discontinuity* between earlier decisions of the Supreme Court defending basic principles of common law morality necessary for the common good and

[26] John Woestendiek, "Gay Teenagers Talk about Coping in School", *Philadelphia Inquirer* (Nov. 6, 1994), pp. B1–2. The Mid-Atlantic Regional Conference of the Gay, Lesbian, and Straight Teachers Network presented teenagers who felt alienated from the other students because they had made it known they were gay or lesbian, and among the remedies proposed for this situation was to teach that the homosexual lifestyle was perfectly acceptable. One teenager said that a curriculum should stress diversity and teach students "there is nothing wrong with being gay or lesbian" (B2).

the decisions on contraception (1965), abortion (1973), and homosexuality (1985), which give unwarranted autonomy to the individual at the expense of family and society.

Concerning the third major claim of professed homosexuals, namely, that same-sex unions should have the same privileges as marriage, Pakaluk points out that there is no real comparison between heterosexual marriage and same-sex unions. Heterosexual marriage flows from the natural complementarity of man and woman, completing each in a permanent bond of love, leading to the procreation of offspring and family, and usually bestowing upon man and wife the rights and responsibilities of being father and mother. The natural meanings of human genital intercourse are in this way fulfilled. In sharp contrast, same-sex unions lack the power of procreation, making no real contribution to family or the human race. Their sexual activity involves a distortion of the physical complementarity of man and woman, because it cannot accomplish a true physical union. For these reasons such unions should not be called "marriages".[27] Unfortunately, however, the term *marriage* is applied to them, leading to uncritical thinking by the public.

The claim that same-sex couples have a right to adopt children or to care for foster children is without foundation in the natural order of human sexuality. Both father and mother, as role models, contribute in different ways to the complete psychosexual development of their children, and the children have a right to male and female parents. There is no adequate substitute for the father-mother family.[28]

[27] Michael Pakaluk, "Why Is Homosexual Activity Morally Wrong?" in *Homosexuality: Challenges for Change and Reorientation, Journal of Pastoral Counseling* 28 (New Rochelle, N.Y.: Iona College, 1993):53–57.

[28] On this issue see Elizabeth Moberly, *Psychogenesis: The Early Development of Gender Identity* (London: Routledge and Kegan Paul, 1983). She sees the origins of homosexual orientation principally in the inability of the young person to identify with the parental figure of the same sex.

Since both sexes are necessary for the proper development of the child, the bond of friendship between man and wife is meant to be indissoluble and as strong as the ties of blood among siblings. This natural permanency of the marriage bond is obscured, however, by our cultural acceptance of divorce, in which the principal casualty is the child. It is thus appropriate for the state to bestow special benefits upon heterosexual marriage as a special kind of friendship that builds good families, thereby contributing to the common good of the state. In contrast, same-sex unions make no contribution to family or to the state.

Like Duncan, Pakaluk sees an ominous connection between acceptance of sodomy, imposition of the state's will in not allowing individuals or institutions to discriminate in matters of housing, and the downgrading of heterosexual marriage to the level of same-sex unions. Once sodomy is tolerated, it is soon accepted, and those opposing it are considered by the media as prejudiced and oppressive. Special protection will be given to the gay lifestyle, while marriage, now dissociated in the minds of the public from the mission of procreation, will no longer be regarded as necessary for the common good of the state but merely another way of exercising one's right to the kind of sex one desires. If faithful monogamous marriage is no longer necessary for procreation, will it be replaced by polygamy or polyandry? Such is the grim picture of the possible redefinition of the family presented by Pakaluk at a Courage conference.

Pakaluk, however, ended on a note of hope, pointing out that this path of social decline is not inevitable. He urges Courage members to spread the message of virtuous and chaste living to the world around them.

Richard F. Duncan

Professor Duncan explores the legal ramifications of gay rights legislation. Considering the relationship of public policy to sexual orientation laws, he shows that gay rights legislation declares homosexual behavior to be good and religiously motivated discrimination to be evil.[29] This issue may force "the Supreme Court to rethink its unwise decision, in *Employment Division v. Smith*, to drastically reduce the scope of the Free Exercise Clause".[30]

It is necessary to give the facts of the Smith case, also known as the "peyote" case, in order to understand Duncan's critique:

> Two members of the Native American Church, Alfred Smith and Galen Black, were denied unemployment benefits after being fired from their jobs as drug counselors. The benefits were denied because Smith and Black had been discharged for work-related misconduct—their illegal use of the hallucinogenic drug peyote for sacramental purposes at a ceremony of their church.
>
> Smith and Black claimed that the denial of the benefits was an unconstitutional burden on their free exercise of religion, because it penalized them for taking part in what to them was a religious sacrament. . . . [T]he United States Supreme Court reversed the Oregon decision [of its Supreme Court], upheld the denial of benefits and, at least for the present, rejected the compelling interest test for most (but, significantly, not all) free exercise challenges.[31]

Duncan foresees conflicts between laws that protect sexual behavior outside of marriage and the faith convictions of individuals and institutions opposed to such behavior. He wonders whether exemptions from such laws will be made for religiously motivated people. In his argument he refers to Dennis Altman's book *The Homosexualization of America*, where the point is made that the homosexual movement has cleverly changed the focus of debate from behavior to identity; thus, opponents are viewed as attacking the civil rights of homosexual citizens rather than attacking specific antisocial behavior.

[29] Duncan, "Who Wants to Stop the Church", 393–445.
[30] Ibid., 398.
[31] Ibid., 418.

Rejecting the claim of gays to minority status, Duncan shows that sexual behavior and orientation give us much information concerning what a person does, or is inclined to do, whereas race tells us nothing about a person's character. Sexual conduct and preferences, moreover, are fraught with moral and religious meaning. At least one can say that homosexual behavior is morally controversial. Thus, a landlord or employer who makes a distinction concerning another person's sexuality is really making a judgment about the other's character.

Since landlords and employers may regard homosexual behavior as immoral, it is up to professed homosexuals to prove that the beliefs of such persons are unreasonable and that homosexual practices are in fact morally neutral.[32] But gay rights advocates are not interested in undertaking such proof. There is no consensus in America that homosexual behavior is morally acceptable.

Duncan goes on to show that the other protected categories under antidiscrimination laws—gender, religion, and disability—are different from sexual orientation and behavior. "[R]eligious freedom is a fundamental constitutional right" from the beginning of our nation.[33]

Duncan points out, moreover, that the goal of civil rights legislation is social legitimation. From the literature of homosexual advocates it is clear that their strategy is to change society's antigay attitudes and to vilify those opposing their agenda. Duncan stresses the high stakes involved:

> When government passes homosexual rights legislation it sends a message to society that the homosexual lifestyle is legitimate,

[32] Duncan refers to the late Chief Justice Warren Burger in the *Bowers v. Hardwick* case (1986) saying that we have "millennia of moral teaching" about homosexuality, all of it condemning the act: ibid., 404, n. 40.

[33] Ibid., 411, including notes 64–65. "[R]eligious freedom is expressly protected by the Bill of Rights. . . . In contrast, the Supreme Court clearly has held that there is no constitutional right under the Due Process Clause to engage in homosexual sodomy."

perhaps on a par with marriage and family life, and that the government is so committed to this value that it will bring force to bear against those who wish to manage their businesses in accordance with a different code of ethics. Persons who believe that the homosexual lifestyle is sinful, immoral, or destructive of traditional family values are given a Hobson's choice under homosexual rights laws—either reject these deep personal beliefs as a code of business ethics, or get out of business.[34]

But homosexual rights laws are only one prong of a large-scale campaign to change the way we think about homosexuality. Other strategies are meant to manipulate the media and the public school curricula. Two favorite buzz words in these strategies are *homophobia*[35] and *religious intolerance*. (More recently, it is the *religious right*.)

Policymakers must be made aware of the high stakes involved in extending antidiscrimination laws to human sexual behavior. It is not a question of race, gender, or economic disparity. The issue is a choice

> between the values of moral relativism and the sexual revolution on the one hand, and the traditional values of family and religious freedom on the other. . . . Although the issue may be primarily a symbolic one, it is nevertheless symbolism of crucial importance. . . . It is about who we are and what we value. . . .

[34] Ibid., 413–14.

[35] Ralph McInerny relates his experience at Notre Dame University concerning "campus publications inveighing against homophobia—a neologism which requires linguistic as well as moral illiteracy. . . . Students follow suit, urging this Catholic university to apply Catholic doctrine and acknowledge that the Church 'does not distinguish between homosexual and heterosexual persons'. . . . The university, in short, has allowed itself to be recruited into an ideological campaign whose aim is to celebrate homosexuality and treat any misgivings about it as somehow, well, perverse. Of course, the enemy has long been within the walls in the form of wobbling on the part of moral theologians. Homophobia has come to mean the principled judgment that perverted sex is a serious sin, that its practitioners lead hellish lives and nowadays run the risk of a horrendous disease. . . . If this is indeed what homophobia means, let's have more of it." See his "In Defense of Homophobia", editorial, *Fellowship of Catholic Scholars Newsletter* (March 1994), p. 1.

The decision whether to turn our backs on millennia of moral teaching should be the product of careful and thoughtful judgment and not of a subtle and manipulative campaign of propaganda.[36]

Next Duncan focuses our attention on the problems created for "religiously-motivated institutions and individuals" (417) by homosexual rights legislation in 139 jurisdictions (416, n. 83). He carefully spells out the dangerous impact of the Supreme Court's decision in *Employment Division v. Smith* (1990) on the free exercise of religious freedom. In his judgment "the Supreme Court cast aside almost three decades of free exercise jurisprudence."[37] He quotes Douglas Laycock to the effect that the *Smith* decision is inconsistent with the apparent meaning of the constitutional text.[38] More troubling than the *Smith* decision's analytical shortcomings is its impact on the quality of religious freedom. "If the Court intends to defer to any formally neutral law restricting religion," observes Laycock, "then it has created a legal framework for persecution, and persecutions will result."[39]

Duncan believes that if free exercise of religion in the Bill of Rights has been misrepresented, it is important that we understand that the Court does allow some exception to the general rule of nonprotection. Perhaps the exception that seems most compelling is " 'hybrid' claims—i.e., claims under which free exercise is 'reinforced' by another constitutional interest such as

[36] Duncan, "Who Wants to Stop the Church", 415. Andrew Sullivan says that societal acceptance of homosexual marriages "is the highest public recognition of our personal integrity".

[37] Ibid., 417.

[38] Ibid., 419, n. 99 (Douglas Laycock, *The Remnants of Exercise*, 1990). See also note 100 in Duncan.

[39] Duncan, "Who Wants to Stop the Church", 420. Here Laycock mentions that Smith recognizes that the free exercise clause continues to protect the right of religious belief as distinct from religiously motivated conduct. Hence it is called formally neutral.

free speech, association, or the right of parents to direct the education of their children."[40]

The remainder of Duncan's article discusses cases of free exercise, which involve hybrid claims or laws that are not neutral or not of general application burdening religious practice. He describes situations in which there is restriction on religious conscience created by the enforcement of homosexual rights laws. In developing his argument Duncan points out that partial religious exemption from *Smith* is not satisfactory, because it leaves other believers unprotected; there must be equal protection of religious exercise. In one state several Catholic clerics argued for the gay rights bill in the media with the understanding that the Catholic Church would be exempt from certain provisions concerning the "right" of openly gay persons to teach in Catholic high schools. So the Church remained "neutral", while clerics and politicians traded exemptions in support for the silence of the Church. Indeed, such silence may be regarded as implicit approval.[41]

Duncan gives special attention to the case of *Gay Rights Coalition v. Georgetown U.* The District of Columbia Court of Appeals held that the D.C. ordinance was justified because homosexual orientation " 'tells nothing reliable about abilities or commitments in work, religion, politics, personal and social relationships, or social activities'. . . . Unfortunately, the court did not

[40] Ibid., 420.

[41] Ibid., 425, and n. 133. See also the Congregation for the Doctrine of the Faith, "Some Considerations concerning the Response to Legislative Proposals on the Non-Discrimination of Homosexual Persons", *Origins* (Aug. 6, 1992), no. 16. Referring to gay rights bills, the document says that it is inappropriate for the Church to endorse or to remain neutral toward adverse legislation despite the fact that such legislation grants exemptions from its provisions to Church organizations and institutions. It leaves the rest of the faithful unprotected. In no. 17 it says that the Church is concerned with family life and the public morality of the entire civil society and "not simply to protect herself from application of harmful laws".

explain this highly controversial conclusion."[42] As Pakaluk has observed, sexual behavior in general and homosexual behavior in particular do say something about the *character* of the agent. Duncan refers to *Ben-Shalom v. Marsh* (1989), in which the Seventh Circuit Court reasoned that even the orientation itself, which it described as "a propensity to engage in morally controversial behavior",[43] should be taken into account.

It is indeed curious to note that a civil court is more willing to see some connection between homosexual orientation, character, and possible behavior than many moralists. In *Ben Shalom v. Marsh*, the issue was the significance of a person's admission that she is a lesbian. The Seventh Circuit Court concluded that this admission of sexual orientation "can rationally and reasonably be viewed as reliable evidence of a desire and propensity to engage in homosexual conduct. Such an assumption cannot be said to be without individual exceptions. . . . To this extent, therefore, the regulation does not classify [the] plaintiff based merely upon her status as a lesbian, but upon reasonable inferences about her probable conduct in the past and in the future."[44]

Duncan thinks that the Seventh Circuit's reasoning is more persuasive than that of the D.C. court in the Georgetown case, and I agree. After all, this is not a condemnation of an individual person but a realistic appraisal of probable conduct.

Homosexual rights laws seem to be more the result of interest group politicians, sometimes under pressure from gay organizations, than a deep commitment on the part of society to carry out a value of the highest order. With regard to such laws the

[42] Duncan, "Who Wants to Stop the Church", 436.

[43] Ibid., 437. In note 197 Duncan quotes from the Vatican document on non-discrimination against homosexuals, no. 10: " 'Sexual orientation' does not constitute a quality comparable to race, ethnic background, etc., in respect to non-discrimination. Unlike these, homosexual orientation is an objective disorder . . . and evokes moral concern."

[44] Quoted in Duncan, "Who Wants to Stop the Church", 437.

state's interests are far from compelling, as they are in regard to just treatment of racial and ethnic minorities.[45]

Duncan and the many authorities he cites are not alone in their concern that gay rights laws will unduly and unjustly restrict the exercise of religious freedom. Congress, for example, passed the Religious Freedom Restoration Act of 1993 (RFRA), and it was signed into law by President Clinton. This law, supported by liberals, conservatives, and moderates, recognized that *Smith* " 'virtually eliminated' constitutional protection of religious freedom and seeks to restore that protection by creating a statutory exemption for religiously-motivated behavior burdened by governmental action. . . . In effect, RFRA creates, as a matter of national civil rights policy, a statutory exemption for free exercise equal in scope to the pre-*Smith* constitutional rule."[46]

Duncan agrees with Douglas Laycock that "unless the [Supreme] Court gives full scope to the exceptions to the general rule of *Smith*, that general rule of no free exercise protection for religiously motivated conduct will create a 'legal framework for persecution'."[47] First, individual believers will be persecuted for discriminating against homosexuals in housing and employment; after that, persecution will extend to Christian schools and churches who discriminate against homosexuals; and later there will be the withdrawal of tax-exempt status from churches for refusing to ordain homosexual ministers. (I think the latter is unlikely.) In Duncan's view, moreover, RFRA is not sufficient to protect religious freedom from these dangers, because, as an act of Congress, it can be repealed at any time.

Employers and landlords are forbidden by gay rights laws from making judgments of character with regard to whom they hire

---

[45] Ibid., 438. Note 199 gives references to the gay strategies, media campaigns, and sympathetic politicians.

[46] Ibid., 439–40.

[47] Ibid., 442.

or whom they allow to live on their premises. In short, gay rights laws impose one view of sexual morality (sexual relativism) on the people and then enforce this code of morality on orthodox religious believers. It is wrong for a political majority to use the power of government to stigmatize another group. "Through homosexual rights laws, the state chooses sides in the cultural war that has divided our society, and one side—orthodox religion—'is on the receiving end of the law's stigma and consequential material harms'." [48]

Not surprisingly, Duncan insists that gay rights laws should not be passed, and where passed, they should be repealed. [49] If the Court allows such laws to be enforced against religiously motivated persons, it could be the end of religious pluralism in America. This view is supported by the thesis of John Finnis, [50] a distinguished professor of law and legal philosophy at Oxford, who sheds light on other aspects of the gay rights issue.

John M. Finnis

Reviewing British and European law on the issue of homosexual behavior and the various statutes against discrimination, John Finnis notes that "the standard modern position deliberately rejects proposals to include in such lists the item 'sexual orientation.' " [51]

> The explanation commonly given . . . [is that the] phrase "sexual orientation" is radically equivocal. Particularly as used

[48] Ibid., 443, n. 222; this note also refers to the thought of Laurence Tribe, *American Constitutional Law* 989 (1978).

[49] On May 12, 1995, the United States Court of Appeals for the Sixth Circuit found constitutional an amendment to the city charter of Cincinnati that prohibits the city council and other government bodies from granting "minority or protected status" to homosexuals in any law, regulation, or policy: *New York Times* (May 14, 1995), p. A18.

[50] "Law, Morality, and 'Sexual Orientation' ", *Notre Dame Law Review* 69 (1994):1049–76.

[51] Ibid., 1053.

by promoters of "gay rights," the phrase ambiguously assimilates two things which the standard modern position carefully distinguishes: (I) a psychological or psychosomatic disposition inwardly orienting one *towards* homosexual activity; (II) the deliberate decision so to orient one's public *behavior* as to express or *manifest* one's active interest in and endorsement of homosexual *conduct* and/or forms of life which presumptively involve such conduct.[52]

Finnis points out that in gay rights laws in America the tendency is to equate orientation with behavior, but this is *not* so in Europe. In America, moreover, the result is that the law itself ends up teaching that homosexual conduct is a good to which one has a "right". This raises a question Finnis seeks to answer, namely, whether the European position that homosexual conduct is evil can be defended by rational argument.[53]

Finnis opens his argument by pointing out that "Socrates, Plato, and Aristotle regarded homosexual *conduct* as intrinsically shameful, immoral, and indeed depraved or depraving. That is to say, all three rejected the linchpin of modern 'gay' ideology and lifestyle."[54]

Following the thought of the ancient philosophers, Finnis develops his argument that all homosexual conduct or genital activity is evil by proposing three fundamental theses:

(1) The commitment of a man and a woman to each other in the sexual union of marriage is *intrinsically* good and reasonable, and is incompatible with sexual relationships outside marriage. (2) Homosexual acts are radically and peculiarly non-marital, and for that reason *intrinsically* unreasonable and unnatural. (3) Furthermore, according to Plato, if not Aristotle, homosexual acts have a special similarity to solitary masturbation, and

[52] Ibid., 1053–54.

[53] Ibid., 1055.

[54] Ibid. Finnis documents his statement from the writings of Plato and Aristotle and the learned historians of Greek philosophy, demonstrating that the prevailing belief that Socrates, Plato, and Aristotle approved homosexual acts is in fact false.

both types of radically non-marital act are manifestly unworthy of the human being and immoral.[55]

Finnis makes use of the pagan Plutarch's understanding of marriage, that genital intercourse between spouses enables them to experience and in that sense express the marriage itself, "as a single reality with two blessings (children and mutual affection)".[56] All other forms of intercourse have no such meaning and are, therefore, unacceptable. In the Christian era Augustine comes close to Plutarch's thought, but he never quite recognizes that in sterile and fertile marriages alike "the communion, companionship, *societas* and *amicitia* of the spouses—their being married—*is* the very good of marriage, and is an intrinsic, basic human good, not merely instrumental to any other good".[57]

The significance of Plutarch's position then is that he makes sexual intercourse between husband and wife not merely an instrumental good but also an expression of the basic human good of union. From this Finnis concludes that parenthood and family are "the intrinsic fulfillment of a communion which, because it is not merely instrumental, can exist and fulfill the spouses even if procreation happens to be impossible for them".[58]

Turning now to the second thesis, that homosexual acts are radically nonmarital, Finnis shows that in both heterosexual intercourse before marriage, as well as in homosexual acts, the couple cannot experience or actualize a *marital* good. It does no more than provide each person with individual gratification. Their bodies are used as instruments in the service of their conscious selves. Such conduct dis-integrates them precisely as acting persons.[59]

[55] Ibid., 1062–63. The emphasis on *intrinsically* is mine.

[56] Ibid., 1064.

[57] Ibid.

[58] Ibid., 1065.

[59] Ibid., 1066–67. See also Germain Grisez, *The Way of the Lord Jesus*, vol. 2: *Living a Christian Life* (Quincy, Ill.: Franciscan Press, 1993):555–74, 633–80, esp. 634–39.

Finnis' third thesis, following Plato, is that homosexual acts are similar to masturbation, and both are unworthy of humans and hence immoral. Avoiding the sentimentality of homosexual lovers in hard-nosed fashion, Finnis points out that reality is known through judgments and not through emotions. There is no *real* difference between same-sex acts of lovers and those of strangers in a rest room, or a prostitute giving a client some pleasure, or a man masturbating with a fantasy of more human relationships at the end of a day's work.[60]

Concerned with the *objective* meaning of homosexual actions as moral evil, Finnis states that

> there is no important distinction in essential moral worthlessness between solitary masturbation, being sodomized as a prostitute, and being sodomized for the pleasure of it. Sexual acts cannot *in reality* be self-giving unless they are acts by which a man and a woman actualize and experience sexually the real giving of themselves to each other—in biological, affective and volitional union in mutual commitment, both open-ended and exclusive—which like Plato and Aristotle and most peoples we call marriage.[61]

Sexual acts, then, do not truly unite man and woman in friendship unless they are marital, and to be marital they must also be open to procreation in the sense that they are the kind of acts of the reproductive function that under certain circumstances would lead to a child. Thus, Finnis makes room for sterile marriages; at the same time it is painfully obvious that homosexual activity cannot fulfill these two purposes of union and procreation. This brings us to Finnis' next argument.

From ancient Greece and contemporary England he draws the distinction between behavior that is merely offensive, such as eating excrement, and "behavior to be repudiated as destructive

---

[60] Finnis, "Law, Morality, and 'Sexual Orientation' ", 1067. See also the quotation from Plato's *Gorgias*, 494–95 in n. 48.

[61] Finnis, "Law, Morality, and 'Sexual Orientation' ", 1067.

of human character and relationships".[62] The example given is the copulation of humans with animals, which reduces the act of intercourse to a purely animal act. "The deliberate genital coupling of persons of the same sex is repudiated for a very similar reason."[63] Here Finnis goes beyond the arguments of the sterility of same-sex activity and the dis-integrative manipulations of each partner to a *new* consideration, namely, that such activity is *hostile* to the self-understanding of those persons who are willing to commit themselves to real marriage.

This self-understanding of the spouses leads them to perceive the sexual joys of marriage as a way of actualizing and experiencing their intelligent commitment to shared responsibilities in genuine self-giving.[64]

Finnis sees the gay ideology and its use of the term *orientation* in the sense of a deliberate willingness to engage in homosexual activity as deeply hostile to the understanding of human sexuality in the minds of those members of society who are willing to commit themselves to real marriage. Homosexual ideology really denies the intrinsic meaning and value of marital sexual intercourse as something good in itself. If one holds that homosexual acts can be a "humanly appropriate use of sexual capacities", then, to be consistent, one must regard sexual desires and acts *primarily* as instruments for gratifying the individuals themselves.

Finnis sees this focus on self-gratification in gay activity as a genuine threat to present and future marriages. It makes nonsense of the view that adultery is immoral because it is a betrayal of the covenantal unity of spouses. Such a depreciation of marriage, implicit in the gay ideology, poses a tremendous challenge to the political community. If the community believes that the soundness and stability of family life are crucial to the well-being

[62] Ibid., 1069.
[63] Ibid.
[64] Ibid. (paraphrased).

of the state, then "it has a compelling interest in denying that homosexual conduct—a 'gay lifestyle'—is a valid, humanly acceptable choice and form of life, and in doing whatever it *properly* can . . . to discourage such conduct.".[65]

In his conclusion Finnis makes the important distinction between private and public acts of morality in regard to the state's duty to promote virtue for the sake of the common good. He believes that the state should not attempt to control "secret and truly consensual adult acts of vice" by making such punishable acts against the laws of the state; at the same time a law that did not criminalize private acts of sodomy between adults should *not* also

> tolerate the advertising or marketing of homosexual services, the maintenance of places of resort for homosexual activity, or the promotion of homosexualist "lifestyles" via education and public media of communication, or to recognize homosexual "marriages" or permit the adoption of children by homosexually active people. . . .[66]

Personal Comments on Gay Rights Legislation

In practice, in the United States the decriminalization of sodomy laws in twenty-three states and the nonenforcement of sodomy laws in all the other states have contributed to a general attitude on the part of the public that may be described as both passive and hostile: *passive* in the sense that many people tolerate the above-quoted public manifestations of the homosexual lifestyle, *hostile* in the sense that people feel resentfully helpless to change the situation to one of public decency.

Meanwhile, many public officials curry the favor of the loudly articulate homosexual leaders because they are afraid of losing votes, while the mainstream media uncritically accept the goals,

---

[65] Ibid., 1070 (italics in original).
[66] Ibid., 1076.

the activities, and the programs of homosexual activists. For example, in late June 1994, the Gay Pride Parade in New York City was authorized to move up First Avenue—not Fifth Avenue, where St. Patrick's Cathedral is located—nonetheless, without a permit a group of gay activists paraded up Fifth Avenue, coming to a halt in front of the cathedral. Various public insults were shouted at the Pope, the Church, and Cardinal O'Connor. A group of men and women danced in the nude, mocking the Catholic Church. Meanwhile, policemen were told to do nothing. When questioned by the press, the mayor said that the nonaction of the city was meant to avoid further disturbances. There was no protest from the press, such as would be expected were one to insult the blacks, the Hispanics, the Jewish people, or any other minority.

The point is that at the present moment the public, in general, does not understand the gay rights movement. This, however, is only one more manifestation of cultural relativism in the area of sexuality, marriage, and family. In the public square, then, there is need for education on the moral issues involved in the gay rights movement. Arguments based upon revealed truth will not be accepted, while arguments based upon natural moral law, such as those of Michael Pakaluk, Richard Duncan, and John Finnis, will need to be translated into the language of the general public.

We must clearly explain what we mean by "rights" and "the common good", the meaning of human sexuality as it is expressed in marriage, the self-destructive nature of the homosexual lifestyle, apart from the AIDS epidemic, and the increasing empirical evidence that many are able to get rid of the homosexual condition through sound therapy, prayer, and spiritual group support.

An encouraging event took place on May 12, 1995, to which I refer above in footnote 49 of this chapter. A federal appeals court declared constitutional an amendment to the city charter of Cincinnati, which prohibits the city council and other government bodies from granting "minority or protected status" to homosexuals. The court's decision declares that one cannot make a law to benefit or to protect an "unidentifiable group or class of individuals" because their identity is defined by "unapparent characteristics", such as "innate desires, drives and thoughts". Those claiming a homosexual "orientation" simply do not comprise, as such, an identifiable class. The decision goes on to point out that many homosexuals successfully conceal their identity, and that those who *become* identifiable become such by their *conduct. It is their conduct that makes them identifiable, not their orientation.* In other words, they are not a minority in the true sense, as has been pointed out previously. One can hope that other communities will follow the lead of Cincinnati with similar amendments to city charters.

Document from the Congregation
for the Doctrine of the Faith

With this background I should like to review the CDF 1992 document on discrimination and homosexual behavior, because one of its concerns was gay rights legislation. Its counsel on this question was roundly criticized by various gay writers; thus, after explaining its counsels, I shall reply to a representative critic of the document.

The full title of this controversial document is "Responding to Legislative Proposals on Discrimination against Homosexuals" (LPDH). It was originally sent out as a private statement to the bishops of the United States, but its content was released to the press by New Ways Ministry. This led to a revision of the original, published by the Vatican.[67] The statement is divided into two parts. The first part reviews relevant passages from the 1986

[67] See *Origins*, no. 2 (Aug. 6, 1992):173–77. Robert Nugent holds that the original version was probably written in the United States by consultants of

letter of the Congregation for the Doctrine of the Faith (CDF) to the Bishops of the Catholic Church on the Pastoral Care of Homosexual Persons (PCHP). The second part provides some practical applications of the norms found in the first part.

Part I: Relevant Passages from the CDF 1986 Letter

In the first part of the document on discrimination (LPDH 1992, also known as "Considerations"), the distinction is made between homosexual orientation and activity, the same as we have made throughout this book. It reiterates the position of the CDF letter on pastoral care (PCHP) that by 1986 an "overly benign interpretation" of homosexual orientation was widespread. It was noted that the distinction between orientation and activity had already been made in the CDF "Declaration concerning Sexual Ethics" (1975), but some had gone so far as to call the orientation neutral or even good. The 1986 statement, however, says that the inclination itself must be seen as an "objective disorder", because "it is a more or less strong tendency toward an intrinsic moral evil" (PCHP, no. 3).

The point is made that any criticism or expression of reservations concerning a homosexual lifestyle is regarded as a form of *unjust* discrimination. Pressure groups seek to manipulate the Church, presenting the homosexual lifestyle as "harmless or even good"—as an alternative way of living. The CDF believes that placing the homosexual lifestyle on the level of marriage will have "a direct impact on society's understanding of the nature and rights of the family and puts them in jeopardy" (PCHP, no. 9).

---

the CDF. The official version ("Some Considerations concerning the Response to Legislative Proposals on the non-Discrimination of Homosexual Persons") was printed in English in *L'Osservatore Romano* no. 30 (July 29, 1992), p. 5. See "The Civil Rights of Homosexual People: Vatican Perspectives", *New Theology Review* 7, no. 4 (November 1994):72–86.

Part II: Application of Principles in Part I concerning Discrimination.

To review section 10 of the 1992 document: the CDF provoked a storm of criticism in the United States by repeating the judgment found in no. 3 of the 1986 letter, namely, that sexual orientation is, as such, an "objective disorder". Section 10 also asserts that sexual orientation is not comparable to race or ethnic origin. Although condemning crimes against homosexual persons, it pointed out that society should not introduce legislation to protect homosexual *behavior* "to which no one has any conceivable right". If society enacts such protective legislation of homosexual conduct, it should not be surprised if distorted notions and practices gain ground, leading to violent reactions from other parts of the citizenry (LPDH, no. 10).

Section 11 of the 1992 document says that it is not unjust discrimination to take sexual orientation into account in the placement of children for adoption or foster care, in the employment of teachers, in the appointment of athletic coaches, and in military recruitment. It should be noted that taking sexual orientation into account is not the same as excluding the person from employment or housing. It is only one of the factors. In practice, moreover, both the employer and the future employee recognize the deeply equivocal meaning of the term *sexual orientation*.[68]

Section 12 of the 1992 statement states that rights are not absolute, and therefore the state can legitimately limit objec-

---

[68] Duncan, "Who Wants to Stop the Church", 397. As used in gay rights legislation, the term "sexual orientation" generally means *practice* as well. Such legislation includes "sexual orientation and practices among the protected categories" (n. 13). See also John Finnis, "Law, Morality, and 'Sexual Orientation'", 1053. Speaking of the standard European politico-legal position on antidiscrimination laws, which deliberately refuses to accept the proposal to accept in such lists the item "sexual orientation", Finnis gives the reason for such rejection. The term "'sexual orientation' is radically equivocal" (1053–54).

tively disordered external conduct, and that it may have the obligation to do so in certain circumstances. Section 13 says that lack of discrimination against public homosexual behavior amounts to regarding homosexuality, as such, "as a positive source of human rights, for example, in respect to so-called affirmative action or preferential treatment in living practices."

The document adds that there is no moral right to homosexual behavior, and, therefore, the orientation itself should not be a basis for judicial claims for nondiscrimination. To give homosexual behavior legal protection is equivalent to preferential treatment, promoting the homosexual lifestyle. Then the claims of homosexual persons to their active lifestyle would be defended precisely as an affirmation of the homosexual condition, while opposition to such claims would be understood as violations of basic human rights.

Section 14 discusses several situations. (1) Those who do not disclose their sexual orientation usually do not have any problem with the civil law,[69] but those who assert their gayness usually put pressure on the Church to support them in changing civil statutes (LPDH, no. 5). (2) Those who view the homosexual lifestyle as harmless or as entirely good and worthy of public approval consider all criticisms of their lifestyle as "diverse forms of unjust discrimination" (PCHP, no. 9). (3) Civil legislation that makes a homosexual lifestyle the basis for entitlements could actually encourage a person with homosexual orientation to declare his gayness and even to seek a partner to exploit the provisions of the law.

Section 15 advises that careful attention should be paid to the simple provisions of proposed measures, such as a homosexual

[69] "As a rule, the majority of homosexually oriented persons who seek to lead chaste lives do not publicize their sexual orientation. Hence, the problem of discrimination in terms of employment, housing, etc. does not usually arise": LPDH, no. 14. This is my experience with the members of Courage, as well as with many other homosexual persons living alone.

couple adopting a child or acting as foster parents for a child. Provisions such as these raise questions concerning the rights of the child to have both father and mother in his formative years. Again, domestic partnerships of same-sex couples are given the privileges of heterosexual marriage under certain forms of gay rights legislation. Should this be? Should gay couples have the same rights as a heterosexual married couple in regard to housing? Should the domestic partner share in the health benefits of the partner who is working, as would the ordinary married person? Obviously, the CDF answers in the negative to these questions, but gay rights legislation will give an affirmative response to the above questions. The CDF wants American bishops to be fully aware of the implications of such legislation (PCHP, no. 9). Section 15 also states that public authority should forbid both public and private acts. Finnis believes that good jurisprudence should restrict itself to the public domain, promoting public morality. Strictly private activity between adults cannot really be controlled.[70]

Sections 16 and 17 raise questions for American bishops. The CDF believes that it is inappropriate for a diocese to remain neutral or to endorse adverse legislation despite its making exemptions for Church organizations. There is good reason: "The Church has the responsibility to promote family life and the public morality of the entire civil society on the basis of fundamental moral values, not simply to protect herself from application of harmful laws" (LPDH, no. 17).

Criticism of the 1992 Document

I have referred to this 1992 document as "controversial" because it was greeted with much criticism within English and American Catholicism. This criticism is epitomized in a recent

---

[70] Finnis, "Law, Morality, and 'Sexual Orientation' ", 1049–51.

article by Robert Nugent.[71] The author refers to the 1992 document as "Considerations", and I shall do the same in my response.

Nugent is correct that "Considerations" does not accept the analogy between "orientation" and race and gender. I believe that the insights of Pakaluk, Duncan, and Finnis have demonstrated that there is no true analogy between "sexual orientation" and truly innate characteristics of persons for the very good reason that many homosexuals make themselves a minority by their active lifestyle. "Orientation" still leaves one free to act out the tendency or not to do so. Again, I did not find in Nugent clear definitions of "orientation" and gender.

On page 77, Nugent makes homosexuality a positive endowment of a person and not an "objective disorder" (PCHP, no. 3.) Elizabeth Moberly, Gerard van den Aardweg, and a host of other writers see the condition as a psychic "deficit". On page 78 and throughout the article, the implication is that the homosexual orientation is fixed for life, and one must simply accept it. Yet a whole school of thought and a body of literature have demonstrated that some can move out of homosexuality and into heterosexuality.[72] In short, what does "accepting" homosexuality mean? Does it exclude the hope that one can get out of it?

Nugent implies that keeping one's homosexual orientation secret leads to self-destructive repression and many suicides.[73]

[71] "The Civil Rights of Homosexual People", pp. 72–86.

[72] See chapter four, above.

[73] Vincent Genovesi, S.J., criticizes me for holding that if a homosexual person keeps his orientation secret he does not suffer any discrimination and can exercise his civil rights with no difficulty. He calls my opinion and that of the Congregation for the Doctrine of the Faith "invidious". He goes on to ask whether keeping one's orientation private is a "form of oppression". He says those who keep their orientation to themselves "live in silent deceit, pretending to be other than who they truly are". Living in this way would seem to be demeaning. See his "Human and Civil Rights for Gays and Lesbians", *America* (April 22, 1995), pp. 15–19, esp. 16.

In my work with young people over many years I have not found this to be so. To assert that not coming out of the closet probably puts one in danger of suicide is to make a gratuitous statement not based on empirical evidence. There are many homosexual persons who, with the help of spiritual direction and the support of Courage or similar organizations, have been able to be chaste and, in some instances, have been able to move out of homosexuality. When Nugent argues on the basis of lack of "empirical evidence" to indicate that there are not many individuals with homosexual tendencies who practice chastity in the sense of avoidance of illicit sexual desires (lust) and sexual-genital acts, he reveals his ignorance of a whole body of Exodus literature as well as the Newsletters of Courage, indicating that there are many such who, while concealing their orientation from the public, lead chaste and healthy lives.[74] The Courage office in New York City, moreover, is filled with letters witnessing to persons of all ages who are leading chaste lives. It is clear that Nugent is not aware of the many people in Exodus and Courage who not only lead chaste lives but also stay far away from the advocates of "gay rights".

Again, Nugent assumes that the analogy between homosexual orientation and race and gender is valid. Referencing a list of authorities found in Michael Pakaluk, Richard Duncan, and John Finnis, I argue that it is invalid. Furthermore, in the context of "Considerations", it is clear that the document argues on the basis of the Church's teaching found in the CDF 1986 letter, namely, that homosexual acts are *intrinsically immoral*, and, therefore, one does not have a *moral* right to such acts. Since the condition of homosexuality is not an attribute that one freely wills to have, one can hardly speak of a moral "right" to "homosexu-

---

[74] For excellent book lists on this and related issues: Regeneration, Inc. Allan Medinger publishes a monthly newsletter. See also Courage Newsletters.

ality". On the contrary, one has a moral right to seek to get out of the condition.

Nugent finds fault with "Considerations" because it says that protection based on one's sexual orientation easily leads to protection and promotion of "homosexuality" and homosexual acts. But, Nugent says, homosexual behavior is not the "focus of civil rights legislation which is worded primarily in terms of orientation".[75] According to Nugent, the CDF argument fails to make clear and precise distinctions between homosexual orientation and homosexual behavior.[76]

In reply, I point out that "Considerations" must be read in the context of the CDF 1986 letter, which clearly distinguishes between the above terms; furthermore, as I have already indicated in analyzing the positions of three eminent Catholic professors of philosophy and law, Pakaluk, Duncan, and Finnis, the word *orientation* in many gay rights bills includes activity as well.[77] It is foolish to believe that the primary intent and purpose of such legislation is to protect *only* "orientation". That is why Nugent uses the adverb *primarily*, because he knows that wherever such statutes have been passed—and they have been enacted in at least 65 cities—the protection and promotion of the homosexual lifestyle also takes place.[78]

An entirely baseless charge that Nugent launches against "Considerations" is that one is "making obligatory the performance of a direct evil (discrimination) without a proportion-

---

[75] Whatever the wording of gay rights legislation, sexual orentation is interchangeable with orientation *and practice* in American gay rights legislation. See n. 52, above.

[76] Nugent, "The Civil Rights of Homosexual People", p. 80.

[77] Finnis, "Law, Morality, and 'Sexual Orientation' ", 52, 65.

[78] See Congressman William Dannemeyer, "Homosexuality and the Law", *Shadow in the Land* (San Francisco: Ignatius Press, 1989), pp. 57–87, esp. 66–73, where specific instances of the promotion of homosexual lifestyle are documented. One can also read the personal ads in the *L. A. Advocate*, the leading gay newspaper.

ately grave justifying reason".[79] The focus here is on section 12 of "Considerations", with which Nugent agrees in part, that human rights are not absolute; but he disagrees with the document's assertion that these rights can be limited in certain cases, because homogenital acts are "objectively disordered external conduct". The document says that such limitations can be both licit and obligatory. I think it is necessary to look at the types of situations in which, according to "Considerations", one may have a right to discriminate against such conduct: employment of teachers or athletic coaches; military recruitment; cases involving landlords and tenants; and so on (section 12).

What Nugent and John Tuohey (whose argument Nugent uses) fail to consider is that there can be *just* discrimination in situations where there is a conflict of rights or alleged rights. Does a Catholic landlord of a small apartment complex, believing that any genital sex outside of marriage is immoral, have a moral duty to refuse rental to an openly gay couple? Or to an unmarried heterosexual couple? I believe that such a landlord can justly discriminate against such couples. It is his private property, and he does not want immoral practices taking place therein. The issue in this case is not what dangers to family or the commonwealth are involved but whether the landlord has a right to exercise his Catholic conscience or whether he can be forced to rent to individuals who will probably be involved in immoral activity. If that were to happen, then those individuals would be imposing their cultural morality upon the landlord.

Actually, some gay rights bills make exemptions for landlords of small complexes and for religious schools with regard to the employment of openly gay teachers or athletic coaches. Other situations are discussed in Richard Duncan's article, where he

[79] Nugent, "The Civil Rights of Homosexual People", p. 81. He takes this argument from John Tuohey, "The CDF and Homosexuals: Rewriting the Moral Tradition", *America* (Sept. 12, 1992), pp. 136–38.

sees an oncoming conflict between the claims of gay rights advocates in applying such legislation and the religious freedom not only of Catholics but of all those who in conscience will not be able to abide by such laws.[80]

One can agree with Nugent that the state should not legislate *strictly private* behavior of adults, heterosexual or homosexual, but it can, should, and does make regulations concerning *public* sexual behavior, and it is rightly concerned with the impact of such behavior upon families, particularly upon youth.[81] Public authority in city, state, and nation has statutes concerning pornography, prostitution, and the like. Why is *public* support of homosexual activity exempt from such regulation?

Nugent's attempt to compare homosexual activity with the practice of contraception from the perspective that the civil law cannot legislate against either type of *private* activity is valid, but when it comes to the consideration of the effect of public homosexual activity upon family life, it is not valid.[82] The attempt of homosexual activists in New York City to influence the minds of children by writing into curricula the notion that the homosexual lifestyle is on the same level as marriage is hardly a private matter any more than homosexuals dancing nude in front of a Catholic church.

"Considerations" does not tell American bishops what to do

---

[80] Duncan, "Who Wants to Stop the Church", 393–401.

[81] Finnis, "Law, Morality, and 'Sexual Orientation' ", 1049–51, cites examples from British law regulating public sexual conduct, or even forbidding advertisements in periodicals concerning one's availability for private homosexual acts, and this long after the decriminalization of adult private sexual conduct (1967).

[82] John C. Callahan, "A Liberal Case against Gay and Lesbian Rights", *New Oxford Review* (December 1994), pp. 8–15. Arguing from the need to preserve the stability of family life and the protection of those who are not able to protect themselves, namely, children and adolescents, the author thinks that the legal and social acceptance of the homosexual lifestyle would have a deleterious effect upon the young, particularly youths who have homosexual inclinations and are vulnerable to seduction.

in regard to specific gay rights legislation, but it offers some salu-
tary warnings concerning the future effects of such legislation
upon the family and the common good. Already in the authorities reviewed in this study as well as in my review of "Considerations", I have presented arguments against gay rights bills in
general, but I have not focused on any one bill in particular. It is
the contention of Duncan and Finnis, for which they present
evidence, that such bills have already created situations in which
the homosexual lifestyle is promoted: witness San Francisco,
New York City, and Washington, D.C. As already observed,
Duncan foresees conflicts of conscience for Christians who hold
that homosexual activity is immoral when confronted with gay
rights statutes concerning housing and employment of individuals who publicly assert their homosexual lifestyle.

Again, I agree that offering religious institutions exemptions
from various provisions of gay rights bills should not persuade
the ordinary of a diocese to accept such bills. Should he be silent, for example, on domestic partnerships or same-sex couples
adopting children? There is little doubt, moreover, that homosexuals regard same-sex coupling as equivalent to marriage.
Surely, the public recognition of same-sex unions lowers the
esteem of society for the sacred meaning of heterosexual marriages and families.

Conclusion: Although I have presented authorities who argue well against gay rights legislation, I believe that the culture
war concerning the morality of homosexual activity will go on.
It is a human issue affecting all of us. In a letter to *First Things*,
Clifton L. Brinson writes:

> In the area of public opinion the homosexuality debate falls
> along remarkably similar lines as the abortion debate. A small
> group is unequivocally opposed to it. A slightly smaller group is
> unequivocally in favor of it. The majority of the public main-
> tains an inconsistent stance in which they are personally op-
> posed to it, but don't feel that they have the authority to impose

their beliefs on others. . . . However, this battle is quite win-
nable for the orthodox. . . . their task is to . . . equip the American populace to translate its private revulsion into public
policy.[83]

While it is true that some bishops have not opposed gay rights
legislation, it seems that the majority are rightly cautious about
such bills. It might be imprudent to condemn all provisions in a
particular bill, but it might also be imprudent to endorse any gay
rights bill presented to the ordinary of the diocese. In general, a
bishop ought to seek advice from professional moralists who are
known for their support of Church teaching before giving any
kind of support to a proposed gay rights bill. There is far more
wisdom in "Considerations" than there is in Nugent's critique
of the CDF's document. I recommend that bishops read the
solid arguments of Duncan and Finnis against gay rights legislation.[84] While providing good natural moral law arguments
against homosexual activity and propaganda. they also present a
realistic view of the current situation.[85]

[83] December 1994, pp. 4–5.

[84] Ernest Fortin focuses on the importance of natural law in these debates:
"For centuries the cornerstone of moral theology was not the natural or human *rights* doctrine, but something quite different called the natural *law*.
Rights, to the extent that they were mentioned at least by implication, were
contingent on the fulfillment of prior duties. Far from being absolute or in-
alienable, they could be forfeited by the individual who failed to abide by the
law that guaranteed them. Simply stated, what the church taught and tried to
inculcate was an ethic of virtue as distinct from an ethic of rights": "The
Trouble with Catholic Social Thought", *Boston College Magazine* (Summer
1988), p. 38.

[85] On June 18, 1995, the U.S. Supreme Court ruled unanimously that the
private sponsors of Boston's St. Patrick's Day parade had a constitutional right
to exclude marchers whose message they reject, including those who seek to
identify themselves as gay, lesbian, and bisexual Irish-Americans: *New York
Times* (June 19, 1995), pp. A1, B16.

9

A CATHOLIC PERSPECTIVE ON
SAME-SEX MARRIAGES

On NBC evening news, September 20, 1994, Tom Brokaw pointed out that there are at least 175,000 gay couples in America. The persons interviewed on that program viewed their lifestyle as being on the same level as marriage. This is certainly a challenge to Roman Catholic teaching on homo-sexual activity. As was noted in the previous chapter, on gay rights legislation,[1] the social approval of same-sex unions as equivalent to heterosexual marriages is one of the goals of the homosexual movement. While there is no way that the Catho-lic Church can give any approval to two persons of the same sex expressing their love for one another through sexual-genital acts, it is still necessary to consider the various moral aspects involved in such unions. This, in turn, calls for a review of pertinent historical, sociological, and psychological studies concerning these unions. Such research does not treat the theological and moral aspects of same-sex unions; that I will do when I consider John Boswell's *Same-Sex Unions in Pre-modern Europe*,[2] a book that will be used by many homosexual persons to justify their same-sex unions. Finally, I shall study

[1] See chapter eight, above.
[2] John Boswell, *Same-Sex Unions in Premodern Europe* (New York: Villard Books, 1994).

Homosexual Partnerships? Why Same-Sex Relationships Are Not a Christian Option, by John Stott.[3]

From the secular literature on same-sex couples I have chosen several representative works on male and female couples. The first study I present is that of David P. McWhirter and Andrew M. Mattison, *The Male Couple: How Relationships Develop*, a serious sociological study about the development of male couple relationships.[4]

The authors studied 156 couples whose relationships lasted from one to thirty-seven years, leading to the general conclusion that male same-sex unions last longer than the public thinks they do. They discovered, however, that an explicit or implicit assumption that 75 percent of the couples had made before entering into a mutual agreement to live together turned out to be false. That assumption was that their union would be sexually exclusive.

After five years, all the couples had come to the conclusion that some outside sexual relationships had to be accepted for the survival of the relationship. These couples viewed emotional stability with each other as more important than sexual fidelity. The couples did not come to this conclusion easily, say the authors, because they had accepted the "cultural" bias that fidelity is necessary for a good "marriage". But gradually the couples developed their own concept of fidelity, which is explained in these terms: "It is only through time that the symbolic nature of sexual exclusivity translates into the real issues of faithfulness. When that happens, the substantive, emotional stability of the partner, not sex, becomes the real measure of faithfulness."[5]

[3] John Stott, *Homosexual Partnerships? Why Same-Sex Relationships Are Not a Christian Option* (Downers Grove, Ill.: InterVarsity Press, 1984). Stott is director of the London Institute for Contemporary Christianity.

[4] David P. McWhirter and Andrew M. Mattison, *The Male Couple: How Relationships Develop* (Englewood Cliffs, N.J.: Prentice Hall, 1984).

[5] Ibid., p. 252. The authors asked the men in the study why they wanted sex outside the relationship. One typical response was: "All my sexual needs are

The authors find a partial explanation for the change in attitudes of the couples after a few years in the concept of *limerence*, which is being in love with the other person together with all the characteristics of this state—an emotional high in which all reality is seen in roseate colors. When the high wears off, relationships often crumble, or at least the other partner becomes less attractive, and other men become more attractive in fantasy and in reality.[6]

As I understand the authors' data, when a couple's union seems in jeopardy, they resort to a curious rationalization. Desiring to preserve the emotional bond between them despite the fact that either or both desire genital sex outside their union, they separate their friendship from their sexual "needs", miminizing its sexual meaning as if it were purely an animal instinct when done outside the relationship, even agreeing to a third person in their sexual activity or to group sex at bathhouses. As long as neither partner becomes involved *emotionally* with another sex partner, they consider that their union will be preserved. The authors sum up this aspect:

> The majority of couples in our study, and all of the couples together for more than five years, were not continuously sexually exclusive with each other. . . . We found that gay men *expect* mutual emotional dependability with their partners and that *relationship fidelity* transcends concerns about sexuality and exclusivity.[7]

It is important to understand that many of these couples consider sexual intercourse a form of recreation, not to be taken too seriously. As one partner put it: "Sex can be like a recreational sport and still maintain its specialness for us between ourselves.

---

not met by my partner. Sex together got boring at times, and I need new material for my fantasies" (p. 253).

[6] Ibid., pp. 27–31, 52–55. Decline of "limerence" occurs usually after the first year.

[7] Ibid., p. 285 (italics in original).

Our relationship is maintained by our love and willingness to make it work, not what we do with others in bed."[8]

Actually, 85 percent of the couples had great problems with the concept of sex with others besides their partner. They come to compromises with sexual exclusivity—what is called *fidelity* in traditional marriage—ending up with a "mutual promise to avoid emotional entanglements with sex partners".[9] One can see how such compromises with fidelity are contrary to the concept of marriage in most religions, not only in Christianity and Judaism. It is likewise a form of dualism to separate sexual activity from human emotions, thereby depriving it of its special meaning in marriage. The very compromises of fidelity by homosexual couples indicate that they do not trust either their partners or themselves to be capable of chastity.[10]

II

This leads us to the Mendola Report, a study based on a nationwide survey of approximately four hundred homosexual and lesbian couples, some of whom Mary Mendola interviewed in depth as a follow-up to mailed questionnaires. The author, a former nun who has completely rejected the teaching of the Catholic Church—indeed the whole Judeo-Christian tradition —makes use of her study to minimize the differences between heterosexual marriages and same-sex unions, male and female, which she terms *homosexual* and *lesbian*, respectively. From the responses to her questionnaire sent to fifteen hundred recipients (with 27 percent return), she draws the conclusion that there are no significant differences between lesbian and homosexual same-sex unions.[11]

[8] Ibid., p. 254.
[9] Ibid., p. 258.
[10] Ibid., p. 259.
[11] Mary Mendola, *The Mendola Report* (New York: Crown, 1980), p. 8.

Before beginning her process of nationwide interviewing of gay and lesbian couples, she stated: "The essence of permanent relationships is the same for both gay and lesbian couples."[12] Throughout the book, in commentaries on the interviews, the author stresses the equal goodness of same-sex unions with heterosexual couples or marriages. It is my purpose to focus on several moral aspects of these phenomena. The first is the concept of *fidelity*.

Like McWhirter and Mattison in *The Male Couple*, Mary Mendola reports that many homosexual and lesbian couples distinguish between sexual exclusivity and emotional exclusivity. In traditional thought, sexual and emotional exclusivity are necessary elements of fidelity between husband and wife, but many gay and lesbian couples permit occasional affairs with a third party provided that nothing more is sought than strictly sexual satisfaction, or, in other words, as long as the partner does not become *emotionally* involved with the sex partner.[13] In some unions one of the partners, while permitting the other to have sex outside their relationship, remains sexually faithful.[14] The "faithful" one makes this compromise because the friendship, as she conceives it, is more important than sexual fidelity.

It is clear from the details of the interviews recorded that Mary Mendola was out to prove her underlying conviction, namely, that the morality of a relationship between two persons has little to do with sexual-genital relationships or with the gen-

[12] Ibid., p. 246. The quotation is taken from the note that accompanied the questionnaires sent across the nation. Therein she adds that "there are millions of other gay people like myself who live happy and full lives with the partner of their choice."

[13] Ibid., p. 17; see also p. 31: "Neither woman (Ann and Kate) believes in sexual fidelity"; p. 33: "Charles has sex mostly with Richard, but does have occasional sexual affairs outside the relationship."

[14] Ibid., p. 33: "Richard has sex exclusively with Charles." See also pp. 64–66, where the author refuses to promise that she will be sexually faithful, while her partner, Valerie, holds firmly to sexual fidelity, because that was the way she was raised.

der of the person with whom one has a sexual relationship. It has much to do with their ability to share thoughts and feelings. The only moral norms (not explicitly stated) are what pleases the individual and what is accepted by the couple.

These moral norms are found in the attitudes of the gay and lesbian couples interviewed by Mendola and by Charles Silverman in a subsequent study, *Man to Man, Gay Couples in America*,[15] not only in regard to their coupling but also in the way other moral problems are confronted. How does a *father* who has left his wife and children to enter into a same-sex union regard his decision and his continued obligations toward his children? This is not a rare problem. Seventeen percent of the couples in the Mendola Report had been married with children.[16] However well intentioned such fathers are with their children, who usually live with the heterosexual spouse, they are not able to relate adequately to them. Visiting by the children is often hindered by distance, by the terms of the divorce, and by the reluctance of the heterosexual ex-spouse to allow the children to visit. Many times the father does not know how to relate to his children in the presence of the other partner, often not wanting the children to know about his homosexuality for fear of their subsequent rejection.

The moral question, moreover, which Mendola does not raise, is: How does such a father become a virtuous role model for his sons and daughters? How also does a *mother* who, divorcing her husband, has entered into a union with another woman relate to her three teenage sons? Can two women relate properly to such sons for months on end? With what masculine role models will the three sons identify? How do two lesbians provide a fatherly influence in rearing a daughter? How do children explain to their classmates that they have two same-sex

[15] Charles Silverman, *Man to Man: Gay Couples in America* (New York: William Morrow, 1981).

[16] Mendola, *The Mendola Report*, p. 84.

parents? These are some of the questions unanswered in the Mendola Report and similar studies. Again, the right of children to have the combined influence of father and mother in their psychosexual development is violated in such same-sex arrangements.

Another facet of same-sex coupling is the general tendency of the participants to shy away from "institutionalized" religion, like the Roman Catholic Church, many Protestant denominations, Orthodox Judaism, and other religious groups, in favor of a private spirituality. Indeed, one notes on the part of the homosexual movement downright hostility toward Roman Catholics and so-called fundamental Protestants because of the clear positions they take against homosexual activity.[17] Some of this hostility is evident in the interviews conducted by Mary Mendola.[18]

To be sure, many gay and lesbian couples harbor no resentment toward the "institutional" Church, which they leave regretfully, or in which they remain, while continuing to attend Mass and receive Holy Communion, relying on "pastoral" advice that their way is the only practical way of living with their sexuality. They see their lifestyle as a decision of their conscience, superseding the authentic teaching of the Magisterium. While it is possible that some individuals are in good faith on this matter, that does not absolve the Church from continuing to inform the faithful on her authentic position.[19]

A third study of gay male couples replicates the findings of the Mendola Report on the issue of sexual fidelity.[20] After pre-

[17] Actually the Metropolitan Community Church, which approves the homosexual lifestyle, flourishes in large urban centers. Many of its members are fallen-away Catholics. ACT-UP is the best-known example of hostility.

[18] Mendola, *The Mendola Report*, pp. 44–47.

[19] John F. Harvey, *The Homosexual Person*, "Major Dissenting Views", pp. 79–93. See also chap. 6, "The Morality of Homosexual Activity". There is much confusion among clergy and laity on the issue of good faith, conscience, and homosexual unions.

[20] Silverman, *Man to Man*.

senting several instances of gay couples who believe in sexual exclusivity, Charles Silverman describes more who see strict adherence to sexual fidelity as too restrictive. One twenty-six-year-old said, "Gay relationships are very exciting because there are no rules. Each relationship has at its disposal an infinite number of rules that it can create."[21] Another speaks of the terrible quest for sexual adventure, which cannot be satisfied by one person. Sex is seen as challenge, hunt, conquest, and excitement.[22] Silverman, moreover, makes another point: among homosexual couples there are many conflicts over the issue of sexual exclusivity. Their relationships suffer from jealousy, envy, and deep feelings of insecurity concerning their partners—a fact that McWhirter and Mattison and Mendola also note.[23]

From the data of these three representative studies of gay and lesbian couples, one can see that such unions present many moral problems besides the immorality of same-sex genital acts. The images and views presented are a far cry from the idealized representations of Catholic authors attempting to justify such unions as monogamous, not on the level of Christian marriage, to be sure, but much better than promiscuity. We have seen how sexual exclusiveness and traditional fidelity are rejected by many same-sex couples. We have seen problems of homosexual spouses in their care of children—children deprived of proper relationships to father and mother in a normal family life. Jealousy, insecurity, anger, and envy are bound up in most of these

[21] Ibid., p. 143.

[22] Ibid., p. 144. These two young men are representative of the general attitude toward morality found in the active homosexual lifestyle: there are no rules. It is found among lesbians, as well, as Mary Mendola asserts concerning her own lifestyle (*The Mendola Report*, p. 75 and passim). It is not surprising, then, that Edward Malloy draws the conclusion that the homosexual lifestyle is incompatible with Christianity. See his *Homosexuality and the Christian Way of Life* (Washington, D.C.: University Press of America, 1981).

[23] Silverman, *Man to Man*, pp. 144–57.

relationships; nevertheless, the late John Boswell[24] attempted to use his allegedly historical research to indicate that same-sex unions "have been sanctioned and even idealized in Western societies for over two thousand years"—so says the jacket copy of his book *Same-Sex Unions in Premodern Europe*.

Since Boswell has influenced the lifestyle of homosexual advocates so powerfully, it is necessary to give serious attention to this book. Like his previous book on homosexuality,[25] the present work is erudite, and, as one reads it, one is aware that his points are plentifully footnoted in Greek, Latin, and many other languages. The first reviews in the popular press and on talk shows spoke of Boswell as a master linguist and painstaking researcher who has drawn startling conclusions from the study of original manuscripts from the eighth century onward. Same-sex unions in the sense of two males committed to living together in a sexual-genital relationship, he alleges, were not only widespread in premodern Europe but also blessed by the Church; from the late medieval period, however, liturgical manuscripts giving evidence of the Church's blessing of such unions were destroyed.[26]

Before reading scholarly reviews of Boswell's book, I read the text with an open mind, and I found myself making frequent notation of his tendency to select certain incidents or certain writings out of context to make his main point: that at

[24] John Boswell died of AIDS on Dec. 24, 1994 (*New York Times*, Dec. 25, 1994, obituary).

[25] *Christianity, Social Tolerance, and Homosexuality* (Chicago: Univ. of Chicago Press, 1980). Boswell builds many of his theses on this book, failing to benefit by the criticisms of his colleagues. See also his *Same-Sex Unions in Premodern Europe*.

[26] Trudeau gave a week's worth of "Doonesbury" to asserting that the Church had blessed homosexual unions. See Liz McMillen, "Same-Sex Rituals", *Chronicle of Higher Education* (June 29, 1994), pp. A6–9; Bruce Holsinger, "Dearly Beloved", *The Nation* (Sept. 5–12, 1994), pp. 241–45. The latter is an uncritical review of, almost an advertisement for, Boswell's book.

one time the Church had a liturgical blessing for homosexual unions, which were regarded as on the level of heterosexual marriage. I noted that he did not say that the Magisterium of pope and bishops gave any approval. It was some early medieval clerics. But they were portrayed as the "Church", and the unwary reader might fail to note the difference. Having already read his 1980 volume, I perceived that Boswell was out to prove a point through his research, and so I was not surprised that he gave his own meaning to terms when it fitted into his argument; for example, *adelphos* (*frater*, brother) is taken to mean "homosexual lover". I found him making gross generalizations about marriage in late pagan Roman antiquity. He maintains it was mainly a legal arrangement for property and dynastic succession, which was the main reason for children. The advent of Christianity did not change this. If affection showed up in a marriage, it was *only* after the fact of marriage. Married men found their female (or male) lovers on the side, so to speak. Meanwhile, in the Roman military, particularly, one found same-sex lovers who had made full commitment to one another, and so their lives were fulfilled, in sharp contrast to the married. Again, celibacy is downgraded as a kind of escape from the responsibilities of real life.

As I read, it became increasingly clear to me that Boswell remained an *advocate* of the homosexual way of life, with the result that his mind was so completely obsessed with proving that the homosexual lifestyle is *good* that he could no longer see the full truth about it. This preoccupation helps explain the tendentious quality of his writing. In this regard, he is like John J. McNeill, who gave up being a moralist to become an advocate of a cause, the homosexual way of life.

Now, a closer look at Boswell's form of advocacy is in order, and, since he claims to present a thesis based upon historical-liturgical documents, I find it necessary to consult the reviews of scholars of the pertinent periods of history and Church history.

Brent D. Shaw,[27] who teaches history at the University of Lethbridge in Alberta, Canada, points out:

> Boswell's argument stands or falls on his interpretation of a series of documents relating to a singular ritual practiced in the Christian church during antiquity and the high middle ages, principally in the lands of the eastern Mediterranean. The bonds that are confirmed in these church rituals are cautiously (and a little coyly) labeled by him as "same-sex unions". For his arguments to have the force that he wishes them to have, however, the words "same-sex" and "union" must be construed to mean "male homosexual" and "marriage". If they signify other sorts of associations that happened to be same-sex in gender, or unions that were meant for purposes other than marriage, or a permanent affective union, then his claims fail.[28]

Like Brent Shaw, Robin Darling Young, after examining the texts adduced by Boswell to demonstrate that the Christian Church had blessed same-sex unions during the Middle Ages, concludes that

> neither Boswell's reconstruction of them nor his method of argumentation can possibly support the interpretation that he proposes: first, it is highly implausible that homosexual unions either in antiquity or in the Middle Ages would have been blessed by a religion that promoted ascetic devotion to the kingdom of God rather than that condition which contemporary Americans understand as the healthy expression of erotic drives. . . . Furthermore, early Byzantine law codes contain extremely harsh punishments for homosexual intercourse.[29]

Both Shaw and Young contend that the ecclesiastical texts that Boswell interprets as same-sex unions, or marriages, mean no such thing. Both hold that the Greek term for brother,

[27] Brent Shaw, "A Groom of One's Own", *The New Republic* (July 18–25, 1994), pp. 33–41. It is refreshing that *The New Republic*, often regarded as liberal, would provide such a thorough review of an important book.

[28] Ibid., p. 34.

[29] Robin Darling Young, "Gay Marriage: Reimagining Church History", *First Things* (November 1994), p. 47.

adelphos, and the Greek term for the creation of brothers, *adelphopoiesis*, do not mean an erotic same-sex union.[30] Shaw invokes the authority of Gabriel Herman, professor of history at the Hebrew University in Jerusalem, who has also studied the same rituals found in the appendix of Boswell's book. Herman agrees with Shaw and Young in that the ritual ceremonies for the creation of brothers do not mean the union of marriage. They "meant the making of brothers who were not brothers by nature. Men often entered into such relationships, not out of love, but out of fear and suspicion. For this reason one finds in these documents references to the right of 'protective asylum' and 'safe conduct'. . . . These links were never mistaken or confused with the union of marriage."[31] Both Shaw and Young hold that Boswell misinterprets and mistranslates the Greek texts, trying to force a meaning on the texts that is not there. Shaw finds "tendentious" translations throughout the book, a finding that other reviewers of Boswell stress.[32] Young holds that the book has only a façade of scholarship, with unwarranted a priori assumptions and "outrageously false translations of critical terms" and a carelessness about historical accuracy that would be "unacceptable in an undergraduate paper."[33]

Shaw goes on to explain that these rituals are "same-sex" in the sense that two men are involved, and that they are "unions" in the sense that the two men are joined together as "brothers".

[30] Ibid., p. 45, n. 37; see also Shaw, "Groom", p. 35.

[31] Gabriel Herman, *Ritualized Friendship and the Greek City*, quoted in Shaw, "Groom", p. 35.

[32] Shaw, "Groom", p. 34. Other reviews: David Wright, "Do You Take This Man?" *National Review* (Aug. 29, 1994), pp. 59–61: "Yet as in the earlier book Mr. Boswell's extraordinary skills and industry are deployed with such tendentiousness, exaggeration, special pleading . . . that the work deserves, at very best, the distinctive verdict of the Scottish courts: not proven" (p. 59). (Wright is senior lecturer in church history at the University of Edinburgh.) Kenneth Woodward says that "Boswell's main problem is his tendentious interpretations of the evidence": *Newsweek* (June 20, 1994), pp. 76–78.

[33] Young, "Gay Marriage", p. 44.

But that is all. There is "no indication in the texts themselves that these are marriages in any sense that the word would mean to readers now, nor in any sense that the word would have meant to persons then".[34]

Most historians who have studied these ritualized relationships believe that they deal with a kind of ritualized kinship best described as "brotherhood". This would explain why the texts concerned with the making of brotherhood found in the prayer books are within the sections dealing with "other kinship-forming rituals, such as marriage and adoption".[35]

Shaw takes Boswell to task for joining two documents as if they were one, so that in the main text of his book he could appeal to the totality of the documents, "as if they are all variant types of a marriage ceremonial, which they are not".[36] Boswell also misleads his readers on the meaning of the Greek term *agape*, love. As found in ecclesiastical documents, such as those in Boswell's appendix, the term never means erotic love, although Boswell tries to give it that meaning in his "same-sex documents". Likewise, he gives to the term *adelphos*, brother, the meaning of "homosexual lover", but there is no warrant for understanding *adelphos* as homosexual lover in the liturgical texts cited.[37]

Boswell also distorts the meaning of marriage in the Greco-Roman world, giving the impression that there was some form of homosexual marriage recognized by the state, whereas there

[34] Shaw, "Groom", p. 35.

[35] Ibid.

[36] Ibid., p. 36. Admittedly one section of one document contains a liturgical service designed for a marriage ceremony, but there is no mention here of a same-sex union. What Boswell did was to join together the text of a brotherhood ceremony with that of a marriage, that is, separate and different documents.

[37] Ibid. Young, "Gay Marriage", p. 45, also takes issue with Boswell on his translation of certain terms, such as *adelphos*. Boswell tried to build a case for the word to mean "lover", whereas in a Christian context it signifies simply "belonging to Christ's family, one of the adopted sons of God".

never was any formally acknowledged alternative to marriage. Marriage itself he caricatures as primarily concerned with dynastic property arrangements in which children are not important. From the definitions of marriage and family in both pagan and Christian times and from our canonical understanding as well, marriage is defined invariably "as a union of opposite sexes: male and female".[38] The sexual definition was constant and explicitly related to children, while the affective elements were seen as variable (as they still are today). It was not conceivable, moreover, that two males could possibly constitute a family.

Boswell's response to the nineteenth- and twentieth-century scholars who refuse to interpret close friendships among men as homosexually erotic is to accuse them of denial. He regards them as not wanting to admit the existence of homosexual marriages—to which Shaw responds, "This verges on paranoia."[39]

I noticed the same emotional language throughout Boswell's book; for example, he refers to opposition to the homosexual lifestyle as "the Western horror".[40] A few pages later (p. 274), he asserts that any opinion holding that homosexual feelings are "abnormal", peculiar, or inherently unlikely is based upon a "moralistic and empirically mistaken assumption". Then comes the astonishing claim that "only female and gay anthropologists, writers, and historians of nearly any time or place have been able to view the ceremony [same-sex marriage rituals] *objectively and without noticeable reticence*" (p. 276, emphasis added).

In concluding his detailed critique of Boswell's position, Shaw admits that in certain ritualized friendships in the Eastern Mediterranean there could have been homoerotic elements, "but same-sex marriages forged with the approval of the Christian

[38] Shaw, "Groom", p. 37.
[39] Ibid., p. 40.
[40] Boswell, *Same-Sex Unions*, p. 270.

church and with its rituals? No. Such a reading is very misleading."[41]

Young also points out that in two chapters Boswell attempts to make homosexual unions the rough equivalent of heterosexual marriages, mainly by demeaning heterosexual marriage to the level of a purely pragmatic arrangement for property and progeny, while portraying homosexual unions as affectionate and humanly superior.[42] Still later, Boswell attempts to show that early Christianity took over the late Roman customs; it is already clear, however, in Shaw's review that the Romans regarded marriage as far more than a business arrangement.

In presenting the Christian history of homosexual marriage, Young says, Boswell creates the impression that early Christianity *uncritically* accepted late Roman mores with regard to sex and marriage. But anyone acquainted with early Christian documents, particularly the *Didaché*, knows how false this claim is. These countercultural writings stressed salvation through union with Christ in opposition to pagan practices, as the Church continues to do today. Pre-Christian sexual practices were not transferred into Christian rituals.[43]

It is astounding how Boswell "reconstructs" early Christian history, downgrading marriage, distorting the historical mean-

[41] Shaw, "Groom", p. 41. Kenneth Woodward comes to a similar conclusion: "That the 'brotherhood' ritual may have served at times as a cover for homosexual relationships is a real possibility. That it was created for that purpose remains unsubstantiated. That its existence could lead to church-sanctioned gay marriages appears to be an empty hope": *Newsweek* (June 20, 1994), p. 59. David Wright asks at the end of his review: "What are we left with? Certainly, a series of liturgical texts largely unpublished and inaccessible to most scholars in the English-speaking world. . . . In less partisan hands these texts will illumine a little-known relationship of spiritual 'brotherhood' akin to the fraternal adoption of secular law. Beyond that, Mr. Boswell's adventurous forays impress more for their speculative ingenuity than for common sense": *National Review* (Aug. 29, 1994), p. 60.

[42] Young, "Gay Marriage", p. 45

[43] Ibid., p. 46.

ing of Christian celibacy, and asserting that Christianity did not focus on the biological family until a thousand years into its existence! Young points out that, in addition to patristic concern for the religious life and celibacy, the Eastern Fathers gave due emphasis to the family as "the primary way for Christians".[44]

As in his first book, Boswell speaks of Jesus and John as the most controversial same-sex couple in the Christian tradition, adding his list of "paired saints"—Perpetua and Felicity, Polyeuctos and Nearchos, and Sergius and Bacchus. All descriptions are rife with homoerotic implications, and all are without historical proof. [45]

In the last three chapters of his book, Boswell tries to interpret what the texts and ceremonies that he has "discovered" signify. As he has done throughout, he mistranslates "brother", "friendship", "intimacy", and "*koinonia*" as homoerotic terms in order to build his case for homosexual marriages.[46] Commenting on the two appendices, which contain translations and documents that "allegedly attest to same-sex union", Young points out that one finds here different kinds of material: a liturgical hymn to Saints Sergius and Bacchus, a nuptial office, a brotherhood contract, a "heterosexual ceremony" from the *Book of Common Prayer*, and twelve brotherhood rituals. The juxtaposition of canonical marriage rites with "supposed gay marriage rites is undoubtedly meant to suggest their equivalency".[47]

Young concludes that this book does not accomplish "what it set out to do. . . . Indeed, the author's painfully strained effort to recruit Christian history in support of the homosexual cause

[44] Ibid.

[45] Ibid., pp. 46–47. See also Boswell, *Christianity, Social Tolerance, and Homosexuality*, pp. 225–26, where he also reads into Aelred what is not there.

[46] Young, "Gay Marriage", p. 47: "Contrary to Boswell, *koinonia* rarely means sexual intercourse."

[47] Ibid.

that he favors is not only a failure, but an embarrassing one."[48] I am grateful for her scholarship.

IV

Having reviewed and analyzed sociological, psychological, and historical works on same-sex unions, I turn now to an English Protestant moral critic of same-sex partnerships, Dr. John Stott.

Stott appeals at the beginning of his discourse to the common ground on which we all stand: we are humans, Christians, and sexual beings subject to sinful tendencies. He then phrases the question: Are homosexual partnerships a Christian option? To respond to this question, he says, one must make three distinctions.

The first distinction is between sin and crime. Adultery is a sin but not, in most countries, a crime punishable by the state. On the other hand, rape is both a sin and a crime. The point of the distinction is that the Sexual Offenses Act of 1967 in Great Britain declared that a homosexual act between consenting adults over twenty-one in private should no longer be considered a criminal offense. This does not mean that the civil law regards such acts as moral; it simply removes any legal sanctions.

The second distinction is between homosexual orientation and homosexual "physical" practices. One is not responsible for the orientation, but one is responsible for homosexual acts.

The third distinction is between casual homosexual practices, usually anonymous acts of self-gratification, and "those which (it is claimed) are just as expressive of authentic human love as heterosexual intercourse in marriage".[49] Those making such a claim, usually members of the gay Christian movement, argue that a gay Christian partnership is equivalent to Christian mar-

[48] Ibid., p. 48.
[49] Stott, *Homosexual Partnerships?* p. 5.

riage because both are equally tender, mature, and faithful. With these distinctions made, Stott formulates the question: whether homosexual partnerships—"lifelong and loving—are a Christian option".[50]

Working on the assumption that some homosexual partnerships are loving and lifelong, Stott turns to the biblical writers and biblical scholars to discern moral norms given by God to the human race. In considering the biblical evidence, he adverts to Derrick Sherwin Bailey's *Homosexuality and the Western Christian Tradition* (1955), which has had considerable influence on Protestant theologians, advocating a reconstructionist point of view as opposed to a traditionalist understanding of the Sodom and Gomorrah story (Gen 19:1–13).

The traditionalist understanding is that the townsmen wanted to rape the angelic visitors and that Lot proposed instead giving the townsmen his own daughters to satisfy their lust. Bailey, however, holds that it is a gratuitous assumption to believe that the men of Sodom wanted to have sex with the visitors. In Genesis 19:5 the Sodom men say they want to know (*yada*) the visitors. Since, in Bailey's opinion, in the Bible, *yada* usually does not mean sexual intercourse, he interprets the word in Genesis 5 to mean becoming *acquainted* with the visitors. So the sin was one of inhospitality on the part of the Sodom men invading the home of Lot. Bailey adds a second argument against the traditional position, saying that nowhere in the rest of the Old Testament is it suggested that Sodom's offense was homosexual activity.

But Bailey's case is not convincing for a number of reasons: (1) the adjectives "wicked", "vile", and "disgraceful" (Gen 19:7) do not seem appropriate to describe a breach of hospitality; (2) the fact that Lot offered his daughters to the men of Sodom indicates clearly that it was a question of sexual intercourse, in-

[50] Ibid., p. 6.

deed, of rape; (3) the verb *yada* was used of Lot's daughters, who had not known a man (v. 8); (4) the book of Jude (v. 7) is quite unequivocal: "The fornication of Sodom and Gomorrah and the other nearby towns was equally unnatural."[51]

So much for Bailey's theory, with which I disagree. Stott, surprisingly, allows himself to be persuaded that the classical texts of Leviticus (18:22 and 20:13) refer not to ordinary homosexual acts but to acts done in rites of idolatry. Many scriptural scholars do not agree with him.[52] He also dismisses Romans 1:26–27 too easily as referring *only* to promiscuous homosexual behavior, and thus not applicable to loving, faithful same-sex unions.[53]

His reasoning in regard to the other two Pauline texts (1 Cor 6:9–10 and 1 Tim 1:9–10) is open to question; for example, he grants the argument that perhaps Paul had commercial pederasty in mind.[54] From the "Letter to the Bishops of the Catholic Church on the Pastoral Care of Homosexual Persons", previously cited, it is clear that the texts of Leviticus and the Pauline texts of 1 Corinthians and 1 Timothy do condemn homosexual acts without qualification.

At this juncture in his argument Stott makes a strong point, namely, that the specific scriptural texts in which homosexual acts are condemned are open to revisionists' arguments, which, in effect, say that such texts tell us nothing about the morality of homosexual acts done in a faithful same-sex union, and therefore one needs to study what the Scriptures say about sex and mar-

[51] Ibid., pp. 8–9. See also Harvey, *The Homosexual Person*, pp. 98–99. Ruth Tiffany Barnhouse, in *Homosexuality: A Symbolic Confusion* (New York: Seabury, 1979), p. 190, holds that taking the sexual element out renders the whole passage nonsensical. John Mahoney, in *The Month* (May 1977), p. 167, argues that the Sodom narrative is an expression of divine displeasure about the sin of homosexuality of the cities' inhabitants.

[52] George Montague, "A Scriptural Response to the Report on Human Sexuality", *America* (October 1977), pp. 284–85.

[53] Stott, *Homosexual Partnerships?* pp. 10–11.

[54] Ibid., pp. 12–13. See also Harvey, *The Homosexual Person*, p. 99, and nn. 12–13.

riage.[55] That is the line of argument I have used in chapter six on the morality of homosexual acts. I have found it more persuasive than discussing the conflicting interpretations of scholars on the relevance of the classical texts from both Testaments.

Pointing out that professed homosexuals like to compare their unions with those of married people, Stott asks: In what ways are homosexual unions similar to marriage, and in what ways dissimilar? He sees *complementarity* between man and woman as the basis for heterosexual marriage. God has created us as social beings with a capacity to love and to be loved. He intends us to live in community and not in solitude, and so He sends man a "helper" who would also be his sexual partner and with whom he would also become "one flesh", thereby consummating their love and procreating their children.[56]

When in Genesis 2, the Yahwist version of creation, Eve is presented to Adam, he responds with "history's first love poem: This at last (in contrast to the birds and beasts) is bone of my bones and flesh of my flesh" (Gen 2:23).[57] In verse 24 we see the sacred writer's deduction from the preceding verse, namely, "for this reason a man shall leave father and mother and be united to his wife, and they will become one flesh" (RSV).

Stott calls our attention to the fact that "flesh" is mentioned three times, thereby teaching us that heterosexual intercourse in marriage is more than a union of bodies; it is certainly that; "it is a blending of complementary personalities through which . . . the rich created oneness of human being is experienced again. And the complementarity of male and female sexual organs is only a symbol at the physical level of a much deeper spiritual complementarity."[58]

---

[55] Stott, *Homosexual Partnerships?* pp. 14–15.

[56] Ibid., p. 14. Stott qualifies this statement with a reference to 1 Corinthians 7, where Paul proposes consecrated celibacy as another calling for Christians.

[57] Ibid., p. 15.

[58] Ibid., p. 16

Stott sees in verse 24 the elements of heterosexual marriage. It is an exclusive union between two individuals, both of whom leave their families to become one flesh. This means that marriage is a loving and cleaving covenant between a man and a woman, leading to sexual intercourse, which then becomes the seal of their covenant. Stott goes on to state that Christ himself ratified this teaching in his discourse with the scribes and pharisees in Mark 10:4–9. In that passage, referring to Genesis 2:24, Jesus said that a lifelong union between husband and wife was not to be broken by man. Stott continues:

> Thus, Scripture defines marriage in terms of heterosexual monogamy. It is the union of one man with one woman which must be publicly acknowledged (the leaving of parents), permanently sealed (he will "cleave to his wife") and physically consummated ("one flesh"). *And Scripture envisages no other kind of marriage or sexual intercourse, for God provided no alternative* [emphasis added].[59]

While emphasizing that only the union of man and wife is approved by God, Stott also observes that Scripture condemns not only homogenital acts but also any sexual activity outside of marriage, including sexual activity in a so-called monogamous same-sex union. Recognizing that his position is not accepted by many, Stott presents opposing arguments and his own critique of them. The first objection to his position is concerned with Scripture and culture. It may be expressed in various ways. Some question the capacity of the Hebrew writers to understand the nature of homosexuality. They assume that the biblical writers were concerned only with culturally determined problems, such as hospitality to the alien, antiquated fertility rituals, or Greek pederasty. Because these writers were creatures of their own cultures, their biblical narratives have no relevancy today.

[59] Ibid., p. 17.

They further assume, in regard to Paul's statements in Romans, 1 Corinthians, and 1 Timothy, that Paul knew nothing about the homosexual "condition" but only about sexual acts with one's own sex. The very idea of a man falling in love with another man, or a woman falling in love with another woman did not enter his mind. Thus, the situation in our time is regarded as so different that these past incidents can have no meaning for us. Accordingly, Stott believes that apologists for the biblical teaching on the immorality of homosexual behavior must turn to biblical truths, which remain applicable to every time and place, and that the universal principle is the divine institution of marriage, as found in Genesis 1 and 2, Matthew 19:1–9, and various other texts, as I have also pointed out in chapter six, above.[60]

The fact that the ancients were not able to conceive of current sexual problems or the contradictory opinions of sexologists does not cancel out the truth that there is order in divine creation, an order that is heterosexual monogamy, transcending fluctuations of culture while remaining permanent and universal.[61] I agree with Stott that the best argument against homosexual activity is that it is utterly contrary to the divine norm for human genital acts.

Stott also argues well against the spurious argument that when Paul condemned homosexual acts in Romans 1:26–27 he was referring to heterosexual men performing homosexual acts for pleasure.[62] Stott believes that Paul uses the Greek term *physis* to mean the natural order of things, which God had established. The same usage is found in Romans 2:14, 27, and 11:24. What Paul is condemning in Romans 1:26–27, Stott says, is not one specific form of motivation and behavior but "any human be-

---

[60] See also Harvey, *The Homosexual Person*, pp. 95–97.

[61] Stott, *Homosexual Partnerships?* pp. 11–17.

[62] For example, John J. McNeill holds that *heterosexual* men peforming homosexual acts were the objects of Paul's condemnation. See Harvey, *The Homosexual Person*, p. 87.

havior which is against 'Nature', that is, against God's created order".[63]

Stott repudiates the argument that the "love quality" of same-sex unions justifies the relationship. Those familiar with Joseph Fletcher's *Situation Ethics* or Anthony Kosnik's *Human Sexuality* will resonate with Stott's exposition of the compatibility of divine law with divine love. Discerning the major premise of the "love quality" advocates to be that love (undefined) is the only absolute and that "whatever seems to be compatible with love is *ipso facto* good", Stott states that love needs law to guide it. Although Christ and his apostles emphasized the love of God and neighbor, they did not do away with the other commandments. "Jesus said, 'If you love me, you will keep my commandments' (Jn 14:15), and Paul wrote, 'love is the fulfilling [not the abrogating] of the law' (Rom 13:8–10)."[64]

Stott admits that in a same-sex union there may be an element of love, but he says it cannot be true love, because it is *incompatible* with God's law. Since love is concerned with the highest good of the beloved, then one negates the genuine good of neighbor by disobeying God's law in sinning with him.[65]

One of the most prevalent arguments in favor of the homosexual lifestyle is that no one has a right to form a judgment of condemnation concerning another's behavior. To this Stott responds that one does not have to accept behavior that is contrary to the law of God; while one cannot judge the interior dispositions of a person, one can make a judgment concerning external behavior; he may decide not to be in the person's company.[66] He has such a right of discrimination in other matters too.

---

[63] Stott, *Homosexual Partnerships?* p. 20.

[64] Ibid., p. 21. St. Francis de Sales speaks of the primacy of divine love over human love when he says, "Mount Calvary is the mount of lovers. All love that does not take its origin from the Savior's passion is foolish and perilous": *Love of God*, bk. 12, chap. 13, trans. J. K. Ryan (New York: Doubleday, 1963), p. 281.

[65] Stott, *Homosexual Partnerships?* p. 21.

[66] Ibid., p. 22.

In the concluding section of *Homosexual Partnerships?* Stott does not seem to be aware that many young people with homosexual tendencies are seeking the help of both prayer and professional therapy in their desire to be rid of the condition itself. This is not surprising, since, when Stott presented his argument, the literature on change of orientation was not as extensive as it is now.

But he is on target when he says that the only alternative to heterosexual marriage is sexual abstinence, although I would qualify the meaning of such abstinence to include the motivation of the love of Jesus Christ. One may decide to practice such abstinence out of love for Christ and for one's fellowmen, as many members of Courage do. This is not to deny the difficulty of complete chastity; one must trust in the power of God to help one to practice celibacy for the sake of Christ's kingdom. Like other Christian leaders who believe that chastity is a special gift of God, Stott teaches that "sexual experience is not essential to human fulfillment"; and that Jesus Christ was no less human for being celibate; indeed, he was perfectly human. Accepting the yoke of Christ brings peace, not turmoil.[67]

Stott was very aware of the negative influence of Norman Pittenger, who wrote *Time for Consent*, and of the American Psychiatric Association's removal of homosexuality from the category of mental illness, which had the effect of making the homosexual lifestyle "normal"; nevertheless, he believes that

[67] Ibid., p. 23. In general, consecrated celibacy has a poor press in many Protestant denominations so far as persons with homosexual tendencies are concerned. While one may wish that everyone who seeks to become heterosexual will be able to make the transition, one must also face the reality that some are not able to do so; but that does not mean they are not able to be celibate with the help of God's grace. Through group support many lead happy and peaceful lives. One Courage member responded to a reporter asking him why he practiced celibacy by saying, "It gives me peace of heart." See St. Augustine, *Confessions* 6.11, 20, where he describes celibacy as a special gift of God.

God can bring about profound changes in persons with homosexual tendencies. He does not mean necessarily that a person becomes heterosexual in orientation but that one is able to be chaste and to be free from homosexual activity. He refers to an interdenominational teaching and counseling ministry called the True Freedom Trust, founded by Martin Hallett, once an active homosexual. Its members testify to their new freedom in Christ in that they have been freed from homosexual activity, although still suffering some pain from the homosexual condition.[68]

Stott sees wisdom in Elizabeth Moberly's theory of same-sex deficit and of unmet needs in the process of development. He agrees with her that same-sex erotic attraction is not the basic problem but the beginning of the solution of the problem. Accepting her answer to the problem, namely, that such persons need loving and lasting nonsexual relationships, Stott quotes Moberly: "Love is the basic problem, the great need, and the only true solution. If we are willing to seek and to mediate the healing and redeeming love of Christ, then healing for the homosexual will become a great and glorious reality."[69]

Stott, however, makes room for situations of incomplete healing, in that some individuals retain homosexual tendencies despite their best efforts to be rid of them, and he counsels such persons to struggle in Christ to lead a chaste life, believing that our present sufferings in this life do not compare with the glory to come (Rom 8:18). I have heard older members of Courage express the same thought. In other ways as well, Stott's perspective is similar to that of Courage. He believes in spiritual support

[68] Stott, *Homosexual Partnerships?* pp. 25–26. The members of this group are very much like many members of Courage who lead chaste lives despite their orientation.

[69] Ibid., p. 27, taken from Elizabeth Moberly, *Homosexuality: A New Christian Ethic* (Cambridge, England: James Clarke, 1983), p. 2. Harvey, *The Homosexual Person*, pp. 38–48, gives a complete summary of Moberly's thought. See also chapter four, above.

groups, the need in some instances for professional therapy, and the importance of chaste affectionate friendships.[70]

Conclusion: The secular studies of same-sex unions, no less than the major religious studies reviewed in this chapter, indicate that "at the heart of the homosexual condition is a deep loneliness, the natural human hunger for mutual love, a search for identity, and a longing for completeness".[71] John Stott, however, proposes a truly Christian approach to the question, with which Roman Catholics can agree. He makes room for those who through no fault of their own still suffer temptations to homosexual acts, while encouraging those who are trying to become heterosexual in orientation to continue their journey. That is exactly the view of Courage. Stott, however, does not give sufficient attention to the development of spiritual support systems with definite goals and programs to implement those goals, such as Courage among Catholics or Exodus among Protestants. But we must not forget that when Stott wrote *Homosexual Partnerships?*, in 1984, Courage was just getting started.

It is to be hoped that our collective reflections on this difficult task of guiding Christian persons with homosexual tendencies to a life of friendship with Christ and with one another will reach those who are confused by the conflicting messages they hear and read. It is tragic that a scholar like Boswell, homosexual in orientation, was not able to see the emptiness of the homosexual lifestyle, probably because he thought there was no viable alternative for himself or others like him. On our part, we need to continue proclaiming the truth of Christ's teaching on human sexuality.

[70] Stott, *Homosexual Partnerships?* pp. 28–30.
[71] Ibid.

WOMEN WITH
HOMOSEXUAL ORIENTATION

Students of homosexuality over the years recognize that far more research and writings are concerned with male homosexuality than with female. In writing about women with homosexual orientation, I realize that there is much that remains uncertain or unknown. Our purpose in writing about Catholic women with homosexual attractions is to show that with God's grace working in their lives they can and do follow the gospel of Christ. Some of these women are single, some married. Some may be termed *bisexual*, because now they relate well to their husbands, whereas formerly they had great difficulty relating to any male. Since my purpose is not to prove that any one woman became heterosexual but only to show how these women live in accord with their Faith, I shall concentrate on the spiritual aspects of their lives without neglecting psychological phenomena, including movement to heterosexuality.

This does not mean that making the transition to heterosexuality is unimportant but only that it is not the *primary* objective of the pastoral minister. His primary objective should be to help these women, whether married or unmarried, to cultivate interior purity of heart. In this respect our objective differs from that of Joseph Nicolosi in *Healing Homosexuality*,[1] where the focus is

[1] Joseph Nicolosi, *Healing Homosexuality* (Northvale, N.J.: Jason Aronson, 1993). Nicolosi describes his approach as that of "'a benevolent provocateur' who departs from the tradition of uninvolved opaque analyst to become a

to free men from homosexuality and to move them toward the other sex. Each of the eight men presented in that work struggles to develop healthy, nonerotic male friendships as the first step toward heterosexuality. Our goal, however, is to help women with a homosexual orientation live chastely. To the extent that group support and psychological insight make this goal more easily attainable, we will profit by these means, keeping in mind always that God wants us to use the natural and supernatural means available to grow in his love.

Protestant counselors who integrate both psychological and spiritual insights have been of great help to me in my efforts to develop a pastoral program for Catholic women with homosexual orientation. The writings of Leanne Payne[2] and Elizabeth Moberly,[3] of the authors from Exodus mentioned in chapter four, and of Joe Dallas,[4] Bob Davies, and Lori Rentzel[5] have influenced my work in significant ways. Most recently, Mario Bergner offers some valuable insights on the healing process for both men and women with homosexual tendencies.[6]

---

salient male presence". He follows the father–son, mentor–pupil model, which is an essential principle of reparative therapy (Introduction, p. 8).

[2] *The Broken Image* (Westchester, Ill.: Crossway Books, 1982), pp. 46–47 (narcissism), 94; her *Restoring the Christian Soul through Healing Prayer* (Wheaton, Ill.: Crossway Books, 1991) has as its subtitle "Overcoming the Three Great Barriers to Personal and Spiritual Completion in Christ". She lists the three barriers as (1) failure to accept oneself, (2) failure to forgive others, and (3) failure to receive forgiveness.

[3] *Psychogenesis: The Early Development of Gender Identity* (London: Routledge and Kegan Paul, 1983), a scholarly study; *Homosexuality: A New Christian Ethic* (Cambridge, England, 1983; Greenwood, S.C.: Attic Press), a popular presentation.

[4] *Desires in Conflict* (Eugene, Ore.: Harvest House, 1991).

[5] Bob Davies and Lori Rentzel, *Coming Out of Homosexuality* (Downers Grove, Ill.: InterVarsity Press, 1993). Regeneration, Inc., provides a book service at reasonable prices: P.O. Box 983, Baltimore, MD 21284–9830.

[6] *Setting Love in Order: Hope and Healing for the Homosexual* (Grand Rapids: Baker Books, 1995). A student and client of Leanne Payne, now involved in her ministry, Bergner gives far more than an account of his own transition to

In 1969, while working in Washington, D.C., with men and women with homosexual orientation, I interviewed in depth eight such women, and these are some of my conclusions.

One of the reasons that all eight held for their way of life was that it was easier for them to maintain an intimate and total relationship with a woman than with a man. While not excluding physical expressions of sexuality, these women primarily sought emotional security and intimacy.[7] There were variations among them on other matters. One woman was involved in a relationship with another woman but was keeping the door open for a future relationship with a man. Another—a leader of the group—had been hoping for two decades that she would enter a heterosexual union in the future.

A third had formed same-sex relationships from the age of twelve. She made a list of the characteristics she wanted in another person but found them only in women. She believed "that men are notoriously unaware of woman's needs".[8] (I've heard heterosexual women say the same.) Several women held that no one really knows the etiology of lesbianism.

At the time, I noted that each woman came from a different environment, and I agreed that there was no single factor that explained lesbianism. Several pointed out that psychiatry should pay more attention to the present circumstances of the individual than to alleged causes rooted in the past of the person, while another regarded the way her father treated her, as if she were a boy, as the decisive factor. Within the group as well as in the literature on the subject the opinion was then expressed that an only child is more likely to become a lesbian, given, to be

---

heterosexuality, offering insights on lesbians as well as on men with homosexual orientation, truly integrating psychological truth with the truth that comes from revelation.

[7] John F. Harvey, "Female Homosexuality", *Linacre Quarterly* 36 (May 1969):101.

[8] Ibid., 102.

sure, other environmental conditions, such as a father treating her like a boy during her childhood years. (Very recently I dealt with a female only child who knew nothing of girls' games until she was fourteen.)

Ambivalent about the freedom she possessed as a lesbian, another would not marry because marriage was too restrictive. Through the differing particulars a theme emerged that one woman expressed thus: "Homosexual women stay together longer than homosexual men, yet their relationship is less physical, and in some cases the physical action is very infrequent."[9] Generally, there is greater depth to their friendships.

In regard to moral sensitivity, I did not find any difference between male and female homosexual persons. But I found the women who came for counsel more receptive than the men to another point of view. These women did not try to defend their way of life by pseudo-intellectual arguments, but frankly admitted their emotional attachments to their lovers and clung to them, not so much in rebellion against moral principles but rather from fear of loneliness, which they foresaw as the consequence of abandoning their beloved. I discerned in this little group of eight a kind of sad resignation, as if they were saying to those who were willing to listen, "We tried to be 'straight', but it didn't work for us. How do you expect us to live?"

One Catholic lesbian summed up the thought of many of her friends when she said to me, "Father, what can the Church do to help us lesbians?"[10]

That remains a good question, to which I will try to respond. But first I will mention that this group took a very dim view of marriage, out of which some had come. I can understand now how they could be pessimistic, because in 1969 there was very little discussion of change of orientation. It will be apparent that

[9] Ibid., 103.
[10] Ibid.

the Washington women held views that are still current among women with a homosexual orientation.[11]

I believe, however, that many homosexual or bisexual women today do not want to keep their lifestyle secret as the Washington women did; on the contrary, they are glad to appear on TV, parading down the main streets of the city with their gay brothers.

Again, most are not asking the Church for any spiritual guidance, and in this respect they are similar to the majority of homosexual male persons. There are comparatively few women with homosexual orientation who seek the help of the Church, and these come to Courage if there is a Courage group in their locality.

Today, however, there are also other currents of thought influencing women with homosexual tendencies, such as radical feminist movements and propaganda for gay civil rights and same-sex unions. The lesbian lifestyle is viewed as a way of complete liberation from men.[12] As we have already noted, lesbians in 1969 were barely visible; now they proclaim their lifestyle on college campuses, in government posts, and in the media. Like the men, they demand that society recognize their unions as being on the same level as marriage. For this reason young women with homosexual tendencies will find other young women, probably in high school and certainly in college, with

[11] In discussing my 1969 study with a veteran psychiatrist recently, I was pleased to know that he resonated with the responses of the women I had interviewed, seeing similar responses in three homosexual women he was treating.

[12] See chapters eight and nine, above. See also Donna Steichen, *Ungodly Rage: The Hidden Face of Catholic Feminism* (San Francisco: Ignatius Press, 1991), pp. 109–10. Steichen quotes Mary Hunt, a Catholic lesbian and theologian, as predicting that "lesbian and gay people in church will become as common as candles" because "the choice will be welcoming diversity or dying on the vine as the people of God". See also pp. 184–85 and 337–43, where other organizations favoring the homosexual lifestyle are described. One should not overlook *Lesbian Nuns: Breaking Silence*, ed. Rosemary Curb and Nancy Manahan (Talahassee, Fl.: Naiad Press, 1985).

whom to identify. They will find further support in media shows and plays, and they can easily come to the conclusion in our multicultural environment that their way of thinking, feeling, and acting is a welcome *variation* from the traditional family culture. They see no need to move out of their lifestyle. It is another way of expressing love and intimacy, and they see nothing wrong with it. In what way can the Church reach them?

In more recent years some researchers have concentrated on women with homosexual orientation, but, unfortunately, their studies have become politicized by the radical feminist movement, resulting in a blurring of facts with ideology.[13] To be sure, that is also true of current studies of male homosexuality, with a similar bias in favor of the homosexual lifestyle as a normal variant of human sexual behavior. Even the entries in library computer lists include few, if any, studies that run counter to the politically correct stand of the American Psychiatric Association in its attempt to normalize both the homosexual condition and behavior.

For this reason we need research that embodies both a Christian perspective and a careful examination of studies concerning homosexuality in women. As in the case of men with homosexual tendencies, one needs to avoid the term *lesbianism* as much as possible because the term is used with the same connotations as the term *gay*, that is to say, "my same-sex attractions are my identity". As Christians, we know better. We are a new creation in Christ. We believe that one can transcend sexual orientation and sexual desires in favor of identity with Christ as man or as woman whenever we perceive a conflict between grace-filled nature and the effects of Original Sin within us.

[13] Three examples: Mary Mendola, *The Mendola Report* (New York: Crown, 1980), which we have discussed in chapter nine; *Lesbian Nuns: Breaking Silence*, ed. Rosemary Curb and Nancy Manahan; and Robert Nugent and Jeannine Gramick, *Building Bridges: Gay and Lesbian Reality and the Catholic Church* (Mystic, Conn.: Twenty-Third Publications, 1992).

Our purpose, then, is to present Christian women who struggle with homosexual desires while holding fast to Christ as their first love. As a way of entering more deeply into these struggles, I find it useful to review some of the differences between homosexual men and women.[14]

Keeping in mind how little research has been done on homosexuality in women compared with men, I have observed the following differences: (1) women tend to form lasting friendships with other women more easily than men do with other men; (2) they tend to be less promiscuous; (3) they are more inclined to formalize their coupling in some kind of religious ceremony; (4) they express less guilt than men while probably denying such feelings; and (5) they seem more hostile to the Roman Catholic Church than men, though again expressing their anger in a private manner.

Vera, my former secretary, explained some of these differences in this way: "It's the whole psychological makeup of the woman. I was with one person for ten years. It was an emotional attachment. It is harder to make that leap out of it. The men tend to be promiscuous, the women attached."[15]

The differences between male and female homosexual persons have pastoral implications. Both may be driven to certain kinds of behavior by loneliness. The men oftentimes settle for a promiscuous way of life, beginning in the gay bars, the gay movie houses, and the baths. The women tend to form very private clusters with other homosexual women, seeming to settle down into a steady lover relationship more easily than men. Women put much more stress on the emotional fulfillment of the friendship, seeing the physical expression thereof as a natural consequence of the already existing emotional bond; on the contrary, men engaging in promiscuous sex tend to avoid psychological intimacy with their sex partners while at the same

[14] Harvey, *The Homosexual Person*, pp. 147, 152, 169, 185–87.
[15] Ibid., p. 152.

time forming a nongenital relationship of intimacy and sharing with another male, heterosexual or homosexual.

In this respect, male homosexual persons appear less integrated than females. Again, since homosexual women, like heterosexual, place primary emphasis on the emotional quality of their relationships, they are more willing than homosexual men to give up the physical pleasure of bodily acts if that is the sacrifice necessary to return to the sacraments without losing the friendship of the other person.

Having observed some of the differences between men and women with homosexual orientation, we must now consider what the Church can do for lesbians. In the early history of Courage the question was raised whether men and women with homosexual tendencies should meet together. It was feared that members of each sex would be inhibited in the expression of their feelings and desires by the presence of the other sex. One Courage unit actually discouraged a young woman from joining them. There were no women in Courage until Vera appeared in 1982. Most of the group accepted her, and she had no difficulty in accepting them. Over a period of fourteen years the number of women increased slowly to seven or eight in the New York area, with a few others nationwide.

On one occasion in which the mixed group totaled seventeen, with three women, the question was asked how comfortable the women felt in such a setting. All three responded that they were at ease in the various discussions but that they also wanted at times to be alone with each other to consider matters proper to women with homosexual tendencies. (This point is made by the women who give an account of themselves later in this chapter.) The men responded that when the women first appeared they felt uneasy, but after a few months they realized that they were not inhibited by the presence of women.

In the Courage program we continue to have mixed groups

in which the men outnumber the women, but, despite this disparity, the meetings are helpful for both men and women. As has been noted, the women, however, want to meet alone at least once a month because they feel that they have issues to discuss. They meet alone twice a month in the New York area, while continuing to meet with the men during the remainder of the month. They follow the Courage program, including the Twelve Steps of A.A., adapted to the needs of Courage members.

The women receive the same kind of psychological insight and spiritual strength or grace that the male members of Courage derive from taking part in the spiritual and sacramental riches of a religious group support system. Suffering from a similar isolation in daily life, they look forward to each meeting of Courage and are disappointed whenever a meeting gets lost in sterile abstract discussions of issues that have nothing to do with their personal growth in the love of Christ. This both men and women have said clearly at our meetings, and so our leaders try to keep the meetings on track.

The reader, however, may want to know how individual women have benefited from the *experience* of being in Courage or in direct contact with Courage leaders. Accordingly, I shall present the experiences of the following women, all of whom have fictitious names to protect their identities. Identifying and nonessential details are omitted, while the truth of their experiences remains. First I turn to Alice.

Alice

Alice was molested at age ten by her girlfriend's father on several occasions during visits to her friend's home. The experience was the beginning of her feeling of mistrust of men, a feeling of "being only used and abused by men". At age fifteen she was romantically attracted to a girlfriend without acting on the attraction. From a Catholic girls' high school Alice entered a convent, where she remained for eight years. Although she was happy in the religious life, after several years she found herself attracted to another religious, with whom she acted out her desires. After much struggle with this problem and following priestly counsel, she left religious life. Soon after her departure from the convent, she met her future husband. She described herself as "very vulnerable and needy", especially after having been rejected by someone while still in the convent. Their marriage has had a rocky road, partly because her husband also entered marriage with a series of emotional problems. Their lives were full of "mistrust, jealousy, and verbal abuse". His behavior drove her farther away from him, and about ten years into the marriage she became attracted to a married woman who was alcoholic. "I became close to her; she needed me as a friend, but my attraction to her became romantic. We were involved physically on and off for eight years."

It was toward the end of this relationship that Alice joined Courage. After rejection by her friend, Alice began to understand the complex nature of her problem and her need for spiritual direction and proper counseling so that she could fulfill her role as wife and mother of four children. She gave herself over to the care of her children, who, in turn, became a source of her strength, for they kept her busy and occupied. She continues to battle feelings of rejection: "I have come to trust that God will guide me."

In addition to rearing a family, Alice has gone back to teaching, from which she derives a sense of self-worth and "great satisfaction". Reflecting on her past, Alice believes that her attempts to become involved in constructive activity in her home and outside the home, living in the present reality, have helped her combat the yearning for sexual-genital pleasures. In lesbian affairs she sees much dependency, manipulation, and role-playing of masculine and feminine parts. One is so desirous of acceptance from one's partner for every decision that one is drained of all energy to break out of the web of dependency.[16] But Alice has done just that as she comes to Courage meetings to strengthen her spiritual life and to help others who struggle in similar ways.

Betty and Charla

Some years ago I received a letter from Betty, who was in an active lesbian relationship with Charla. Betty, a Catholic, wrote to me from the midwest, not asking for approval for her way of life but simply wanting to have someone with whom to correspond. At the time she and Charla were at college. On one occasion she mentioned that Charla and she were going to have a "holy union" ceremony with a "guru" from the East as the minister. She hoped that I would continue to write to her despite my disapproval. I did continue to write. About a year later, after discussing the matter with me and several Protestant clergy and having studied Saint Paul's references to homosexual acts, Betty and Charla gave up their physical relationship while resolving to remain best friends. They had spent time in prayer before making their decision.

They have taken pains to avoid the circumstances in which they had fallen. Betty describes it thus: "It was not always easy, and we did have slips, but slowly we were able to move past our physical relationship to an actually stronger emotional/nonphysical relationship. . . . We are the best of friends in a nonsexual relationship" (correspondence, Feb. 5, 1995).

Betty is of the opinion that she turned to a woman as the

---

[16] See Davies and Rentzel, *Coming Out of Homosexuality*, pp. 107–15, where Lori describes the dynamics of emotional dependency among women. She shows how defensive detachment can lead to emotional dependency. Dr. Carol Ahrens analyzes the same phenomenon in "Emotional Dependency and Lesbianism", *Desires in Conflict* (Eugene, Ore.: Harvest House, 1991), pp. 203–12.

result of the way she was treated by her "last boyfriend". (From my correspondence with her over ten years, I believe that she has some heterosexual tendencies and some homosexual.) Both Betty and Charla have practiced chastity for the last eight years, sometimes under difficult circumstances, as when Charla helped Betty to dress and undress after an operation on her arm. Betty does not know what she will do in the future, having no interest in dating young men at this time. She has returned to the practice of her Faith, and Charla to hers. I see it as a journey of faith by two people once active in the gay lifestyle. God's grace worked through persons who gave support to Betty and Charla. I believe that Betty and Charla may begin to cultivate their heterosexual interests in the future. They need to examine their ongoing relationship, with the help of a spiritual counselor, to remove any elements of emotional dependency. (There is no Courage group near Betty and Charla.)

Donna

In her late thirties, Donna comes from a background of spiritual and psychological deprivation, beginning in infancy and lasting all the time she was in her parents' home. Both parents were animal lovers who saw children as just another form of animal. Donna was so regarded by her mother and father, who sexually abused her as a child. This abuse, together with similar abuse by an uncle, made Donna feel guilty, worthless, and abandoned. She had dreams of being raped by a male figure, while a woman who she thought was her mother walked nonchalantly by. Other dreams were forms of annihilation anxiety, such as falling through space. Her mother also was afraid of death, denying its existence and hanging on to the remains of her dead pets. From this Donna feels that she has "inherited" a morbid fear of death.

In any case, Donna sought refuge in attaching herself to a pretty, red-haired girl of eight, who died very suddenly in the hospital. Donna was frightened and bewildered by the incident, denying that it ever happened. She picked another special friend, who, after a severe automobile accident, never returned to school. Invited by another classmate to her home, Donna felt rejected again when her friend went off without her after a quarrel. She was so upset that she ran out in front of a passing car, her first attempt at suicide. In her loneliness she sought escape in fantasies about biblical incidents, such as Jairus' twelve-year-old daughter, or Samuel hearing the voice of the Lord. (She was not yet twelve.)

She kept her faith as secret as possible, however, because it seemed to upset her mother. When her mother learned of her praying, she mocked her, claiming that Donna was communicating with the devil and would wind up in an insane asylum.

Donna continued to live in fantasy, imagining that she had been orphaned and adopted by another woman, usually one of her mother's friends or a favorite teacher. She wrote a passionate love letter to one of them and says, "I imagined being held and kissed by them and pretended to be ill at school so that they would put their arms around me." At school she was part of a threesome, but always "feeling the odd one left out".

At secondary school she became close to another girl with "masses of red hair" but then experienced great disappointment when her friend had her hair cut short. Donna recalls that at the time she was unaware why she overreacted, having blocked out the early memory of the little girl with red hair who had died. During this period she had little interest in boys.

At a university she became a Catholic, but she practiced her newfound Faith for only a year before giving it up. Donna tended to be a perfectionist in Catholic observances while finding confession very difficult because she felt a "sort of global guilt".

In the following years, with all kinds of disturbance at home because of her parents' lifestyle and her grandmother's dementia,

Donna took time out with her friends of both sexes, including two who were gay and one who was bisexual. Although she suspected that she herself was homosexual, she decided to ignore her suspicions, settling for, in her words, "emotionally dependent friendships with several women whom I liked to be older and found physically most pleasing if they were well rounded". They were invariably good Christian women.

Donna, however, found it very painful when, because of moving or bereavement, the time for separation came. She was torn apart by these separations. (During the next decade she would become anorexic until her husband helped her overcome the illness.) She worked in a Catholic community during part of this period. At first she was fearful of any long-term commitment, like marriage, but she gradually became less fearful of such commitments. A man with whom she had socialized tried to talk her into marriage, but she found this prospect "completely unbearable", and to get away from him she escaped into the big city and the Catholic community. Although she describes herself as being in a "very bad state" upon her return to the Church, she gradually came to enjoy living in a lay Catholic community. At this time she met her future husband, who had been granted laicization from the priesthood. She says there seemed to be a "marriage of minds, ideals, and spirituality. . . . We married quite quickly without fully knowing each other and had no marriage preparation. Romance and sexual intimacy were not high on the agenda."

Although Donna still found sex "distasteful altogether", it gave them three wonderful children. Both Donna and her husband, Teddy, have had to make considerable adjustments in light of their unusual pasts. On her part, Donna had resolved not to talk about the past, trying to forget its horrors.

For a while, everything went fine, and Donna was told by her doctor that she was the perfect mother. She and her husband were pleased to be complimented on their "holy family". Yet deep inside Donna felt that something was going to go wrong, because, she says, "I was tormented with the secret fear that one day I might go mad and destroy my children". So she took great precautions to protect her children from any kind of situation in which she might possibly lose control of herself. Though she knew she needed help, she did not know where to turn for it, being afraid even to voice these fears. "It was sheer hell."

Donna was able, however, to share some memories of the past with an older female relative by marriage, including the dreadful fear regarding her children. With the help of this person she coped with this "irrational" fear by uncovering certain "root memories", which she regarded as the source of the dread. She was so dependent upon this older woman, however, that when the latter called one day to inform Donna that she was terminally ill, Donna's world began to fall apart. It was a life crisis for her, turning her world upside down.

At the funeral of the older woman Donna wished that she could go down with the coffin, "feeling more afraid to live than to die". This led to the resurfacing of many traumatic memories of the past, and Donna became suicidal. She began to take steps in this direction when (in her words) "I was stopped in my tracks, due mainly to a dream". At the same time she was aware that her "smallest child" was getting separation anxiety, clinging to her and saying, "Mommie, I don't want you to die."

Although Donna turned away from suicide, she did not come through unscathed, because the cumulative effect of these traumatic memories created in her a yearning for physical intimacy with another woman. She described the emotions engulfing her as

> fear, panic, isolation, shame, and guilt, as well as anger, feelings of rejection, despair, and disconnectedness. These strong emotions can assemble into a shame cycle where the person acts out sexually to try to feel better, but this makes her feel worse, and the cycle becomes increasingly difficult to break. I became a

total nervous wreck and was told to try to pull myself together, which was impossible.

Donna tried in vain to get help from a confessor, two so-called Catholic groups of lesbians and gays, and several pastoral counselors who agreed to help her but very quickly changed their minds "when they realized that it was too much for them to handle". She had no guidance.

One night she held her sleeping daughter close to her, thereby gaining sexual satisfaction, although she knew that it was wrong. But afterward she did not yield again to these impulses. Then came the trauma of her father's death. She became afraid to show affection for her children because they might discover her feelings. This fear drove her to methods of releasing her feelings that are "condemned by the Church in its wisdom" (masturbation). She testified later that this did not help.

Turning to clinical psychological help, she found that the "disclosure and subsequent report procedures" only perpetuated the shame cycle. In spite of this downward slide, Donna vigorously denied that her feelings were out of control. She believes, however, that the turning point came when she was "pulled up" to the fact that she "was getting into a state bordering on total depravity". As she began to climb out of this situation, her memory was overwhelmed with all the traumatic fantasies of the past, especially "sexualizing enormous ladies, women in fur coats, sometimes in a masochistic setting".

Still she came through it all with clinical help, prayer, and spiritual support groups like A.A. and Courage. She thanks God that no one came to any real harm. "I know that there is no condition that God cannot cure, and that he is able to save to the uttermost all those who trust in him. I realized beyond any doubt that it is impossible to cure one type of impurity with another kind of impurity." (This is a reference to the advice of one clinical psychologist, who had counseled her to find a same-sex lover.) She recognizes that she must be faithful to her husband.

Donna continues to go to group support meetings, to a spiritual director, and to her family doctor, who has a background in psychiatry. She has found the latter more helpful than the hospital therapist, who did not share her Christian values. Her family doctor also referred Donna and her husband to a female Christian counselor who "underpinned her counseling with prayer". It took many sessions, because Donna had almost despaired of the future of their marriage, having sought divorce, which her husband refused. She noted that both of them went through all the emotions identifiable with the bereavement processes: denial, anger, fear, depression, bargaining, acceptance, and resolution. It was not easy—with acceptance coming toward the end of the sessions, when the counselor was on the verge of giving up. When Donna went "berserk", however, her husband met her at a desperate point of need, recognizing, she says, "how helpless and hopeless I had become". His help led to reconciliation and a completely new start.

During the period of counseling, both observed sexual abstinence, which gave Donna space to reorient herself. She describes her current married life as the resolution stage—an ongoing process and a time of inner peace and serenity, leading her to exclaim, "I'm amazed at where I have been and how I've come out of it. I now want and enjoy his love. If any disordered feelings momentarily threaten to come between us, I immediately cling all the closer to him."

Commentary: I introduced Donna to Courage, where she has found support and spiritual direction in the context of prayer and the sacraments. At present she is in contact with a Roman Catholic psychiatrist of "deep faith", who corrected all the false teachings of the hospital therapist, while giving Donna not only psychological insight but also strong encouragement to practice her Faith. Now Donna spends volunteer time in a nursing home for elderly people. Her husband and the psychiatrist have helped her to look after her children. As a result, the children have been kept safe and secure, with no awareness that there has been a problem concerning Donna's feelings toward them. As Donna continues to grow spiritually, she does not blame all her troubles on her traumatic childhood and living with inaccessible parents, although she recognizes that there is some connection between her childhood and her sexual orientation, which she has been given to understand was predominantly homosexual, with some elements of pedophilia.

Now she realizes that her greatest stumbling block has been her avoidance of the truth about herself. From early days she consistently retreated from painful thoughts and realities until they came to a head. This human tendency to deny the truth about oneself, which Donna has seen played out in her life, causes her to urge others to help persons like herself to open up their hearts and minds to trustworthy counselors, such as she has found in Courage. She really appeals to both counselors and counselees: the counselors to encourage others to trust them and the counselees to be willing to trust their innermost thoughts to those they seek out. In this interaction we all need the help of the Holy Spirit.

Donna's progress is almost miraculous. The fact that with God's help and good friends she and her husband have resolved the very serious problems in their relationship—particularly Donna's difficulties—is a sign of hope for other couples in similar circumstances. Both Donna and her husband recognize that they must continue to work on their relationship through prayer, mutual support, and Courage.

One sees in Donna's history some of the elements that have helped other members of Courage to regain control of their lives as the first step to a spirituality rooted and grounded in Christ: individual spiritual direction, group support, sound therapy, and continual prayer.

Besides the insights gained from professional therapy, which helped her to understand the nature of her fantasies and the strength of her repressed sexual desire, Donna learned something else. She realized that she was powerless over her condition and that a Power greater than herself could restore her to sanity. This brought her into Courage, where she continues to do well. It is significant in Donna's life as well as in the lives of other addicts that *regular participation in group support meetings while working the Twelve Steps is essential for full recovery*.

Another point to be made is that Donna's confiding in the older woman and in the clinical psychologists made it easier for her to open up within a support group. Many people who are involved in any form of sexual addiction dread telling anyone about it. What will my friend think of me? As denial and rationalization feed a compulsion, so sheer honesty will starve it. Donna says, "The one requirement for any person who wants to get out of any compulsive behavior is total honesty with oneself and others. It means stop lying to oneself. To recognize that I was a sinful person and that therefore I was able to take the responsibility for my actions was certainly a great relief."

I can sum up what I regard as Donna's contribution to the members of Courage, and that is her use of all the means available to pull herself from the traps of addiction to the freedom of a new life of grace. She made use of professional therapy (although some of it was not helpful); of friends; spiritual directors; group support systems, particularly Courage; good spiritual reading; and, above all, prayer. Her journey inspires others to struggle on the road to Christ with the help of his Church.

Megan

Megan comes from an Irish Catholic background in which alcoholism was so strong a factor that the first help she sought in her adult life was Al Anon. She does not remember whether in those early years she was a victim of sexual abuse. She remembers very little of her childhood. She received little sex education, and most of that was negative. As a child she played almost exclusively with boys, and as a teenager she experienced crushes and romantic feelings about boys. She is not sure what familial factors may have contributed to her subsequent homosexual attractions. Because of living in an alcoholic household, despite feeling some attraction to the other sex, Megan blocked out the thought of ever getting married. It was more a visceral decision than one thought out. From being around young males, she saw them as a threat, so that whenever she walked past a group of males she would "steel" herself in the expectation of hearing "some vile come-on". This expectation, in turn, affected her self-image. She felt "different" in a negative sense, not seeing herself as attractive and not being able to relax among males. She had no interest in female cosmetics, jewelry, clothing, girlish excitement about male teens, and the like. She spent her high school and most of her college years at women's institutions. She dated no one, and yet she had crushes on the few males whom she came to know. Looking back on this period of her life, she feels that she was both shy and fearful. Although she does not recall being asked out on a date, she remembers having a "yearning for physical closeness with those particular males at that time". She does not believe that she could have allowed them to know that she liked them "in an open way, although some may have guessed".

On the college level, Megan found herself in a little group of "gay" women, one of whom told her about her relationships, although Megan did not herself become involved in a sexual way. After spending considerable time with this one woman, listening to her escapades, Megan "walked away from the friendship, feeling depressed and used". She entered into a "long grieving" period without realizing that she had been in an "emotional attachment". Because of this experience, she agrees with the opinion that "homosexually oriented women get involved more in emotionally dependent relationships".

"After college," Megan says, "I seemed to be in a sexual 'no man's land', perceiving myself as without sexual attractions." But as she came to know herself better, she realized that it had been a long time since she had been attracted to a man and that the feelings she was experiencing were "homosexual". She felt no guilt in having these feelings, because she knew she had not brought them on and that she was morally bound not to act on them. She was able to remain sexually abstinent without difficulty because the feelings were "not constant or irresistible".

Coming from a religious background, she had studied the Church's position on the immorality of homosexual behavior and supported it as a teacher of catechetics. Then she entered addiction-counseling training. In this work she began to notice that gay women, recovering from alcoholism, began to talk to her freely, as if they had guessed that Megan was homosexual, and that these same women were not as open with the other counselors.

She only gradually came to the realization that she had homosexual inclinations and that she should do something about them. Eight years after first hearing of Courage, she attended her first meeting: "I walked in fearful and felt acceptance and peace for who I was, a child of God who struggles." She wanted to deal with the issue. At first she was the only woman, or one of few women, at the meetings. But within a year five women formed their own group, meeting once a month on a different night from the meeting with the men. These women go to both meetings.

Megan relates how much she needed the women's group. After the first one she went to the chapel and cried. "I felt home and no longer alone. Courage meetings have made it possible for me to 'get out of my head', dealing with the issues of emotions and sexuality—not just intellectually." She felt comfortable talking to her brothers and sisters about these matters: "Though I was never sexually active, I am always amazed at the sexual identification I can have with members who have been sexually addicted. This has humbled me and graced me to the point of seeing my own powerlessness and compulsiveness with fantasy and dependency feelings."

Courage members, Megan relates, have taught her how to laugh at herself, to accept her limitations, and to go on striving to live a life of grace. When she first came to Courage meetings, she had no desire to change her orientation. She had no desire for marriage and children, simply wanting to live a chaste life, especially now that she was in a fellowship of persons who knew where she was coming from. But two years later, after becoming friends with the men in the group, she was surprised by

> occasional feelings of attraction for some of these men. About a year ago I started realizing that I would really look forward to seeing and hearing from one male friend in the group. I was pleasantly startled to realize that romantic feelings were developing. . . . I suffered with guilt and frustration for a while until I realized he was bisexual. The friendship has deepened, but only recently did I find out that the romantic feelings are mutual. . . . We're open with our feelings while not taking any action that would endanger our chaste friendship, including dating at this time.

Despite this good news, Megan is concerned with what she terms "obsessive and addictive" fantasy—only now it is about marriage. She constantly finds herself evaluating her motives to make sure that this present friendship is not a form of sick dependency. Wisely, she is going to present her current state of feeling to a reliable therapist. I believe he will encourage her to pursue the present friendship while helping her to deal with other issues in her family background, such as relationships with parents and siblings.

Megan's caution concerning friendships is rooted in a series of negative experiences she has had in same-sex relationships. She usually tended to form relationships with headstrong, masculine women who became the "decision makers" in the friendship. Then came "breakup" and grieving.

She refuses to call herself a lesbian. "I am first a child of God, a daughter of the great King, not defined only by sexual feelings."

Megan concludes her autobiography with an expression of gratitude for the graces that have come to her through her participation in Courage meetings: "Courage has given me stronger impetus to be a Christian, because I feel so much more need of God's help to live a Christian life. . . . I can't state enough my gratitude."

Cynthia

From her earliest years Cynthia displayed leadership qualities of "assertiveness, friendliness, and strength", while having an older brother who was constantly criticized by their stepfather for lacking these very qualities. Cynthia would come to the defense of her older brother by confronting the stepfather. Their mother, moreover, humiliated them both, telling her son that Cynthia should have been a boy and he a girl. As a child, she felt abandoned on the occasion of her mother's second marriage, and throughout her life she has found her mother emotionally inaccessible. At the age of four or five Cynthia was sexually molested by a male babysitter. When she told her mother, she felt that she did not believe her, although she did not bring the same babysitter back again. The perception that her mother did not believe her hurt Cynthia deeply through the years.

She tried in vain to gain her mother's affection: "I used to think that the only way I could get her attention was to be a 'man'. . . . I wondered why she preferred males to females, and noticed that she generally affirmed me for the 'male' qualities that I exhibited. She also complimented me on my good looks, posture, and dress, so I was careful to be well groomed and mannered. It's funny what we will do to earn praise and recognition."

As she grew up, Cynthia felt very comfortable among boys without having the consciousness of being "unfeminine". In school she was always the captain of the team or the class president. At the age of eight, she found herself praying to Christ and finding great joy in the gifts that she believed he had given to her. In the same year she had a baby sister, whom she was to mentor later.

In her adolescence Cynthia continued to have many male friends, giving her mother and stepfather the impression that she was popular, which delighted them. Deep in her heart, however, she says that she was "scared, had low self-esteem, and felt alone and unloved. I felt as though I would be liked only if I were some kind of 'hero', and my fear was that if I was vulnerable, I would be rejected and abandoned. I learned that what *shows* or appears to be reality is more important than what *is* reality."

Her mother interpreted Cynthia's desire for physical affection from her as homosexual overtures. This misperception perplexed and hurt Cynthia "terribly". At sixteen she dropped out of sports because she was having doubts about her femininity. At twenty she married a young man whom she had known in high school because she perceived him as strong and masculine, making her feel feminine. But he turned out to be an alcoholic, violent and verbally abusive, like her stepfather. She felt that she had no one from whom to seek help.

Later, at age twenty-seven, homosexual desires began to arise, occasioned by the sexual advances of her closest friend, which she resisted, but she still found herself obsessed with fantasies of sexual intimacy. To guard herself from giving in to her friend's advances, she put on weight, making herself unattractive: "I no longer believed in myself and couldn't even 'fake' it. I no longer felt in charge of myself."

She became sexually infatuated with her friend, who lived miles away, but since she was not interested in any other woman, she tentatively concluded that she was not a "lesbian". But then she remembered her feelings toward a special girl friend at eleven years and her feelings of sexual confusion in high school, and she began to fear that she really was a homosexual, although she did not want to be one. Whenever she met a woman to whom she was sexually attracted, she would avoid her. She was eating excessively "to help stuff down these feelings", but that was not working. The only thing happening was that she "was getting fat".

Her problems led Cynthia to join two Twelve Step programs—Al Anon and Overeaters Anonymous. There she found direction through her sponsor and cosponsor, who made it clear to her that "there are no victims, there are only volunteers". She began to recognize her woundedness, turning back to Christ "slowly, gradually, painfully". While forgiving her husband, she recognized her responsibility for the kind of life she chose to live. Her husband, however, "did not want, or was unable, to recover" from alcoholism, so, "after years of recovery and prayer", she divorced.

At this juncture, having moved to another city, Cynthia began to realize that the first time she had done Steps Four and Five she had been in denial concerning her homosexual orientation, and now she felt the need to do the fourth and fifth steps "around this issue".[17] She found another female sponsor, but, unfortunately, she was also sexually attracted to her: "She became my most concerned other. I was not only erotically attracted to her but also in love with her." This new friend reminded Cynthia of her mother, but, she says, she "seemed to offer the unconditional love and affection that my mother never did".

---

[17] The fourth and fifth steps of A.A., which are used by most Twelve Step programs, are (4) "Made a searching and fearless moral inventory of ourselves" and (5) "Admitted to God, to ourselves, and to another human being the exact nature of our wrongs".

Both Cynthia and her friend sought the help of a priest, who recommended Moberly's *A New Christian Ethic*, which both read together. Despite the insights from Moberly, Cynthia continued to experience conflicting emotions because part of her wanted to be sexual with her friend. This led to a struggle with jealousy, fantasy, and masturbation. Then, as she and her friend began to quarrel, Cynthia called her original sponsor, who pointed out that Cynthia was emotionally dependent upon her friend and that the first step toward healing was to go "cold turkey", at least for three to six months.

Cynthia said she could not accept the original sponsor's advice then, even though she knew it was sound. She asked her sponsor why she had not mentioned homosexuality when she had done the fifth step with her earlier. Her sponsor replied that Cynthia would not have been emotionally able to cope with the news at that time. She told her, Cynthia says, "that God needed to teach and heal before I could deal with this. She pointed me to God and the Twelve Steps."

At this time Cynthia noticed a Courage announcement in a church bulletin, and, as she read it, she imagined that everyone in church knew she was the "lesbian" being spoken about. It took six months before she called the Courage number. A week later she arrived early at the Courage meeting to meet the director, but the next person to arrive became angry at the sight of her—he thought she was a reporter "about to break his anonymity". "He was just as concerned as I", says Cynthia, "about the secret 'leaking' out. I felt reassured that he didn't 'think' that I was a lesbian. . . . I was the only woman at our group, which suited me just fine. I had never met an 'official' lesbian and was afraid that I might be attracted to one if I did." (Later Cynthia would become more accepting of other women with "this woundedness".)

Cynthia liked the men in the Courage group, looking forward to the weekly meetings. She was not sure how the men were responding to her at first: "My addiction to masturbation and desire to deal with it opened the way for a lot of gut-level sharing on everyone's part, and they hadn't realized that women struggle with the same things they do." She got much help from the meetings, but she also felt the need "to speak to another woman who struggled with this orientation".

So she called a woman in a New York City Courage group, who reassured her that it was "normal" for women with these tendencies to feel this way and that she was not alone. Nevertheless, Cynthia still "beat herself up" with thoughts such as "what kind of freak am I?. . . . Why don't my emotions match my intellect?" Over the years, as Cynthia attended four national conferences of Courage, she was able to learn much about her condition, particularly from meeting with women from all over the United States and Canada; however, she found the first national meeting the hardest:

> When I arrived I went to my room and cried. I felt such shame. . . . I begged God to take this cross away, but by his grace I said, "Not my will but yours be done." I found acceptance and unconditional love. The women from far and wide got together to share experience, strength, and hope. One gal shared her fear that we would all have a sexual orgy together at the conference. Everyone laughed—we laughed out of relief and perhaps because we could all identify with her fear.

Cynthia found numerous helpful and concerned priests at the conferences. She wondered how Father Harvey could understand a woman's pain and suffering. She found herself wanting "an easier, softer way" than Courage, but she also realized that the purpose of Courage is to lead persons to heaven.

Cynthia still tortures herself about whether or not she might be homosexual; she still has not gotten over the attachment to her friend, pointing out how upset she was when her friend announced her engagement to be married last fall: "I feel tremendous loneliness, abandoned by someone very important to me—nothing can replace this loss. . . . I feel the way I did as a little girl when my mother remarried and deserted me emotionally." Her friend, too, is upset and saddened by Cynthia's reaction, and they communicate with one another in a more distant way. After much prayer Cynthia decided to go to the wedding despite the intense emotional pain she has experienced. She felt she could control her feelings.

Cynthia places her hope in Courage. At the meetings she does not feel shame, as she sometimes does at other times. Although she feels she is not the woman God intended her to be, she is willing to give testimony at conferences concerning her struggle: "I think God is funny to use us in spite of ourselves."

Commentary: Courageously, Cynthia keeps turning to the crucified Christ for help. A year ago she told her mother about her struggle but received no real support. Her younger sister, however, has been "extremely supportive". With the help of Courage and spiritual direction, Cynthia is gradually coming to know and to accept herself as the first step toward healing. She sees this as a gradual process under the grace of God. She is honest in admitting her areas of weakness, and, in my judgment, with the help of the kind of therapy proposed by Leanne Payne, she needs to find healing for her past relationships, most particularly that with her mother. Without denying the value of insights gained through psychological procedures, she needs to bring everything of the past to Christ, the Healer, both asking for forgiveness for her own failings and sins and, by the power of Christ working in her, forgiving those who have hurt her. She is already on this journey.

Sarah

Sarah tells us her story this way:

Although I can remember having a desire to be intimate with women at the age of five, I was nineteen years old when I entered the gay lifestyle. The events that led to my decision to pursue a homosexual lifestyle are clear; it is rational for me to conclude that my involvement in homosexual relationships was a choice. Ten years ago I was unable to admit this. Let me begin with my family background.

I am the older of two girls. My childhood was unsettling. I remember periods of peace in my home as well as times that were riddled with anxiety and disharmony. My father was a recovering alcoholic who had been sober for twenty-five years, and my mother was the stereotypical coalcoholic. Although we were raised in a sober household, the pattern of behavior was characteristic of an alcoholic family. Fortunately, however, my sister and I were directed at a young age to seek help from counselors, who guided us in our struggles. There was a sense of enmeshment in my family; dependency was strong. As I matured, I never saw my homosexual tendencies as an outlet for these weaknesses. Mostly I denied my feelings, never discussing the issue.

Adolescence was a trying time for me, as it is for many teenagers. My appearance was feminine, and I never created an image of masculinity. My heavy involvement in sports, however, somewhat fulfilled my need to be around women. But I was not satisfied, desiring a deeper involvement with women. While I consistently dated men, I was never emotionally invested with them as I was with women. The difference was very clear to me, yet I continued to keep my experience secret. Eventually, I found myself closer to certain groups of women whom I suspected to be lesbian. I became excited with the possibility of exploring the lifestyle, so I pursued these relationships.

At nineteen I had my first homosexual experience, simultaneously entering into a serious relationship with a woman fifteen years my senior ("SM"). At the time, I didn't recognize this pattern of behavior, which would later become familiar. Prior to entering into a sexual relationship, I remember going to a favorite chapel of mine and praying to God to help me make the right decision about my involvement. I was struggling with an intense need for intimacy and felt empty without the emotional attachment that I had with SM. Upon leaving the chapel I felt torn, as if my soul was being pulled in two directions. This feeling would not leave me until I left the homosexual lifestyle. I went from one life of secrecy to another. I was not comfortable with "outing", so continual denial of my orientation was an acceptable alternative. Meanwhile, I became isolated from my heterosexual high school and college friends. Although this bothered me, I began to accept that the gay lifestyle demanded such choices.

Two years later, I found myself uneasy in the relationship. I did not want the smothering in which I was entangled but could not escape the attachment, which I had assisted in creating. Avoidance behavior was familiar to me, so once again I employed it. I began going to Boston on weekends to visit lesbian friends, and I began dating several women, without ending the primary relationship. The emotional roller-coaster with SM prevailed for the next year because of my dishonesty. While in Boston on one of my getaways, I received a phone call from my mother. She had found a letter from SM and was aware of my lesbian lifestyle. Immediately, I denied the whole story, resenting her for going through my personal belongings. She was very upset and asked me to return home.

Reflecting on the stress level at the time, I am not sure how I continued to work, maintain my lifestyle, and engage in family discussions. Through constant denial and lack of closure with most of my relationships, I had created a trail of hanging people who were angry and empty, the most severely injured being myself. However, to begin the healing process myself would have been a painful remedy, and I was not ready.

My parents were in touch with Father Harvey within a week or two of becoming aware of my sexuality. The pain that my family was going through was too intense for me. I didn't know how to handle it, because I was not interested in their Christian pursuits and I did not wish to give up my gay lifestyle. Although I planned to move to Boston within the month, I agreed to visit Father Harvey with my mother prior to the move. I agreed to the visit because of a deep love for my mother. I could barely stand to see her so upset, and I felt I was losing her, so I went. Today I am aware that God was touching my heart with a special compassion that I would come to cherish. Our visit was brief, and it only deepened my confusion and rage.

Immediately after my move to Boston, my life turned upside down, forcing me into therapy and recovery. The next two years were tumultuous and painful. Although I pursued lesbian relationships, I remained unfulfilled and searching. I think that "searching" sums it up. Truly, this time was spent on examining my truth and why I had taken this path. I left my parents to care for their own healing, and our relationship was slowly rebuilt on a more solid foundation. We never quite agreed on everything, which was actually healthy. We began with a common ground: *we loved each other*, and we did not want to lose that connection. I had to accept their understanding of homosexuals as well as their approach to the lifestyle: that is, they would not encourage it in any way. As Christians, they took a strong stand in love and compassion as well as the hope that I would "change". This annoyed me, but, interestingly, *I never rejected the possibility* [emphasis added]. The road to honesty and to myself would not fully come to fruition for three years. I never stopped trying and eventually learned from the members of Courage that I was being very hard on myself. At times, trying was the best that I could do. I didn't end up in the lifestyle in a day, nor could I create my life in the same time frame.

I was constantly called back to God. Although I refused a trip to Medjugorje with my mother and sister, I believe that the Lord touched my heart through their intercession. After five years in the lifestyle I began feeling open to spending time with straight friends. Ironically, they entered into or returned to my life. I learned that this reintegration is very important. My desires for intimacy with women did not disappear, but instead my approach was to focus on fulfilling myself in healthy ways. For instance, I went back to graduate school, applied for a more challenging job, and made decisions to place myself in friendships that did not encourage dependence. My father often observed my "fence-sitting" as God's way of knocking at my door. It was clear to my father that my search for peace would end in nothing less than a complete healing.

I made a commitment to remain open to dating men. Of course, my gay friends insisted that I was in "denial" and that I couldn't force such a change. In therapy I continually discussed these challenges, making a commitment to maintain honesty with myself regardless of pain. The severe emptiness was something I never wanted to return.

During this period I attended daily Mass and often Exposition of the Blessed Sacrament. I prayed the Rosary, or at least a decade daily. I was blessed with a sense of clarity that I had never experienced. I found that if I made choices for myself with my best interests at heart I felt healthy and had a clear conscience. Automatically, I gained strength, and unhealthy dependencies slipped out of my life. Strong friendships with men and women were important to me, and since I depended on myself and God for internal fulfillment, the need for others to meet all my needs diminished.

In August 1990 I attended my first Courage conference, although initially I resisted the invitation. Everyone there knew my mother, and I was afraid they would try to change me. At the time I was dating two men and had a floundering interest in one woman. On the contrary, the conference proved to be a turning point for me. The guys complimented me and said that I was beautiful. I had forgotten the power of flattery! The women struggled as I did. Our experiences were almost identical, and we often talked into the morning hours. At the healing service I cried for the first time about my emptiness, the choices I had made, the people I had hurt, and my own pain. It was difficult to look at my heart and figure out what I wanted for my life and my soul in the long run. I left the conference feeling renewed and free.

I maintained contact with many members of Courage, as we helped each other through difficult periods. Almost subconsciously, I made a decision to leave the gay lifestyle. I trusted my continued relationship with a coworker, which eventually resulted in marriage. Not once did I experience doubt or struggle with this relationship. I was completely honest with him about my past and was secure in his acceptance. We have never had a subsequent discussion about my involvement in the lifestyle or my involvement with Courage. He trusts my relationship with the two or three lesbian friends who remain in my life, not questioning my judgment. Truthfully, I can say that I no longer have any desire, physically or emotionally, to be involved in homosexual relationships. The thrill and intrigue that once attracted me no longer exist. The healing power of prayer has given me a great faith that, with God's help, I will never lose. I know that it is a choice to enter into such a life and a choice to resist it.

Today I understand that my experience was not unlike that of many others and that my life could have gone in several directions. I have a special passion for teens who are struggling as I did with the secret of homosexual tendencies. Although today there is encouragement for young adults to discuss these tendencies, I am concerned that they are being led to believe that there is no choice but to accept the gay lifestyle. Through extensive reading and discussion, I have come to believe that each individual has a unique experience. Many unfulfilled needs can be misinterpreted to suggest a homosexual orientation as well as to minimize a very normal curiosity with homosexual behavior that adolescents often experience. I pray that the emphasis will be on guidance to work through these difficulties rather than on encouraging a declaration of homosexuality.

Commentary: In Sarah's account of her movement out of the gay lifestyle into a heterosexual marriage, it is noteworthy that even when she was still very much in the lifestyle she kept herself open to the possibility of change. Her parents' clear wish that she change annoyed her, but she did not reject the possibility. She was open to what God had to send to her. Another factor in Sarah's journey has been the constant love of her parents and sister, which in turn is rooted in a profound faith in God, in Christ, and in the Church. Her parents and sister have always been there. The members of Courage also helped Sarah along the road. The good friendships she formed with both men and women led her to a very special male friend with whom she is now bonded in matrimony. Sarah and her husband had their first baby in July 1995. We thank our loving God for the graces and blessings he gives Sarah.

Susan

Susan tells us her story this way:

When I was a child I used to read a lot of superhero comic books. In those comics the hero was always male. It was always a male who was strong and supportive. The female figure, however, was always in need of rescuing and protection. This pattern seemed to follow in most of the books I read when I was young. I would often fantasize that I, too, was male, because I wanted to be heroic and strong and had come to connect these qualities with maleness. Since I had also come to associate femaleness with weakness, I never liked wearing dresses—that was too "girl-like"—and they were impractical for the activities I was interested in: climbing trees, fishing, turning cartwheels.

My mother was always present company for me when I was a

child. She encouraged me in my interests of painting and music, and she made me feel special and loved. I was not close to my father, however. I loved him, and I know that he loved me, but I was mostly afraid of him. He was often emotionally and verbally abusive toward my mother and me and sometimes struck me in anger. My mother would often come and cry to me at night. It would hurt me to see her hurting, and I would try to console her. At the same time, I think I subconsciously decided that I didn't want to grow up to be like my mother lest I too should be the weak person in a relationship where a man was hurting me. Upon observing how my father treated my mother, I would often think to myself: "If I were a guy, I would never treat a woman that way." I would then proceed to fantasize about how the ideal man would treat a woman, and I would imagine that I was that man. As I grew older and learned about sex, I began to incorporate sexuality into my fantasy; then, with the accidental discovery of the pleasure of masturbation and an exposure to pornography, I soon became addicted to a habit that strengthened my fantasy life.

In high school I really began to struggle with my gender identity. Although I looked like a typical schoolgirl in my kilt and blazer, I felt hopelessly inadequate as a female. Most of my female friends had major crushes on guys and were starting to date. Meanwhile, I secretly had crushes on other girls—and not just crushes but full-blown sexual fantasies about them. I was attracted to guys, but my sense of inadequacy about my femininity kept me from developing good relationships with them. Emotionally, I felt more comfortable with women.

Where was God in all this? Well, I had been raised Catholic, I believed in God, and people were always coming into my life to encourage me in my faith. My struggles with my sexuality as a teenager drew me closer to him as I tried to figure myself out. Through all the wanderings of my mind and heart, I was always drawn back to Jesus and the Church.

I kept myself busy with school and work until I graduated from the university, never entertaining the idea of actually pursuing a relationship with another woman in real life. I even thought of various male friends as potential marriage partners, although I still had a high degree of discomfort around men. I had grown lax, however, in areas of personal discipline, and I was not vigilant in guarding my thought life or resisting the temptations to masturbate; consequently, my sexual fantasies about women were alive and well.

The summer after I graduated, I learned that two male friends of mine were in a homosexual relationship, and a female friend of mine who was pursuing a guy admitted to me that she also had a crush on a woman. This was the first time that others had ever disclosed to me their same-sex attractions. Apparently some of them had been wary about my finding out, because of my strong Catholic beliefs. As these people were school friends with whom I had started to spend a lot of time socially, I didn't want them to feel I was standing in judgment on them, and I finally opened up to them about my own struggle with homosexual desires. They knew, however, that my moral beliefs remained the same.

At about the same time, I heard about Courage through the church bulletin of a parish I was visiting. The timing was perfect, as I was about to deal head on with my greatest weaknesses and would need the strength of a support group. When I started attending the meetings, I found the other group members to be extremely friendly and warm. I was never pressured into sharing, and I felt accepted. I did find it difficult, however, to open up to the group about my personal struggles, despite the fact that the other group members were so honest, open, and candid. Perhaps it was because I was the only female in the group. The two social situations that had often been awkward for me were talking to men and talking in a group, and here I was in a group full of men, needing to talk about the most personal things in my life.

Perhaps that was why I was drawn to A. She was someone I had encountered that same summer. Although I had met her briefly before at the university, I now learned for the first time that she was "out of the closet" and looking for a relationship. I found her to be a very sweet and gentle person, and I was happy to meet someone I felt I could open up to completely. I felt comfortable talking to another female about these personal things, and I also believed that she would understand me in a special way. Perhaps it was risky for me to confide in someone with a secular perspective on homosexuality, but God blessed me through A.

Admittedly, a lot of pain came with the blessings, but the pain was brought on by me alone. I quickly fell in love with her and was willing to compromise my beliefs in order to have a relationship that I thought would be emotionally satisfying and fulfilling. However, although A was at one point attracted to me, she quickly and firmly decided that she didn't want to have anything to do with a neurotic Catholic who would feel guilty afterward; nevertheless, it was her firmness and strength that kept us from getting into a relationship that would have led us into sin.

It took me a long time to get over her, and for months I battled with various issues: Are the Church's teachings right on this topic? Why can't a committed, faithful homosexual relationship be viewed in the same way as heterosexual marriage? Suddenly my thinking was not clear, because I had allowed myself to flirt with temptations and had listened to the arguments of the world. I also battled with pride, because I had a hard time accepting that I had been the weak person in that relationship—me, the Courage member—I was the one who was ready to fall. There was also a sense of loss and failure since I believed that I could have had a special friendship with her if I hadn't been weak, showing a lack of self-control.

During this difficult time, various members of Courage were helpful to me. Although I was still shy about sharing my struggles in a group setting, I had come to know some members well on a one-to-one basis, and I found myself spilling my guts in private conversations as the need arose. One member had previously introduced me to his Rosary group, and I found the daily recitation of the Rosary to be of great help and comfort. I also found powerful help in kneeling before the Real Presence of Christ in the Blessed Sacrament. Through Courage I got in touch with a good Catholic priest whom I asked to be my personal spiritual director. Father D's faith strengthened me when my own faith was low. He always remains faithful to the Church's teachings.

That experience with A humbled me completely, and I have truly come to see that it is only by the grace of God that I get by. It's only by his grace that my thought life and personal habits are being tidied up. I do believe that the Church's teachings on marriage and sexuality, including homosexuality, are correct, and I'm trusting Jesus on a day-to-day basis to work out his plan in my life.

Does this mean that my goal is eventually to be in a married heterosexual relationship? No. My only goal is to rely on the grace of God to follow Jesus every day, wherever he may lead me, whether that be marriage, religious life, or celibate lay life. I have nothing but compassion for anyone struggling with homosexuality, because I know what it's like to have those thoughts and desires. I know what it's like to have a crush on someone of the same sex and even to think of being in love with someone of the same sex. My recent experience has also shown me how easy it would be to fall into a same-sex relationship, and that it is hard to resist such a relationship when you meet someone you really like.

I don't for a second think I've arrived. I'm still journeying like everyone else, and, like everyone else, I sometimes stumble and fall. Yet I know that when that happens I have Jesus to lift me up and help me start again. I also know that I have a mantle of protection around me from that one Lady I do truly love with all my heart, the Blessed Virgin Mary.

Commentary: Susan's story reflects the painful conflict of a woman of deep faith torn between her conscience and her desire for complete fulfillment in a same-sex union. The practice of her Catholic Faith, the support of the members of Courage, and the guidance of a spiritual director are all important factors in her movement toward spiritual and sexual wholeness. It is to be hoped that Susan may find more psychological insight into her past and that this insight will be integrated into an already existing prayer life. Susan is thinking not in terms of complete psychological healing but rather in terms of a more intimate union with Jesus Christ. But I believe with Leanne Payne's way of thinking that, as Susan pursues Christ, she will continue to find healing for the trauma of the past. Without overlooking the benefits of therapy, she will learn to integrate it into the life of prayer.

Jennifer

Jennifer's life illustrates how sexual trauma during childhood can create in the adolescent a state of confusion concerning sexual orientation that usually leads to seeking emotional and physical intimacy with same-sex persons. The important point is that over the years Jennifer has worked her way through these traumas, principally with the help of prayer, group support, and spiritual direction. It has been a rough journey, but today she is leading a life of chastity. Now to Jennifer's story:

I was about twelve or thirteen years old when I first began to realize that my feelings for girls were "different" from those of other girls my age. Sometimes I would have a sudden urge to kiss one of my friends when we were hanging out after school. Although I never acted on these urges, I was still afraid that my friends or other people would eventually be able to tell that I was "different" or to discern how I felt. I remember how once in my teens, in preparation for joining the girls' soccer team, I was given a physical by a woman doctor. She commented that my heartbeat was unusually fast. I tried to explain it away by saying that I had run to that location, but she said that because of the waiting period before I saw her, the heartbeat should not have been so elevated. I felt terribly awkward. I could not tell the young intern that I was attracted to her and was aroused when she placed her hand over my chest to measure my heartbeat.

As a teenager, I was not so attracted to boys as I felt I should be. I didn't really date until my senior year in high school. My sexual identity was something I had difficulty understanding—a fact that still causes me a good deal of tension and pain. Still, I have been attracted to men in varying degrees throughout my life, usually in inverse proportion to my feelings for women.

I believe that the primary reason for my lesbian tendencies—and why I have found it hard to become more emotionally involved with men—is that before I was ten years old I was sexually abused by teenage boys in my neighborhood. This made it extremely hard for me to trust men, since I probably unconsciously presumed that they have a secret "bad" side just waiting to come out and oppress me in some way.

I observed this reaction when I was molested twice by the older brother of a friend of mine. I was playing hide and seek at a friend's house, and his teenage brother joined the game. The older brother proposed that he and I "hide" together, and he would let me in on the secret of the best place to hide. When we were in this place, his facial expression changed to something extremely hard. He fondled me, and I felt totally paralyzed with fear. I froze up, trying to ignore what was happening, especially the physical sensations. Later, I suffered another experience of molestation involving a group of teenage boys.

These traumatic events affected my emotional responses to men in the future. I was not able to respond adequately to a man in intercourse. Although I may have been physically aroused, I was not able to give myself *emotionally* to a man because I did not want to be hurt again. I felt anger toward men and even toward God. I recognized that I was not following the Church's teaching, but at the time I did not feel guilt or shame. True spiritual contrition would come later. I believe I was still under the baneful influence of the earlier molestations. I also found it hard to trust God and his care for me, but now I am learning to trust him. I still struggle with doubts about God's care for me. Why did he allow this to happen to me?

Over the twenty-some years of my life I have experienced loneliness, despairing of having a satisfying relationship with a man. I have been tempted to consider finding a woman with whom to have an intimate relationship. It was in one of these moments that I went to a lesbian bar and conversed with other women. Nothing romantic or sexual happened, and I did not go again because I joined Courage, and I was discouraged from going to such places. I indeed wanted to commit myself to the ideals of the group, not wanting merely to "talk the talk".

I am pleased that I joined Courage, though in moments of loneliness I question my choice. Still, I continue to go to Courage meetings. It is good to share my feelings with people who have similar feelings, because it is hard to deal with this issue alone. Since I have joined Courage, my feelings of isolation and bitterness about the past have diminished. I see improvement in several ways; for example, I don't fantasize about women to the same extent as in the past, when my thoughts bordered on obsession. I can share my feelings with women who have had similar temptations but now are committed to chastity in the Lord.

Women appeal to me in large part emotionally. Most are in touch with their feelings, expressing them quite well. Most do not try to dominate a conversation, a relationship, or a person, as men do. Women seem more interested in people as people and appear to be less selfish. They seem more warm and caring.

Many of my romantic fantasies focus on these aspects of women, rather than on physical aspects. Along with decreased fantasies about women has come less frequent masturbation, as well as a growth in my heterosexual "side". The hope that this would happen, along with my religious viewpoint, is another incentive for sticking with the "program". They don't push "change" in Courage but present it as an option. (Actually, for myself I view it more as an "expansion" of already existing feelings rather than as true change.) I really don't like labels, but I don't consider myself to be a lesbian; my guess at the moment is that I am bisexual, but that may change.

It is important for people to "deal" with who they are and not to run away from themselves. It is a struggle to have lesbian tendencies and to be someone who tries to incorporate the Church's teaching in her life. I have always had the gift or virtue of faith, and I find it difficult to convince myself of the truth of something that is against Scripture or the teaching of the Church I really tried to do that about two years ago, when I began to have another strong wave of lesbian tendencies. I would put forward arguments in my mind, such as: Well, isn't God all about love, anyway? Shouldn't I be a person of love? Then countervailing "arguments" would sometimes pop into my head, such as: "If you love me, then keep my commandments" (perhaps they were movements of the Holy Spirit). Or I would recall Jesus' statement that whoever wishes to be his disciple must deny himself, pick up the cross, and follow him (very apropos for people with homosexual/lesbian tendencies).

I remember being out jogging one day and having strong thoughts/fantasies about entering the lifestyle. I was not thinking of anything religious at all—in fact, quite the contrary! Suddenly, I seemed to have a mental impression of something outside myself, but I heard within myself these words from Revelation: "I am the Alpha and the Omega, the first and the last." And then, quickly, my mind reached a conclusion, almost like an argument in logic: "Therefore Christ must be the beginning and the end of everything I do." This occurrence, which took place before I joined Courage, has stayed with me, making it easier for me to reject temptations to enter the lifestyle.

CONCLUSIONS

From my ongoing analysis of the situation among Roman Catholics with apparent homosexual orientation, I draw the conclusion that there is a great spiritual hunger not only for the truth of Catholic teaching on homosexuality and homosexual behavior but also for the inspiration to live a new kind of life with Christ. I have no way of knowing with certitude what percentage of the Catholic homosexual population desires to lead a chaste life, but I do know it is a considerable portion, as the gradual and steady growth of Courage units throughout the United States and Canada attests. In tandem with the growth of Courage has been the spread of Encourage, a group support system for parents and relatives of persons with homosexual orientation.

Unfortunately, Courage and Encourage have been confronted with scandalous opposition from Catholics, both clergy and lay, who do not believe in the teaching of the Church as it is spelled out in the "Letter to the Bishops of the Catholic Church on the Pastoral Care of Homosexual Persons". Our response to our opponents is to continue to spread the good news of magisterial teaching and to encourage homosexual persons to live chastely in Christ.

Four hundred twenty-five members of the National Association for Research and Treatment of Homosexuality agree with Father Jeffrey Keefe in his explanation of the homosexual condition as a psychological disorder. It is true that the majority of the members of the American Psychiatric Association claim that no change in orientation is possible or that it is possible very rarely. The minority view, however, with which I agree, is that one can grow into heterosexuality and that there is a wealth of empirical evidence for this position. The process involves much prayer, group support, and sound therapy. Some, however, who have not been able to change their orientation have been able to live a life of sexual abstinence by divine grace and group support.

The only effective motive for sexual abstinence is the love of Jesus Christ. For those who sincerely desire to be chaste, God's grace is always present. The development of chaste friendships within a spiritual support system is also an important element in one's plan of life.

Young people are far more likely to want to be chaste if they have a vision of hope for the future. If the young person, however, believes that he cannot get out of the homosexual condition, he becomes vulnerable to gay propaganda telling him that the homosexual lifestyle is a natural variant to marriage. Young persons need to focus more on spiritual healing through union with Christ than on becoming heterosexual.

The moral argument against homosexual activity flows directly from the revealed teaching on marriage, namely, that the two purposes of human sexual activity are the permanent union of husband and wife and the procreation of children—two purposes inseparably connected. Since homosexual activity cannot achieve either of these purposes, it must be immoral by its very nature. This argument is more persuasive in demonstrating the immorality of homosexual activity than using specific passages from sacred Scripture that condemn homosexual acts.

With regard to the personal responsibility of the homosexual person, two extreme attitudes should be avoided: (1) that the homosexual person cannot help acting out his homosexual desires, and (2) that he has full freedom to rid himself of homosexual fantasies and feelings. On the contrary, to achieve personal responsibility it is necessary to develop a spiritual plan of life within a spiritual support system. After more than four decades of pastoral counseling, I am convinced that, when advising persons with a homosexual orientation, one must integrate individual counseling with some form of group spiritual support. Within such groups the person can learn to accept himself as a child of God with hope for the future.

Courage recommends that professional therapists and spiritual directors work together in helping individuals who come to them. With explicit permission from the client, the spiritual director and the therapist can facilitate the process of healing. There is a difficult pastoral problem in parishes with a large number of openly gay persons who regularly receive Holy Communion despite their active homosexual lifestyle. Such persons should be informed gently but firmly that they are not to receive the Holy Eucharist until they have reformed their lives.

For thousands of years world cultures have disapproved of sodomy, but now it is regarded as a natural act for persons with homosexual desires. Gay rights laws, moreover, fail to distinguish between homosexual orientation and practice, thus actually teaching the licitness of the homosexual lifestyle. There is no way that the Catholic Church can sanction same-sex genital unions.

While scientific research on female homosexuality is limited, it is now generally known that it is easier for female homosexual persons to maintain intimate relationships with women than with men and that they put more emphasis on emotional security and intimacy than on physical satisfaction. Their relationships seem to have greater depth than those of homosexual men. I have also noted that comparatively few women with homosexual orientation seek the guidance of the Church. It is not surprising that the media regard female homosexual persons (lesbians) as symbols of female liberation. In all its forms the media has served to confuse issues and manipulate emotions to

give the distinct impression that homosexual persons are dis-
criminated against because of their orientation, when it is really
the lifestyle to which the public objects.

It is my hope that this volume will provide clarification and
guidance for its readers.

Appendix I

THE ORIGINS AND HEALING
OF HOMOSEXUAL ATTRACTIONS
AND BEHAVIORS

Richard P. Fitzgibbons, M.D.

At the present time most Catholics have little to no understanding of the emotional causes of homosexual attractions and behavior or of the powerful role that Catholic spirituality can play in the healing of this disorder. The reasons for this state of ignorance are numerous and include the scant literature available on the value of the Catholic Faith and sacraments in the resolution of homosexual attractions and acts; failure of traditional therapy to resolve homosexual behavior; views within the American Psychiatric and Psychological Associations that homosexuality is not a disorder; and the influence of powerful groups within the media and educational, social service, health, and political fields. In addition, there are many factions within the Church herself that oppose and are attempting to undermine traditional Catholic moral doctrine on this issue.

The failure to understand the actual causes of homosexuality impacts those who counsel teenagers and adults with this disorder. Therapists regularly tell those seeking help that the Church's teaching on homosexuality is insensitive to homosexuals, unscientific, and erroneous. They are advised to accept themselves as being created homosexual by God. Unfortunately, those giving such counsel usually have little awareness of the emotional conflicts leading to homosexual attractions nor of the healing power available with forgiveness and Catholic spirituality.

In my clinical experience over the past twenty years, I have witnessed the resolution of the emotional pain that caused homosexual temptations and behavior in several hundred males and females. Their process of healing occurred, first, through insight-oriented psychotherapy to identify the origins of their conflicts and then through the use of forgiveness and Catholic spirituality. Such a treatment approach is similar in ways to the employment of spirituality in the treatment of substance abuse disorders. In fact, major breakthroughs were made in the management of addictive disorders only after a reliance on God was made the cornerstone of the treatment plan. Prior to that time, traditional psychotherapy alone resulted in minimal improvement. The use of Catholic spirituality in the treatment of homosexuality follows a similar pattern.

The Origins of Homosexual Attractions and Behaviors

The most common conflicts at different life stages that predispose individuals to homosexual attractions and behavior are loneliness and sadness, mistrust and fear, profound feelings of inadequacy and a lack of self-acceptance, narcissism, excessive anger, sexual abuse in childhood, and a lack of balance in one's life coupled with overwhelming feelings of responsibility. During times of stress these inner difficulties are activated. In an attempt to seek relief or to escape from this unconscious emotional pain, strong sexual temptations and behavior can occur. This dynamic of inner emotional suffering leading to homosexual desires and activity rarely can begin during childhood, but usually it develops in early adolescence. However, adult life may be the first time for the emergence of this disorder.

Sadness and Loneliness

The most frequently seen cause of sadness in the past leading to homosexual attractions in males was the result of childhood and adolescent rejection by peers because of very limited athletic abilities. Many children who have poor eye-hand coordination are not good in the most popular sports and are on the receiving end of harsh and cruel criticism and rejection by their peers. Subsequently, powerful feelings of loneliness, sadness, and isolation develop. The craving for acceptance and love from peers results in strong emotional attractions to those of the same sex, which leads many youngsters to think they may be homosexuals.

More recently, the collapse of the nuclear family, with almost 40 percent of children and teenagers living apart from their fathers,[1] has resulted in serious problems with sadness and loneliness in our young. Pope John Paul II in his "Letter to the Family" described the tragic plight of these youngsters, identifying many of them as "orphans with living parents". When the need for warmth, approval, physical affection, and praise from a father is not filled, an inner emptiness develops, often referred to today as "father hunger". In an attempt to overcome this pain, some adolescents and young adults seek comfort in being held by another male.

Ted grew up in a home in which his father had very little time for anyone in the family because of his demanding career. Ted's dad left early in the morning for work, returned drained most nights, and also worked Saturdays. In Ted's childhood he felt very lonely and wished that his father were more available and more loving. In early adolescence, in an unconscious attempt to seek relief from this pain, Ted experienced homosexual attractions to older males and later homosexual fantasies of being loved by them.

[1] D. Blakenhorn et al., *Fatherless America* (New York: Basic Books, 1995).

While many males who did not receive praise and physical affection from their fathers never develop homosexual attractions, those who are particularly vulnerable are those who, because of limited athletic abilities, also did not receive peer acceptance. In my clinical experience, the earlier the father abandonment, the greater the likelihood of homosexual temptations developing. Finally, in some very sensitive males, ongoing harsh treatment by older brothers produces an inner loneliness, leading to homosexual desires.

The failure to receive warmth, affection, and praise from a mother can result also in a terrible inner emptiness and sadness. Some females will attempt to fill this void for gentle, comforting maternal love through homosexual behavior. This maternal loneliness is not seen as often as father loneliness because mothers generally have a much greater freedom to communicate love and praise to their children than do fathers.

Sue was the youngest of three children, and her mother left the family when she was four. She saw her mother intermittently through her childhood but never felt close to her. Sue dated several times in high school, and in her early twenties she engaged in homosexual relationships. She entered therapy in an attempt to resolve her sadness and anger with her mother. As her insight grew, she realized that none of the males she had dated could provide the affection that the little girl within craved from her mother. For a period of time the warmth and love from girlfriends was comforting. However, these relationships were unfulfilling. Sue slowly recognized that the little girl within needed to be healed of her pain of maternal loneliness before she could have a stable adult loving relationship.

Some adults who are very frustrated and lonely because they have not yet met the right person to marry retreat into homosexual behavior in an attempt to seek relief from their loneliness. Married persons may engage in homosexual acts as a result of stress and loneliness in their marriage. Also, the sadness and loneliness that occur after the ending of a marriage or a serious heterosexual relationship may result in homosexual behavior because these individuals are fearful of becoming vulnerable to someone of the opposite sex. In my clinical work I have seen this pattern occur more frequently in women.

Since loneliness is one of the most painful of all life experiences, significant amounts of energy are expended in attempting to deny the presence of this debilitating pain. As a result, many individuals have no conscious awareness that they struggle with this deep emotional wound. Also, they regularly fear facing this sorrow, in part, because they do not believe that it can be healed. In point of fact, those with such views are correct if the attempts to bring healing have excluded spirituality, since no amount of adult love can make up for what one did not receive from one's father, mother, siblings, or peers in childhood and adolescence. Understandably, many men and women with these painful emotional wounds of loneliness may prefer believing that they are homosexual rather than face their terrible inner sadness.

The failure of any adult love to fill the inner loneliness from childhood and adolescence is the major reason for the extraordinary promiscuity in the homosexual lifestyle, with some studies showing an average of sixty sexual partners per year. Unconsciously, they do not seek stable commitment because of the realization that no single adult can satisfy the inner child and adolescent. The powerful unhappiness and despair in these individuals result in the highly reckless sexual behavior and explains the reports of 30 to 46 percent of men engaging in unprotected anal intercourse and anilingus.[2] Such compulsive and pathological behavior supports the view that homosexuality is a serious emotional, mental, and behavioral disorder.

Conflicts with loneliness and sadness can be manifested in many ways other than through sexual acting-out behavior.

[2] J. Nicolosi, *NARTH Bulletin* 2 (1994):10.

These include dependent and childlike behavior, a constant need for attention and affection, an excessive sexual fantasy life, compulsive masturbation, attraction to adolescents, dependence upon pornography, narcissistic behavior, exhaustion, and symptoms of depression.

Weak Masculine Identity

Another important cause of homosexual temptations and acting-out behavior is the result of strong feelings of insecurity. A lack of confidence may arise from rejection by parents, peers, siblings, and other significant people in whom one wants to invest trust. In an unconscious attempt to undo the earlier life rejection, a person may seek validation and acceptance from members of the same sex. In my clinical experience this painful emotional conflict is seen much more frequently in males.

Self-esteem is based primarily on acceptance of the role model in early childhood, the boy with his father and the girl with her mother. Every male child yearns for acceptance, praise, and validation from his father in order to establish a positive sense of well-being and a degree of comfort with himself. While a mother's love is essential for boys, it is not as important as the father's love and affirmation to the formation of a healthy male identity. Failure to receive positive feedback from one's father results in serious weaknesses in the masculine image and a lack of self-acceptance. Many of those with homosexual attractions grew up feeling that they could never please their fathers.

Older male siblings can also play an important role in the establishment of a positive masculine identity in childhood. Rejections in such relationships can produce serious weaknesses in male self-esteem.

However, the most common early life disappointment leading to homosexual desires is the result of peer rejections because of a boy's poor eye-hand and athletic coordination. This is a very difficult weakness to have in a culture obsessed with successful athletic performance to the point where it is seen as the major measure of masculinity. Children who are not athletically coordinated are regularly the last to be chosen to join teams and are often the victims of rejection and ridicule. They are referred to regularly in a feminine manner through the use of such painful names as sissy, fairy, and queer. Also, they may be told that they run or act like a girl. As the betrayal pain by their peers continues year after year, these males feel increasingly inadequate, confused, isolated, lonely, and weak. This harsh treatment by peers results in these youngsters having a very poor body image and a poor sense of their masculinity.

Such males often become scapegoats for their peers, who insult them in an attempt to enhance their own self-esteem. At school these children are victimized particularly during gym class. They often report feeling tortured by their peers. This anguish can be so damaging to masculine identity that it can even override the psychological benefits of having a positive father relationship. For many of these youngsters the homosexual attractions and temptations begin in the sixth or seventh grade. The appeal is usually toward strong and athletic teenagers.

In the 1950s and 1960s, when it was possible to do research on the causes of homosexuality, a study of 500 males in New York who viewed themselves as homosexuals revealed that over 90 percent of them had problems with athletic coordination and were subjected to various degrees of humiliating rejection by their peers when young. Many of these males related that not only did they feel as if they were failures as males because they either were not good at or did not like sports, but they also felt that they had disappointed their fathers, who, they thought, hoped that they would do well athletically. The lack of interest in sports interfered with the father–son closeness and bonding.

The need for male acceptance is essential for the development of a positive male identity, and it precedes the adolescent stage of development. If self-acceptance is not attained through peer affirmation, rarely will a boy find himself attracted to girls.

Lou was a very bright college student who had thought from his early adolescence that he might have a vocation to the priesthood. However, the major obstacle to this life path was the presence of homosexual attractions, which began when he was thirteen. He sought the advice of a priest at his college, who told him to pursue the priesthood and to try to accept his homosexuality and be comfortable with it, since this was how God had created him. At that time neither Lou nor this priest was aware of the influence on his homosexual desires of the constant peer rejection that he had experienced through childhood and early adolescence. His peers often referred to him in feminine terms because, according to them, he threw a ball like a girl. He was also scapegoated because he was the brightest boy in his class.

Lou decided that he could not pursue priestly training because he would not be able to live with himself if he tried to lead a double life of being engaged in homosexual acts while at the same time presenting himself to the Catholic community as a celibate priest. For several years he attempted to live as a homosexual. Later he sought therapy because he was repulsed by many aspects of that lifestyle, especially the extreme promiscuity and substance abuse. He could not accept that this was God's plan for his life.

The influence of peer rejections on the development of homosexual desires was confirmed again to me several years ago at the national Courage conference at Rosemont College, outside Philadelphia. After giving a talk on the origins and healing of loneliness and anger in those with homosexual attractions, the following hour-long discussion with the audience focused almost exclusively on their sharing the wounds to their masculine identity and their various types of sexual acting-out behaviors related to sports rejection in childhood and adolescence. These men believed that the rejections by their peers played a much more important role in the development of their homosexual attractions than hurts from their fathers.

The basic conflicts with low self-esteem are manifested in a number of ways in males with homosexual attractions. These include an obsessive attraction to muscular, athletic men; fantasies of having another body; an excessive need to act in a strong or aggressive manner; a compulsive need to work out; and a profound sense of being unlovable.

Fear and Mistrust

Fear of vulnerability to heterosexual relationships is another important factor in the development of homosexual attractions. This inability to feel safe loving someone of the opposite sex is usually unconscious and originates most often from traumatic experiences within the home. In males this may be a consequence of having a mother who was overly controlling, excessively needy or dependent, angry and critical, unaffectionate and cold, narcissistic and insensitive, mistrustful, addicted, or ill. In females the fear of trusting males in a loving relationship may arise from having a father who was very angry, rejecting and distant, insensitive toward the mother, abusive, harsh, selfish, addicted, or unloving. Today, abandonment pain by the father from divorce is one of the major sources of mistrust of males in females who develop an unconscious dread of being hurt as they saw their mothers wounded by their fathers. Subsequently, such females for a period of time may only feel safe being comforted in love by another female.

Diane was a young architect whose father was an angry alcoholic. She had witnessed years of emotional and physical abuse toward her mother by him. In her early adolescence she was attracted to males and went out with them, but she found herself much more comfortable with females during her college years. She came to realize that she had a very powerful fear of being hurt like her mother if she made a commitment to a man. Diane was not fully satisfied emotionally, physically, or spiritually in her homosexual relationships. She recognized in therapy that her father controlled her relationships with men and decided to work to break his domination over her relationships.

Pete's mother was a very sarcastic woman who was the daughter of an alcoholic father. He rarely saw his mother show any affection to his father, and she was regularly critical of him. Pete came to understand that her compulsive need to be in control in the home stemmed from the fear and powerlessness she had experienced in her own family background as a result of her father's drinking and the chaos that surrounded it. Pete found her control to be suffocating and, subsequently, did his best to keep her at a distance. Since she was his foundation for relationships with females, Pete did not feel comfortable being emotionally close to the girls he found attractive. He feared that if he became vulnerable they would be as insensitive as his mother was to his father and to him. His homosexual temptations developed because of his fear of trusting in female love and his need for affection from someone whom he could trust.

Mistrust can also develop as a result of living in a home with frequent conflict and fighting between parents. Since this relationship is the model or basis for the child's view of a heterosexual loving relationship, a marriage marred by turmoil and pain can lead to a son's or daughter's developing a fear of becoming vulnerable to those of the opposite sex. This fear can lead some to retreat into homosexual relationships. A similar dynamic is sometimes present after divorce, when many adults have a fear of being hurt by those of the opposite sex and withdraw into a homosexual relationship. It should be noted, too, that the epidemic of divorce in our culture is resulting in a significant fear of commitment to heterosexual relationships among young adults.

Mistrust and fear of complete commitment to one person are extremely common in those with homosexual attractions.

Rampant promiscuity with fidelity to no one is one of the most striking manifestations of such a fear of commitment. According to Dr. William Foege, director of the Centers for Disease Control, the average AIDS victim has had sixty sexual partners in the past twelve months.[3] Spiritually, this mistrust shows itself in Catholics as a mistrust of the Lord and of God the Father as a loving father or Mary as a loving mother.

Addictive Disorder

The sexually compulsive, highly reckless, and life-threatening behavior in a large percentage of homosexuals would indicate the presence of an addictive disorder in these individuals. While the specific diagnostic category of sexual addiction has not been officially accepted yet in the mental health field, clinical programs exist in various parts of the country for the treatment of sexual addictions, and a journal of sexual addictions now exists. These addictions resemble substance abuse disorders in that individuals engage in compulsive behaviors that are medically hazardous. Also, powerful denial is present in regard to the serious danger to their health and the health of others from these sexually compulsive behaviors.

This clinical view of much homosexual behavior as being addictive in nature is supported by numerous studies of the sexual practices of homosexuals and by the recent best estimates that one-half of all homosexual males in New York City are HIV positive.[4] In spite of the danger of acquiring AIDS, enormous numbers of males do not protect themselves sexually. Reports of this highly dangerous behavior include a 1991 study of homosexuals in sixteen cities that revealed that 31 percent of the respondents had engaged in unprotected anal intercourse within

[3] J. Gudel, "Homosexuality: Fact and Fiction", *Christian Research Journal* (Summer 1992), p. 32.

[4] C. Horowitz, *New York* (Feb. 22, 1995), p. 30.

the previous two months. The National Institutes of Health esti-
mated that at current rates of infection, a majority of twenty-
year-old gay or bisexual men nationwide will eventually have
the AIDS virus.[5] A study of 425 homosexual or bisexual men
ages seventeen to twenty-two in San Francisco and Berkeley
revealed that about one-third reported having unprotected anal
intercourse within the past six months. A national survey of gay
men showing that 41 percent performed anilingus (tongue on or
in the anus), 47 percent received it in the past year, and 46 percent of the men sometimes had sex that they considered riskier
than they should be having.[6] Also, Michael Warner's article in
the *Village Voice*, "Why Gay Men Are Having Risky Sex" (Jan.
31, 1995), describes similar compulsive, self-destructive, and
irresponsible homosexual acting-out behavior without protection. The addictive nature of much homosexual behavior explains why HIV infections have quadrupled in San Francisco
since 1987.

These studies support the clinical view that homosexuality is
a disorder with extremely compulsive, highly reckless, and self-
destructive features. Many therapists view this addiction, like
others, as being driven by numerous emotional conflicts. In
many individuals their homosexual behavior is frequently preceded by the use of alcohol or drugs.

Father Mike became involved in compulsive and dangerous
homosexual behavior following consumption of alcohol, usually
in the evenings and on Sunday afternoons. Such activities were
always followed by enormous guilt, because Father Mike truly
desired to follow the teachings of Jesus Christ and the Church.
He saw the value of celibacy and wanted to live it. Fortunately,
he was able to understand and work on his alcohol and sexual
addictions.

[5] *Newsweek* (Sept. 19, 1994), pp. 50–51.
[6] *The Advocate* (Aug. 23, 1994), p. 20.

Narcissism

Narcissism or selfishness is another major factor influencing the attraction to the homosexual lifestyle. The appeal here is multifaceted and includes not having to make a total commitment to one person and not having to give oneself completely as a parent. There is a desire to remain childlike with minimal obligations in relationships and few limitations to the pursuit of pleasure. Hedonism is associated with many people involved in the homosexual behavior.

Another serious manifestation of narcissism in the homosexual lifestyle is grandiose thinking. Such thought processes lead to the belief that one is far superior to others and so special and exceptional that he is even immune to acquiring the AIDS virus. Grandiose delusions and extreme irresponsibility are important factors in the unsafe sexual practices of a large numbers of homosexuals today. Not only do these persons fail to protect themselves sexually on a regular basis, but they are so self-absorbed that they do not warn their partners of their HIV status.

Anthony was a young man who was extremely selfish and in this regard was very much like his mother. In his childhood he felt deprived emotionally and materially, because his mother spent most of the family's modest income on herself. He recalled always feeling ashamed of his attire. In response to this deprivation he believed that life owed him a great deal. His world became totally centered on himself. Anthony believed in using people in his drive for constant pleasure and had no conscious moral conflicts about having sixty to a hundred sexual partners per year.

Attempts to Flee from an Excessive Sense of Responsibility

Some people attempt to escape from excessive pressures and burdens by engaging in homosexual activities in which there is no commitment, obligation, or responsibility. Married men sometimes struggle with intense insecurity after experiencing the stress of a negative boss, a lack of success in work, or a sense of overwhelming anxiety from financial worries. Then they begin to view their wives and children as burdens and difficulties rather than as gifts from God. They engage in homosexual behavior in an attempt to flee from their stress and to feel more lovable and special.

A lack of balance in life, along with perfectionistic thinking, regularly leads to a feeling of excessive responsibility. This conflict interferes with the ability to be quiet and to receive the gift of love that is available from family and friends and even more from God—the Father, the Son, the Spirit—and from Mary.

Jim was a pleasant married father of two children. He enjoyed his work; however, it was extremely demanding and pressured. His wife, Jean, also had a busy, stressful career. In the evenings, in addition to caring for their children, both of them spent time on their careers, with the result that they had little time for each other. Under such stress, Jim began to visit adult book stores near his work and there engage in anonymous homosexual acts. These actions were followed by tormenting guilt because he felt that he had betrayed his wife and children as well as God.

When a husband is emotionally distant or absent from a family, the wife may feel an intense loneliness and, subsequently, become emotionally dependent upon a son. Often she will discuss with him concerns and worries that would normally be shared with her spouse. While most males in such a family home enjoy the relationship with their mothers when young, unconsciously they begin worrying excessively and feeling overly responsible for her. Later, an unconscious view of female love as burdensome and draining may develop.

Ralph was the oldest of three children and grew up in a home in which his father had great difficulty communicating his love. His father's need to distance others was the result of the alcoholism of both of his parents. This man's childhood wounds resulted in an inability to give himself because he did not feel safe and relaxed in loving relationships. Subsequently, Ralph's mother was extremely unhappy in her marriage and divorced when Ralph was twelve. He recalled feeling that, as a result of the divorce, he had become the little man of the home and was responsible for his mother and his younger brothers.

When Ralph was thirteen, he had a crush on a girl in his class. He was confused, however, because he had no desire to be physically affectionate with her, nor did he feel sexually aroused. He continued to be puzzled by his limited desires, and although he did not want to be attracted to men, he experienced his first homosexual desires when fifteen. Ralph entered therapy in his mid-twenties. He had never engaged in homosexual behavior and hoped that he would be able to overcome his homosexual temptations and marry someday.

Early in his treatment Ralph realized that he had felt overly responsible for his mother's happiness for many years and that this had taken a very high toll on him. The pressures had resulted in an unconscious fear of intimacy with females. Under the tension of these conflicts, homosexual relationships felt appealing because they appeared to be free of excessive responsibility and accountability. His growing insight into his fears of commitment to female love was liberating and filled him with hope for his future.

Sexual Trauma in Childhood

A number of males who were raped or sexually abused by older males in childhood develop confusion about their masculine identity. As with other victims of rape, they think that their behavior must have in some way led to the abuse. Such traumatic experiences can create self-hatred and the false belief that they must be homosexual. As adolescents, their relationship with girls is often undermined by their shame and the belief that no female could possibly love them if she knew of their sexual experiences.

Anger

The most significant type of anger influencing the development of homosexual attractions in childhood is anger with oneself. As a result of ongoing rejections by peers, many boys acquire an intense dislike for their bodies and view them as weak, unattractive, and unmasculine. They are so uncomfortable with their physiques that it is not unusual for them to spend a great deal of time fantasizing about escaping from their own bodies by assuming the body of another. This daydreaming can begin when they are very young and may lead to a strong physical attraction for those of the same sex.

The experience of being held by someone of the same sex may diminish self-rejection for a period of time. However, awkwardness with or dislike for one's body perdures in spite of homosexual affirmation, affection, and sexual activity. This occurs because late adolescent or adult love and acceptance cannot undo the childhood and early adolescent self-hatred. In many homosexuals, highly reckless, promiscuous, self destructive, addictive, and sadomasochistic behaviors arise from an intense dislike of themselves. Also, anger with oneself as a male can lead to cross dressing. Finally, the ultimate expression of self-hatred and aversion for one's body is seen in those who undergo sex-change surgery.

Paul was sensitive and painfully shy in regard to his small stature. Although he did not feel directly rejected by his peers, he felt weak and inadequate. Because he was not strong physically, he thought he could not compete in any sport. As his sense of isolation from his male peers grew, so too did his dislike for his body. He was very self-conscious about his appearance, and, in fact, he was never comfortable removing his shirt in the locker room at school or at the pool in the summer.

Prior to adolescence, Paul began to be obsessed with the bodies of his peers who were well-built and muscular. His obsessional thinking was followed by strong feelings of attraction for these males and then by sexual desires. When he began engaging in homosexual activity in college, he regularly fantasized being absorbed into the body of his sexual partners and emerging with a different physique. His early sexual encounters gave him fleetingly a sense of being special and lovable. While his sexual behavior produced brief emotional highs, it did not lead to greater self-acceptance. In fact, as he slipped into sexual promiscuity, he became increasingly uncomfortable with himself, and then he entered therapy.

In a small group of people, homosexuality originates from a strong need to rebel against parents, peers, the Judeo-Christian culture, the family unit, or God. As with many angry people, they derive a deep sense of pleasure from their rebellious behavior. This anger-driven homosexual conduct is seen in those whose parents of the opposite sex were extremely controlling, emotionally insensitive, physically abusive, or profoundly narcissistic. Some males delight in their mothers' knowledge that their lifestyle is the ultimate rejection of female love, whereas some females enjoy that their fathers are aware that they would appear to have no need for an ongoing loving relationship with a man.

Finally, excessive anger is seen in a number of other areas in the homosexual lifestyle. Most important, passive-aggressive anger—the quiet venting of hostility while pretending not to be angry—is manifested in the failure of HIV-positive individuals to inform their sexual partners of their illness. These men and women often feel that, since they have to suffer, others should also. Intense anger is also seen in homosexuals within the media or in the educational, political, ministerial, and mental health fields when they attempt to force our culture to change its views on homosexuality. Their approaches are often direct assaults against Judeo-Christian morality, the nuclear family, and the basic differences between men and women.

The Healing of Homosexual Attractions and Behaviors

The healing of those with homosexual attractions involves a process of understanding compassionately the emotional hurts they have experienced, resolving the anger with those who have inflicted pain through a process of forgiveness, utilizing cognitive and behavioral techniques, admitting powerlessness over their emotional suffering, and relying upon Catholic spirituality and the sacraments. While each of these steps is important, in my clinical experience over the past twenty years of treating several hundred adolescents and adults, the cornerstone to recovery is the combination of forgiveness and spirituality. No amount of insight, adult love and affirmation, assertiveness, or behavioral and cognitive changes can resolve the profoundly deep emotional wounds present within these individuals. Only God's love is powerful enough to overcome the painful loneliness and sadness, insecurities and fears by providing a feeling of being deeply loved, special, and safe at every life stage. As the emotional wounds are healed, homosexual attractions and behaviors diminish and eventually disappear.

In regard to the success of psychotherapy in treating homosexuality, in 1962 Bieber[7] reported a cure rate from psychoanalysis of 27 percent. A recent survey of 285 psychoanalysts who had treated 1,215 homosexual patients revealed that 23 percent of their patients changed to heterosexuality.[8] These traditional

[7] I. Bieber, *Homosexuality: A Psychoanalytic Study* (New York: Basic Books; 1962).

[8] H. MacIntosh, "Attitudes and Experiences of Psychoanalysts in Analyzing Homosexual Patients", *Journal of the American Psychoanalytic Association* 42 (1995):1183–1207.

treatment approaches did not utilize either a process of forgiveness for resolving the inner resentment or Christian spirituality and meditation for the sadness, low self-esteem, and mistrust. In marked contrast, when forgiveness and Christian spirituality are essential parts of the treatment, it has been my clinical experience that the recovery rate from the emotional pain and subsequent homosexual behavior approaches 100 percent in those who are truly committed to the process.

Understanding

Increasing numbers of males with homosexual attractions are entering therapy because of their fear of AIDS. Many of these people may resist initially working to recognize their emotional hurts because they fear facing their pain or because they have been influenced by our culture to believe that there are no psychological conflicts associated with homosexuality. However, most who seek counseling are searching for the truth and are open to exploring their life disappointments. Their openness is enhanced by the therapist's optimism and confidence in regard to the healing of the emotional wounds that produce their temptations and behavior.

Identifying and understanding the various types of emotional conflicts at different life stages are the first steps in the recovery process. These wounds are inflicted most often in childhood and early adolescence and arise from disappointments with parents, siblings, or peers. This pain is regularly denied and then emerges in masked ways as homosexual temptations early in adolescence. However, for some, the homosexual attractions may not come out until their twenties or thirties. In such cases, some adult trauma associated unconsciously with unresolved childhood and adolescent conflicts has usually occurred.

The major difficulty identified in this understanding phase of treatment, influencing homosexual attractions in more than 70 percent of the males I have treated, is that of a weak masculine identity. This insecurity is most often the result of repeated peer rejection and sometimes father rejection because of poor eye-hand coordination leading to limited athletic abilities in baseball, basketball, football, and gym activities.

The next most common hurt is that of an emotionally distant, insensitive, or unaffirming father. While there is usually little resistance in recognizing the sports wound, many males have great difficulty admitting how much they have wanted emotionally from their fathers and how deeply hurt they have felt when these needs were not met. This resistance can be overcome in part by the therapists sharing their own struggles in facing disappointments with their fathers.

These two areas of emotional trauma are not being identified in many males because of the failure of therapists to recognize the powerful influence on masculine identity of athletic abilities and experiences and of the father relationship. Neither of these important issues has been described extensively in the literature in the counseling fields for various reasons.

Mistrust of those of the opposite sex is the next most common cause of homosexual attraction. This is often the result of childhood and adolescent hurts with a parent who was overly controlling, too dependent, intensely selfish, emotionally distant or manipulative, absent, addicted, or otherwise dysfunctional. Also, an adult betrayal experience can result in severe fear of being hurt by those of the opposite sex.

In the understanding process in women the most common hurts that emerge, predisposing them to homosexual attractions and behavior, are a mistrust of male love because of trauma with their fathers or other males and a lack of love and affirmation from their mothers. In marked contrast to males, rejection by peers in childhood and adolescence is rarely seen as a significant factor in the development of female homosexual attractions.

Narcissism and excessive anger play a significant role in driving compulsive homosexual behavior. Finally, childhood sexual trauma and an excessive sense of responsibility for others are the least frequently seen causes of homosexual behavior.

As the understanding process progresses, a number of emotional changes occur. Initially, many report a sense of relief, happiness, and gratefulness because for the first time they can identify a cause for their ego-dystonic temptations and acts. The emotional pain may intensify for a period of time as the person recalls and emotionally relives the hurts of the past. Often, for the first time, the true depth of the emotional pain of sadness, insecurity, mistrust, and anger is felt. Some patients may need the support of medication during this phase of healing. Most do not but do experience relief as they move on in the healing journey by working to forgive those who have hurt them and by being open to meditate upon the reality of God's powerful love.

Forgiveness

The resolution of excessive anger is essential in the healing of various emotional and addictive disorders[9] and in the healing of homosexual attractions. The painful disappointments in important relationships during childhood and adolescence result in very strong anger, as well as sadness, mistrust, and low self-esteem. It is not possible to resolve the loneliness, fear, compulsive behavior, and insecurity without removing the closely associated resentment. The childhood rejections by peers and fathers lead first to sadness and next to anger. The emotion of anger then encapsulates experiences of sadness at different life stages. In order to dislodge the sadness, the capsule of anger must be removed. This can be done only through a process of

---

[9] R. P. Fitzgibbons, "The Cognitive and Emotive Uses of Forgiveness in the Treatment of Anger", *Psychotherapy* 23 (1986):629–33.

forgiveness, because the sole reliance upon the expression of anger does not truly free individuals from their inner resentment and bitterness.

Unfortunately, the young mental health field has relied almost exclusively upon the expression of anger as the primary mechanism for dealing with this powerful emotion. While expression is important at times, when solely relied on for relief from anger, it has limited value, because mere words or behaviors cannot make up for the depth of resentment and bitterness that has been denied in significant relationships in childhood and adolescence. Those who pursued therapy for their homosexual impulses in the past were rarely challenged to resolve their hostile feelings toward their parents and peers, nor were they counseled to use forgiveness. The failure to address and to recommend an effective treatment approach for buried anger is one reason why therapy did not produce more significant clinical improvement in these individuals, with the other being the lack of understanding of the value of spirituality in the recovery process.

After analyzing the specific childhood, teenage, and adult disappointments and betrayals, a forgiveness exercise is recommended in relationships where indicated. Patients are informed at the onset of and regularly during treatment that without the resolution of the anger associated with hurts of the past it is unlikely that their homosexual temptations or behavior will end. Then they are given the option of trying to forgive on one of three levels. These are cognitively, in which the decision is made to forgive even if the individual may not feel like forgiving; emotionally, in which there is understanding of those who inflicted the hurt, with the result that the person truly feels like forgiving; and spiritually, in which the person has been wounded so deeply that he cannot forgive and asks God to forgive or to remove his anger.

At the beginning of the forgiveness process, the person tries to picture himself during a painful event of the past making a decision to let go of the anger toward whoever inflicted the pain. At the same time he endeavors to begin to understand the motives of the individual who hurt him. This process usually begins as a cognitive or intellectual exercise in which a person makes the decision to forgive in order to overcome his pain, even though emotionally he may not feel like forgiving at all. Frequently, a considerable amount of time and energy is spent on this level of forgiveness before he truly feels like forgiving.

Often the forgiveness exercise is recommended in relationships in which the person has either limited or no conscious awareness of the presence of anger. If indicated by the history, the individual may be asked to try to forgive family members or peers daily for ways in which they may not have met certain needs, such as being accepted, loved, praised, or held at different life stages. This process often brings immediate emotional relief; however, some individuals discover that they may have to spend weeks, months, or even years thinking of themselves as children or adolescents and forgiving others for specific disappointments.

In a number of severe emotionally traumatic events from childhood and adolescence, the betrayal pain is so profound that forgiveness on a natural level is impossible. In such cases, spiritual forgiveness exercises are recommended. Here the individual reflects that revenge belongs to God, or that God will forgive him because he didn't know what he was doing, or that someday God will punish him, or that he is powerless over his anger and wants to turn it over to God. These spiritual forgiveness responses are particularly effective with those who were severely scapegoated by peers; profoundly betrayed by a parent, sibling, or spouse; or sexually abused. Also, many people find themselves at times simply unable to forgive, for example, a controlling or angry parent, and discover relief in being able to give their anger to God.

The regular use of the sacrament of reconciliation for Catholics has enormous benefit for those who discover intense inner rage and violent impulses of revenge or who need more grace to facilitate the resolution of their anger. I regularly recommend the use of this sacrament in the healing of the anger associated with this disorder, particularly that meant for parents, peers, or self.

Employing forgiveness exercises in those with homosexual attractions frees them from the subtle control of individuals of the past, helps them forget the painful past experiences, expedites the resolution of sadness and loneliness, improves self-esteem as anger decreases, diminishes guilt, leads to a decrease in anxiety as anger is removed, enhances the ability to trust, results in more compassion toward those who inflicted hurts, and produces a greater acceptance of the past. As the understanding grows of those who caused pain, there is a growing awareness that the behavior of many individuals can be attributed to their emotional scars, that significant others have loved as much as they were capable of loving, and that rarely was the pain deliberately inflicted.

The most frequently seen and strongest resentment is in those who were victims of scapegoating, rejection, and ridicule by peers, usually because they were not athletically coordinated. The victims of such ridicule often respond by developing both intense self-anger and violent fantasies of revenge, including, in some, murderous impulses. I have never treated anyone who acted out these furious daydreams; however, in the present culture of violence, the inhibitions to the release of these hostile impulses have decreased, and a few teenagers are now bringing guns to school and shooting those who torment them.

For those with violent impulses as a result of being scapegoated, resolving their deep resentment can be facilitated by a process that begins with the physical expression of anger in a manner in which others will not be hurt, for example, using a punching bag, breaking nonvaluable objects, or doing strenuous exercises. This is followed immediately by cognitive or spiritual forgiveness exercises aimed at relinquishing their desires for revenge. Also, relief from violent impulses is felt when patients imagine expressing these impulses and then try to think that revenge belongs to God. Finally, the sacrament of reconciliation is extremely helpful in the healing of this specific betrayal resentment.

Many men who felt emotionally abandoned by their fathers and unconsciously sought to fill the emptiness for father love in homosexual behavior have great difficulty initially forgiving their fathers. When a man comes to understand his father's childhood and realizes that *his* role model often was also emotionally distant, he grows in his ability to experience compassion for his father. He may come to see that he loved as much as he was able to love, and then he begins to feel truly like forgiving him. However, a man who was physically abandoned by his father usually experiences relief from his rage only through the use of spiritual forgiveness exercises.

The process of father forgiveness in both males and females is facilitated as these individuals grow spiritually in developing their relationship with God the Father as their other loving and caring father at every life stage. His love diminishes their feelings of being cheated and makes it much easier to let go of resentment toward their fathers.

Some individuals, aware that forgiving will lead them into the painful truth of disappointment in relationships, will not forgive until they can be reassured that there will be some love for them to hold on to that will comfort them and ease the pain that may arise with forgiveness. This fear of the forgiveness process is one of the reasons that I communicate early in treatment that an awareness of the truth and reality of the love of the Father as another father, Jesus as a best friend and brother, and Mary as another loving mother is essential to the healing of childhood, adolescent, and adult wounds.

Catholic Spirituality

The major aspects of Catholic spirituality that play an essential role in the healing of the emotional wounds leading to homosexual attractions and behavior are prayers of petition, meditation, the Scriptures, the Rosary, holy hours, the Eucharist, the sacrament of reconciliation, and spiritual direction. Once the basic conflict has been identified and understood, most individuals regularly employ each of these aspects of spirituality in their recovery. However, some find one particular method of prayer particularly helpful. For example, those who were rejected repeatedly by their peers often discover that spending time daily meditating upon and visualizing Jesus being at their side through childhood and adolescence as their best friend, when they felt very lonely and isolated, to be particularly comforting and strengthening.

The Sports Wound

In the initial stages of treatment, people with this painful hurt regularly find so much inner rage toward those who rejected them that they are unable to forgive. This resentment, while primarily meant for peers, is also often with God for failing to give them athletic abilities. In attempting to resolve this anger, Lou, who was the victim of sibling and peer ridicule because of his lack of coordination in sports and who held back pursuing priesthood because of his homosexual attractions, expressed to God his profound disappointment with him for withholding those gifts. He verbalized to God a strong sense that he had abandoned him to the terrible suffering of peer ridicule, loneliness, and profound masculine insecurity simply because he was not given athletic abilities. Lou first needed to let go of his anger with God before he could release his rage toward his peers.

He accomplished this by taking his anger to the sacrament of reconciliation on a regular basis. After his trust in God increased, he was able to give up the multiple levels of peer resentment by reflecting that revenge belongs to God and that he was powerless over his anger and wanted to turn it over to God. These spiritual interventions into his childhood and adolescent rage brought him significant emotional relief and slowly broke the control those who had hurt him had over his self-esteem. As his anger decreased, his insight and understanding grew concerning those who had made him feel inadequate. Lou came to see that the peers who had tormented him were jealous of his superior intelligence, were themselves very insecure, and came from troubled families. This understanding later enabled him to feel compassion for his childhood tormentors, enabling him later to want to try to forgive them.

Making inroads into Lou's deep resentment was an essential part of the initial stages of his recovery. Then he needed healing of the wound of peer rejection, loneliness, and masculine insecurity. Traditional therapy cannot resolve these emotional wounds. Fortunately, Catholic spirituality can, through a process of growing in an awareness of the reality of the accepting and loving presence of the Lord with the individual during the painful times of isolation in childhood, adolescence, and adult life. This knowledge of Jesus as a loving best friend begins by meditation. The individual tries to picture the Lord with him on the sports fields, in the gym, and in the neighborhood, accepting and affirming him. This meditation is often combined with reflecting upon the Lord's communicating scriptural passages to the person, such as John 15:9, "As the Father has loved me, so I have loved you." At times Lou would visualize the Lord being between himself and those who were ridiculing him, telling him that he loved him very much and that he would never betray him.

Lou also became more aware of the Lord's unique love and

friendship by making regular holy hours. During those times he gave to the Lord his masculine insecurity and loneliness and tried to be open to receive his love. As he became more aware of the Lord being with him as a young adult, his trust in Jesus grew, enabling him to become more open to his loving presence earlier in his life. Also, his trust in the Lord's love increased by going to the Eucharist more often and there specifically asking for healing of his homosexual attractions and the emotional pain causing them. Finally, a spiritual director helped him in numerous ways, especially in hearing the Lord speak to him through the Scriptures.

Slowly, Lou grew in an awareness of the Lord's being with him when he was a very insecure and lonely boy and teenager. The flow of the Lord's love into him strengthened his masculine identity by making him feel special even though he didn't have athletic gifts, healed his profound sadness, and filled the emptiness of the past. As this occurred, Lou's homosexual temptations gradually diminished. He no longer needed to engage in sex with other men to feel accepted and complete as a young man. Before his childhood and adolescent wounds were completely healed, he experienced periodic temptations. His response to them was to ask the Lord to heal the loneliness of his past, to protect him from loneliness, and to strengthen his confidence in the special male gifts he had been given by God. He also found prayer to Mary to be helpful when tempted during the earlier phase of his healing, and he became devoted to saying the Rosary daily for his healing. Lou's healing took several years. Then he was able to pursue training for the priesthood.

Over the past twenty years I have seen large numbers of single and married men, seminarians, religious, and priests who were severely rejected in childhood and adolescence set free from their pain and homosexual behavior through the use of forgiveness and Catholic spirituality. The Eucharist, the sacrament of reconciliation, meditation, spiritual direction, the Scriptures, holy hours, and the Rosary have made these healings possible. In their journey toward wholeness most individuals regularly encounter times of strong discouragement, slips, intense anger, and even hopelessness. However, with perseverance and grace the emotional wounds and the homosexual attractions and behaviors are resolved.

The Father Wound: Sadness, Insecurity, and Fear

Loneliness and a lack of affirmation in the father relationship is the second most common cause of homosexuality. In order to be psychologically healthy, children need to experience a flow of love and praise from their fathers. When this does not take place, they develop an inner sadness and insecurity. The latter occurs because children idealize fathers and tend to believe that something must be wrong with themselves if their basic emotional needs are not being met. The wound of insecurity is particularly painful in males because they are not being validated by their role model. This father wound is very prevalent, particularly today with the collapse of the nuclear family.

 The majority of males with distant fathers do not struggle with homosexuality because their masculine identity has been validated through acceptance by male peers and in athletic competition. However, some males will have strong homosexual attractions to men in an unconscious attempt to fill the emptiness created by an angry, absent, or negative father.

 In exploring disappointments in the father relationship, one often encounters very powerful defense mechanisms, particularly in males. An effective way to deal with this resistance is for counselors to share ways in which they have worked at forgiving their fathers for disappointments in their past. The process of forgiving the father is extremely difficult for many people, so difficult that they feel that there is no possible way in which they can do it. In such cases, spiritual forgiveness is very effective for the resentment. Here, too, it is essential that, in healing the father wound, the anger be removed in order for the underlying sadness to be resolved.

Many men will engage in extremely promiscuous homosexual behavior in a frustrating unconscious attempt to fill the childhood and adolescent craving for father love. In an effort to help these men, some therapists suggest that the adult try to heal the wounded child within by loving him more. This approach does not bring lasting emotional relief because the child within craves a father's love, not self-love, and because the adult was not present at the time the child yearned to be accepted and loved by his father. Only a knowledge of God the Father's presence during childhood and adolescence can fill the emptiness and heal this wound.

The initial spiritual approach is to suggest that the person begin working on his relationship with God the Father. Since grace builds on nature, most of those with distant or troubled fathers have great difficulty trusting God the Father. They did not feel safe with their own fathers and, subsequently, struggle to be open to God the Father. Because fear is rooted in unconscious anger, as they work at forgiving their fathers, their mistrust will diminish.

Growth in trust in God the Father is facilitated by praying to Jesus, asking specifically for this gift. Some implore Jesus to help them to trust in Abba's love, just as he did. Once the trust begins to increase, the person is asked to try to meditate for two fifteen-minute periods daily upon God the Father as their other loving father at each life stage. Some are helped by imagining the Lord's taking them by the hand as children and teenagers and leading them into a greater closeness to the Father. Others ask the Lord simply to help them to come to a greater knowledge of the Father. Reflecting through the day that "God is my father" is strengthening for many. Reading the Scriptures, slowly praying the Our Father, and seeking healing at the Eucharist enable growth in the knowledge of the Father's love. What is essential here is an awareness of the Father's love for them as children and as teenagers.

The experience of Abba's love flowing into them dispels the loneliness, insecurity, and mistrust that they have acquired from their fathers. Slowly, the homosexual temptations diminish and ultimately leave, as the father wound is healed in this manner. These individuals become strengthened by God the Father's love, and, when tempted to act out homosexually, they don't give in immediately as they had done in the past. Instead, they ask the Lord to show them the emotional stress causing the temptation and then to heal it. They are regularly pleasantly surprised by the Lord's faithful response to such prayer. These tests increase their confidence in God's power to assist in the complete healing of their homosexuality.

Females who withdrew into homosexuality because of a fear of male love arising from childhood and adolescent trauma with their fathers grow, as their sense of the Father's love for them increases, to be open to trust male love. When they can be comfortable entrusting themselves into the providential care of God the Father, they regularly find themselves more willing to try to become vulnerable to males. This stage is followed regularly by feelings of attraction and then love.

Diane's homosexual feelings were the direct result of a family life with an explosive alcoholic father. For years she was involved emotionally and sexually with women, yet felt very unfulfilled. Early in her recovery Diane had great difficulty in forgiving her father for all the ways in which he had hurt her mother and had created chaos in their family life. Realizing that she could not forgive him, she became comfortable reflecting upon the words of Christ on the cross and applying them to her father, "Father, forgive them, for they know not what they do." As her anger decreased, she came to know Abba more as her other loving and protective Father. This love warmed and comforted her and diminished her father's control over her relationships. She grew to feel safer and more attracted to men, and she believed that the Father would protect her as her own father had not.

In response to his love, a strong desire developed in Diane to serve the Father and to do his will in relationships. Also, a growing knowledge of her faith led to a deeper understanding of the sinful nature of homosexuality[10] and the desire to avoid such sin. His providential care became a strong foundation on which Diane believed she could base a loving relationship with a man.

The Mother Wound: Sadness, Mistrust, and Insecurity

The childhood and adolescent wounds with mothers who were unaffectionate, distant, angry, insensitive, selfish, controlling, overly dependent, emotionally ill, or addicted regularly lead to homosexual temptations and behavior in some individuals. After recognizing these wounds and beginning the process of forgiveness, the next step in the healing journey is that of asking the person to consider the spiritual reality of Mary as another loving, giving, joyful, and trustworthy mother and friend at every life stage. The experience of Mary's love can fill the emptiness and loneliness in the mother relationship, become a new foundation to trust females, strengthen confidence, and resolve homosexual attractions and behaviors.

Sue had great difficulty thinking about trusting Mary initially as another loving mother because her own mother had been so insensitive to her. Even though understanding the little girl within her mother, who had not been properly mothered, and forgiving her had been emotionally liberating, she continued to be fearful of Mary's love. Sue felt discouraged because she knew that only another mother's love could heal the childhood sadness

---

[10] Congregation for the Doctrine of the Faith, "Letter to Bishops of the Catholic Church on the Pastoral Care of Homosexual Persons", Oct. 1, 1986, nos. 4–7.

and the longing for maternal affection that fueled her homosexual temptations. Fortunately, when she daily asked the Lord to help her to rely on the love of his mother as he did, her ability to trust in Mary slowly increased. Sue was helped by meditating in front of a picture of Mary holding the Christ Child and by praying the Rosary. When tempted, she would meditate upon Mary as the truly loving and joyful female in her life.

Pete had difficulty in trusting Mary initially because he feared that she would be as demanding and controlling as his own mother had been. He had retreated into homosexuality because of his fear of becoming vulnerable to and being dominated by a female. Pete made great strides in his recovery by trying to picture Mary as a very gentle, safe, and trusting mother who did not want to dominate his life and by reflecting that she had never betrayed him. As his trust in her love grew through prayer, spiritual direction, and the Rosary, his fears of female love decreased. Mary became for him a loving companion who helped him open his heart to women.

Ralph's mother's excessive dependency on him, because of an absent father, produced an unconscious negative association with female love. While attracted to females and hoping someday to marry, he viewed closeness to females as being draining and burdensome. Ralph meditated first on picturing the Lord being between his mother and himself, lifting from him the heavy burdens he had experienced because of feeling overly responsible for her. At Mass he would place his mother on the altar and reflect that Jesus was her Savior, not himself. Slowly the Lord set him free from his excessive sense of responsibility for his mother. After being unburdened, he was greatly comforted by meditating upon Mary as a joyful, giving mother at his side in the past. With this healing came a new openness to dating relationships and a strong desire to marry.

The Anger Wound

Paul remembered hating his body, which, since the third grade, he had viewed as small and weak. He was ashamed of his lack of muscle and his short stature. His overwhelming need for acceptance led him into an extremely promiscuous homosexual lifestyle.

Paul began to experience remorse after realizing that he had not accepted the body that God had given to him. He asked the Lord to forgive him and to help him to embrace his body. His healing progressed by his being thankful for his body, by rejecting the desire to be other than who he was, by viewing his soul as much more important than his body, and by being thankful for his special male gifts. When meditating upon Jesus being with him and loving him, just as he was, at every life stage, Paul sensed the Lord telling him what masculinity truly is in the eyes of God. This experience of the Lord's affirming love for him when he was a boy and a teenager freed him from his self-hatred and deep sense of male inadequacy. Finally, the graces from the Eucharist and the sacrament of reconciliation were of enormous benefit in his growth in accepting himself.

Addictive Disorders

Alcohol, drug, and sexual addictions often are seen in those with promiscuous homosexuality. Father Mike's homosexual behavior was always preceded by excessive drinking as a result of his struggles with loneliness. He overcame his sexual acting-out behavior completely by regular attendance at Alcoholics Anonymous meetings; by cessation of drinking; and by the use of meditation, spiritual direction, and the sacraments for his loneliness.[11]

[11] R. P. Fitzgibbons, "Identifying, Resolving Loneliness in Priestly Life", *The Priest* (September 1989), pp. 10–17.

For those who are truly sexually addicted, the initial steps in treatment are to help them to accept their addiction, to embrace their powerlessness, to believe that they cannot recover without God's assistance and love, and to attend a Twelve Step sexual addiction group, such as Sexaholics Anonymous. Also, weekly participation in Christian homosexual recovery groups, such as Courage, Homosexuals Anonymous, and Harvest, can be very helpful. Those who are too embarrassed to attend such groups may be given the names of individuals who are more advanced in their recovery and who can act as sponsors for them. Then, when they struggle with strong temptations, they can turn to these sponsors for needed support, prayer, and encouragement. While Twelve Step sexual addiction groups are helpful, it has been my clinical experience that the addictive behavior is not brought under control until the underlying emotional wounds are healed.

Narcissism

Narcissism is a very powerful disorder that fuels the homosexual behavior in many people. This personality weakness is not easily overcome because of the reluctance to give up a life of unchecked, irresponsible self-indulgence. This clinical disorder is the major reason for failure in recovery from homosexuality. Many people begin their healing journey only to be pulled down into a superficial life of hedonistic pleasure-seeking.

If those with this disorder are to recover, they need to commit themselves to a highly disciplined spiritual life. Such a program would include weekly confession, growth in the virtues of self-denial and humility, regular meditation upon the Lord's Passion, spiritual direction, regular retreats, a close relationship with Mary, the ending of unhealthy friendships, daily reading of the Scriptures, and daily attendance at Mass.

The Excessive Sense of Responsibility

Jim's anonymous homosexual behavior developed as an attempt to escape from the excessive pressures and demands in his professional and personal life. As he daily sought God's will for his life, he was able to see a clear path out of the darkness. With the help of God's grace he placed the Lord, not work, first in his life, gave his responsibilities back to the Lord daily, asked to be healed of his tendency to feel overly responsible, read Scriptures each evening and, most important, worked to strengthen his loving friendship with his wife. Taking these steps removed the exhaustion and inner emptiness and enabled Jim and his wife truly to enjoy their married life together.

Childhood Sexual Trauma

Those males whose sexual identity is confused as result of childhood rapes and other sexual abuse regularly harbor unconscious violent impulses against their abusers. These vengeful thoughts can be removed by surrendering them daily to God and by reflecting that revenge belongs to God. Next, the specific recollections of abuse also can be very tormenting and confusing. These recurrent memories can be overcome by giving them to the Lord daily and by asking him to heal these memories.

The identity confusion diminishes as the severe emotional pain surrounding the traumatic memory decreases. Also, the masculine identity is strengthened by being thankful for one's male gifts, by growing in a sense of divine filiation, by identifying with the positive qualities in one's father and other male relatives, and by asking for healing at the Eucharist.

Conclusion

An urgent need exists to examine the truth in regard to homosexuality, both morally and psychologically. Pope John Paul II has stated, "We need now more than ever to have the courage to look the truth in the eye and to call things by their proper name, without yielding to convenient compromises or to the temptation of self-deception."[12] As the teacher of truth, the Church affirms in the *Catechism* that "homosexual acts are acts of grave depravity, are intrinsically disordered, and under no circumstances can be approved."[13]

Psychologically, homosexual attractions and acts arise from a number of very specific emotional hurts and conflicts in childhood, adolescence, and adult life. In the past these wounds were not clearly and fully identified by mental health professionals, nor, in the majority of cases, were they healed. The reasons for this are that the mental health field in its early stage of development failed to understand and to incorporate forgiveness into removing the significant betrayal anger in these individuals and did not provide Christian spirituality to resolve their sadness, mistrust, low self-esteem, and addictive behavior. Fortunately, Catholic spirituality, combined with good psychotherapy, can result in a complete healing of those with this disorder.

---

[12] John Paul II, encyclical letter *The Gospel of Life* (March 25, 1995), no. 58.
[13] *Catechism of the Catholic Church*, no. 2357.

Appendix II

HOLISTIC TREATMENT PROCEDURAL MODEL FOR HEALING THE HOMOSEXUAL CONDITION

Maria Valdes, Ph.D.

This Appendix will mainly present a holistic treatment procedural model for healing the homosexual condition. The title of the Appendix was deliberately chosen because this writing is not about changes in the homosexual orientation but about an arrested or incomplete psychosexual development, i.e., the homosexual condition. The format, components, and stages of treatment presented apply almost the same to the treatment of this condition in males as in females. However, since the psychodynamic causes combine differently in males than in females, the choice had to be made as to what would be presented and the examples to use.

Homosexuality is a very complex phenomenon, and, if we keep in mind the complexity of human sexuality itself, we can perhaps begin to appreciate its complexities in terms of not only its causes but also its development, treatment, and outcomes. It could be said that the complexity of homosexuality is related to the innumerable combinations of possibilities within any of the identified main causal categories expressed by the following:

1. Those who adhere to biological, hormonal, genetic, and hereditary causes for homosexuality.

2. Those who emphasize environmental or social factors. Learned theory—homosexuality is viewed as a learned preference.

3. Those who emphasize psychosexual, developmental, and/or psychosocial factors, referring to the different psychodynamic interactions that may affect a person's life.

Some Descriptions and Dynamics on Homosexuality

I shall highlight my views on some of the most important concepts and dynamics to be considered in trying to understand what homosexuality is, for treatment purposes. In the traditional consensus, homosexuality has been described as a predominant, persistent attraction of a sexual-genital nature to persons of the same sex.

Elizabeth Moberly, however, speaks of the homosexual condition as "one of same-sex ambivalence", a defensive detachment with the urge for renewed attachment.[1] By sex ambivalence she means that, for example, on one hand a boy wants to be attached to his father, and on the other hand he has developed a detachment as a defense against being hurt.

I would like to introduce the following description of homosexuality as it relates to the person: A person with a homosexual condition is one with an incomplete or arrested psychosexual development that manifests itself by the need of that person to stay at a homopsychosexual stage of development rather than to complete the psychosexual cycle and become heterosexually oriented. Psychosexual development is meant to include attitudes and ways of perceiving and relating to others, in other

[1] Elizabeth R. Moberly, *Homosexuality: A New Christian Ethic* (Wiltshire, England: Redwood Rose Ltd, 1983).

words, a kind of mind set that is more than sexual. The importance of this description is to help the understanding that when a person with a homosexual condition attains heterosexuality, homosexuality has not been reversed; rather, the psychosexual development has been completed.

A number of clinicians and theorists, including myself, view homosexuality mainly as the result of a deficit in the relationship with the parent of the same sex: boy with father, girl with mother. This deficit brings about a lack of identification or disidentification with one's own gender. Lack of gender identity is the inability to feel, think, and act in accord with one's own physiological makeup. For example, a man may have the capacity to have sexual intercourse with a woman but not have the emotional satisfaction of doing so. A man may beget a child but not think that it is his principal duty to protect the child rather than to be motherly to the child.

If the gender identity is not developed and integrated with the physical sex, it becomes an unmet need of that individual, for which he is not responsible at all, and it will remain so until it is met. In my practice I have seen either or both parents involved in the development of the deficit. Due to personal difficulties or conflict between husband and wife, the mother may present a very negative image of the father to the boy, whether by direct verbal communication or in nonverbal ways. This makes it difficult for the boy to move toward identification with a man whom he perceives as negative or hurtful.

Every child has certain basic needs that have to be met so that he is able to attain full psychological development; psychosexual development is included. Some of those needs are affection, individuation, autonomy, independence, acceptance, and gender identification with one's own physiological make-up. Further, most clinicians and theorists agree that several of these needs occur within the same developmental period. For example, a boy is faced with two major developmental objectives during his first three years of life. The first is concerned with autonomous identity formation: the young boy becomes conscious that he is distinct from his mother. He begins to see himself as an individual with a sense of this individuality—who I am—a person. The second is that of gender identification: the boy is aware that he is not only separate but also different from his mother. He also realizes that he is like his father—what I am—a male. Thus the young boy's needs of autonomy, individuation, independence, and gender identification occur during the developmental period of one to three or four years.

The emotions and feelings experienced by the boy during this period in which he struggles for independence, autonomy, and gender identity tend to become fused with each other, making them appear to the child as if they were the same. For example, a boy feels rejected by his father as he tries to assert himself by doing something; or he feels overly dependent on his mother as she does not allow him to do something; or the mother is overprotective of him; he also feels a failure in self-esteem. He feels powerless as a boy. As these developmental objectives are interrelated, he feels that he is not accepted by his parents. Since he feels that he is not accepted by them, he feels that his gender identity is not accepted either; he feels it as not established or incomplete, as though his gender identity has not been established or accepted by his parents.

When the boy attains puberty, he uses his sexual drive, strongly perceived at this time, not to relate to the opposite sex, but to satisfy an unmet need for gender identity. However, since his gender identity needs remain fused with some other basic needs (independence, autonomy, individuation), when the adolescent feels a sense of failure, rejection, lack of acceptance, powerlessness, and so on, he is inclined to meet these needs by eroticizing them—usually resulting in some form of sexual acting out, as if by this acting out he would gain acceptance by males in general. Most of the time, after acting out, he discovers that he feels worse and that the sexual gratification did not satisfy any of his needs.

The fusing of unmet basic needs with sexual needs might be one possible explanation as to why so many men report that they have felt the lack of gender identity from a very early age and have experienced themselves as different from other male peers as long as they can remember.

In a boy some of the basic needs that may not have been met and get fused together are:

1. emotional need to identify with same sex—gender identity

2. emotional need of autonomy

3. emotional need for independence

Later, as an adolescent or young male adult, the same needs remain unmet and fused, and the sexual drive is added. At this time the following occur:

1. He is not able to identify with same sex.

2. He has the emotional need of autonomy.

3. He has the emotional need for independence.

This leads to

4. The need to have sexual activity with another male, as he directs his sexual energies toward males. Thus, the global or total experience of these needs is the homosexual experience.

The fourth characteristic, that is, the need to have sexual activity with another male, makes the homosexual experience come to the surface or consciousness. Since this combination of needs resembles the basic emotional needs that he felt as a boy, he concludes that he is a homosexual, rather than recognizing that he has not attained gender identity.

Psychosocial Treatment Procedural Models

First, I will mention a few psychosocial treatment models frequently used in the treatment of homosexuality. Group and individual therapy have been the traditional methods of choice. Then I will briefly present to you a holistic treatment procedural model that I utilize in my approach to healing the homosexual condition, since I view it as one of psychosexual development.

1. *Psychoanalytic.* Involves cognition, feelings, and insight. Its weak points are that it mostly excludes the therapist's intervention and that it offers almost no room for individual free choice.

2. *Behavioristic.* It does not address the problem that underlies the behavior of the person. It offers a simplistic solution: elimination of the behavior, i.e., homosexual acting out.

3. *Religious.* It is more holistic in that it includes faith and grace. However, it sometimes deals mostly with the control of behavior. If so, it needs also to examine the origins of homosexuality and the person's motivation.

4. *Eclectic contemporary.* In the eclectic contemporary treatment, there is more understanding of the need to deal with insight, cognition, and feelings, as well as behavior.

5. *Holistic.* What I want to share with you is a form of treatment that is more inclusive than those previously mentioned. It is a holistic approach where philosophy, theology, physiology, and psychology come together. It is an integration of psychology and spirituality. This holistic therapeutic procedure includes the participation of the spiritual director. The therapist and spiritual director work hand in hand with the client/directee for his psychological development and spiritual growth.

Holistic Treatment

For homosexuality, the purpose of the treatment is to complete the psychosexual development and help the individual attain heterosexuality. In doing so, both conscious and unconscious material are dealt with.

During this treatment:

1. One is helped to distinguish each of the unmet or unsatisfied needs underlying his homosexual condition.

2. One is guided to meet these needs.

3. One learns to identify with one's own sex and to establish relationships with the opposite sex.

4. One starts meeting each need independently so that the sexual need is ordered to relate to the opposite sex and thus it can meet its own need of complementarity.

When all the preceding objectives have been achieved, the individual attains his gender identity or completes his psychosexual development. When all the unmet needs underlying his homosexual condition are appropriately met, he has reached psychosexual growth.

Stages of Treatment

In order to present the stages or phases of treatment, I will take the example of a young boy who was not allowed or encouraged to develop autonomy due to family interactions that occurred between the ages of one to three. He developed as an adult in a way that made him feel powerless and inferior to his male peers.

He had a homosexual condition. Due to the complexity exhibited by his intertwined emotions, feelings, subjective ways of viewing reality, and so forth, I will have to choose only one of the conflicts that led to the lack of sexual identity. Other existing conflicts are dealt with, often simultaneously, as the treatment progresses through the various stages. The conflict chosen is powerlessness and inferiority. All the aspects involved in the different stages are not covered here since only those related to the example are included.

Phase I. During Phase I of the treatment we review all the individual's conscious material as he presents it. He comes for treatment at age twenty-nine. He expresses his feelings of failure and powerlessness at the company where he works. He feels he cannot compete with other males and/or develop close relationships with them as he is afraid of their rejection, and so he does not spend too much time with them. This is similar to his relationship with his father, with whom he does not get along at all. He states that his concern is not only about acting out with other men but also about masturbation, pornography, and fantasy life.

Phase II. During Phase II we work at identifying past and present emotions that lead him to have the sexual genital contact. He expresses that he does it because it is a way in which he feels accepted by other males. It makes him feel powerful. Let me mention here that he feels he cannot compete or make any form of emotional contact with other males in any way except through homosexual acting out.

Phase III. We work through the defense mechanisms to identify the emotions and/or feelings associated with his sexual-genital activities with one of the top executives of his company. He develops the insight that the emotions of alienation, lack of acceptance, or failure are present when he feels the sexual need to act out. At other times he identifies the emotions of powerlessness, dependency, and inferiority. He does not know why he feels the sexual need when he has these other emotions. As he progresses through this phase, he is able to stop sexual activity with men but continues with masturbation, pornography, and fantasy life. We now start working on the conflicts with father and/or mother.

Phase IV. By working in therapy with his father, he becomes aware of his father's love and acceptance of him. As he becomes stronger and more defenses are dropped, he is able to start separating the two needs:

> the need to develop gender identity through sexual activity with other males

from

> the need to be accepted, to become independent, the need for power, and so on.

As we progress through this phase, he starts developing nongenital relationships with other males and good relationships with members of the opposite sex. He begins to experience heterosexual arousal. By the end of Phase IV, masturbation and pornography are seldom to nonexistent. Homosexual fantasy is still alive.

Phase V. He is able to express physical love to members of same sex without physical genital arousal. This is another indication of his ability to separate love and acceptance needs being met, without their being intertwined with sexual needs. He attains self-assurance in his gender identity, which at the same time allows him to relate to members of the opposite sex in a more physical and emotional manner. Homosexual fantasy life is seldom engaged in by the end of Phase V.

Phase VI. During this phase, with his own self-acceptance as a male, he experiences greater possession of his gender identity and seldom feels homosexual arousal. Instead, he is learning to handle heterosexual arousal and is developing a capacity for expression of physical nongenital love toward the opposite sex.

Phase VII. In this phase he reports no homosexual arousal or fantasies. He is so happy with his masculinity and his accomplishments relating to his father, mother, and other men and women that he feels very confident. He has new interest in learning and working with people. He is ready to use all his gifts and talents to lead a fulfilling, happy life, whether as a single person or in married life.

Phase VIII. We set up the schedule for follow-up appointments.

One important aspect of this holistic treatment, which is not included above in any one of the specific phases since it occurs throughout the different stages, is the participation in Open Focus[2] Biofeedback-Assisted Attention Training Workshops. These workshops include group attention training sessions as well as individual biofeedback sessions. There are three levels to these workshops: introductory, intermediate, and advanced. The intermediate and advanced levels include neurofeedback, which is a process by which a person receives information regarding the brain's electrical activity. The use of neurofeedback enables the individual to train, modify, and enhance his brain waves. With the advent of neurofeedback, new avenues are being opened up to us for assessing the changes in brain activity before and after healing of the homosexual condition. Perhaps we can look here for a success similar to that accomplished with neurofeedback in the treatment of alcoholism, drug abuse, attention deficit disorder (ADD, ADHD), insomnia, and so forth.

Structure, Format, and Components

Initially, one or more consultation sessions are held between the therapist and the individual. During these consultations, the individual presents his problems, and the therapist explains the treatment procedure. The person's reasons and goals for entering treatment as well as his commitment are identified and discussed.

---

[2] Open Focus is a registered trademark of Biofeedback Computers, Inc.

If the therapist and the individual reach an agreement on these issues, then treatment begins.

There is a comprehensive psychological examination, which includes an interview, a clinical history, an intake or assessment form, self-reporting inventory tests, projective tests, and intelligence tests, as needed. The purpose of this psychological examination is to identify the specific causes of the individual's condition and his conflicts in order to make a diagnosis and the treatment's prognosis.

The components of this holistic treatment procedural model are psychological, spiritual, physiological, and educational. For the purpose of this appendix, the interactions and activities that occur during treatment are classified under each one of those components.

Psychological

— Weekly individual sessions between therapist and individual.

— Development of specific plans for behavior control when needed.

— Participation in group sessions when appropriate.

— Encouragement of several friendships and intimate relationships with heterosexuals of the same sex.

— Parent involvement whenever possible.

Spiritual

— Encouragement of frequent attendance at Mass and reception of the sacraments for Catholics or attendance at other religious services according to the belief system of the individual.

— Encouragement of daily meditation and prayer.

— Encouragement to include the contents of the psychological session with its insights in one's development of the spiritual life, whether it be as part of meditation or as writing a journal.

— Involvement in works of charity and of helping people.

Psychological and Spiritual

— Three-way meeting with individual, spiritual director, and therapist. The role of the spiritual director may be assumed by the confessor, minister, or rabbi.

— Signed consent for the release of psychological information and the treatment's progress to the spiritual director.

— Discussion of results of the psychological examination. These would include personality traits, conflicts, defenses of the individual, as well as his diagnosis and the prognosis for his treatment.

— Sharing of any information pertinent to the discussion. Initial plans for both spiritual director and the therapist are drawn.

— Subsequent meetings are scheduled at the request of any of the three parties (usually every three to four months).

— Regularly, information is shared, and consultations take place between the spiritual director and the therapist.

Physiological

— Generally, there are specific programs for physical activity, nutrition, and recreation.

Psychological and Physiological

— Stress management workshops are introduced early in the treatment.

— Appropriate biofeedback training is used, including neurofeedback. Emphasis is placed on the interdependent relationship between the psychological and physiological realms, based on this psychophysiological principle: "Every change in the physiological state is accompanied by an appropriate change in the mental-emotional state, conscious or unconscious; and, conversely, every change in the mental-emotional state, conscious or unconscious, is accompanied by an appropriate change in the physiological state."[3]

— Behavior modification is used as needed.

Educational

— Readings, movies, workshops, and so on are recommended as appropriate.

Outcomes

It is difficult to address the issue of outcomes in the treatment of homosexuality. The difficulty arises from various reasons.

First, we would have to consider whether the rate of success or failure reported in the literature refers to individuals who are ego-dystonic (they see homosexuality as negative) or ego-syntonic (they see homosexuality as a condition to accept and one where nothing should be done). Second, do the reported statistics include individuals who continue treatment to justify themselves even though they really do not believe they can develop into heterosexuality? Do they take into account the individual's age, motivation, and commitment?

In addition to these reasons, which refer directly to the individual's internal forum, we have to add external reasons.

---

[3] Elmer and Alyce Green, *Beyond Biofeedback* (Ft. Wayne, Ind.: Knoll Publishing, 1977), 58.

How does society view this condition so as to be supportive or detrimental to its healing? Are those who are successful in treating homosexuality, whether in clinics or in private practice, devoting their time to helping people rather than to writing about their successes?

In my over thirty years of clinical practice, I have treated many individuals with a homosexual condition, and the success rate has been very high. However, I must express that I work in treatment only with individuals who are ego-dystonic and show high motivation and commitment to heal their condition and fully develop psychosexually. The others drop out of treatment. Experience has taught me that there is still much to learn about this condition and its treatment. In each individual there is a multiple combination of genetic, environmental, social, and psychological factors. To accept the influence of some and not others would be to miss some important aspects for understanding the human person. The combination of factors is so varied and the external influences so multiple that learning and discerning for each individual involved are ongoing tasks for the therapist. The fact that not one single cause/effect has been found to explain homosexuality should only serve as encouragement for further investigation into all the possible factors that contribute to the onset of the homosexual condition.

Successful Holistic Treatment Case History

Below is a successful treatment case history of one of my clients, a white, twenty-five-year-old seminarian named Rich. He had majored in philosophy and had three years of graduate school in theology. His father was forty-eight and his mother forty-seven. He had four sisters, two older and two younger. Rich was referred by his spiritual director on account of serious doubts regarding his ordination to the priesthood based on his acting out behavior just a month and a half after having been ordained as deacon.

After a complete psychological examination had been administered to Rich, he signed a consent for release of confidential information to his spiritual director. The diagnosis was a high level of generalized anxiety with a homosexual condition (egodystonic feelings) and acting out behavior. Rich's intellectual functioning was bright normal with the potential of very superior. In his conflict areas he revealed serious difficulties with parental figures, both father and mother. Treatment lasted for three and a half years and consisted of two hours per week for about forty-two to forty-five weeks per year. Some additional sessions were scheduled for interaction with his father, and father and mother together. The follow-up to the treatment was four times in the first year, twice in the second year, and once a year for the next five years.

The following is the conscious material reported by Rich. He had two close friends with the homosexual condition. He had a very poor relationship with his father, whom he perceived as not caring, loving, or accepting of him, and an excellent relationship with his mother, whom he perceived as truly understanding and accepting of him. He became aware of his homosexual condition at the prepubertal stage, and he reported not having been good at sports and not being well accepted by his peers. During adolescence he had become involved in homosexual acting out—frequently attending bars and parties for homosexuals, mutual masturbation, high fantasy level, mouth-genital contact, and anal sex. He reported having had occasional heterosexual encounters (two or three times), mainly mouth to genital, once actual intercourse. When Rich entered the seminary he stopped most of the external sexual activity; however, he developed a rich fantasy life, autoeroticism, and, later on, mutual masturbation with others at the seminary.

Based on Rich's psychological examination and in consultation with his spiritual director, it was decided that he should postpone indefinitely the continuation of his studies at the seminary and, therefore, his ordination to the priesthood. Rich left the seminary, went back to live at home, and worked in the administration department of a college. With the involvement of the spiritual director, a treatment plan was developed that included, but was not limited to, a program for spiritual growth, physical exercise for improving self-image, and a nutritional program geared to eliminate excessive social drinking and the use of stressful foods (those capable of producing a physiological stress response, such as caffeine, theobromine, sugar, and salt).

During treatment there were regular three-way meetings with Rich, the spiritual director, and the therapist, usually every three months. In addition, as needed, there were consultations between the spiritual director and the therapist.

After a few months of treatment, with the consent of Rich and his father, it was agreed to have his father participate in an undetermined number of sessions with him to work out their difficulties. There were a total of five meetings of four hours at a time. New understandings and insights were developed between Rich and his father. Healing took place, and a new relationship was born.

As the meetings with his father progressed, Rich became aware of the much greater role his mother had played in the development of the problem and in the separation between him and his father. As soon as Rich had worked out the relationship with his father, he started feeling better about himself. However, he became very angry with his mother, as he could not understand the level of dominance and control she had exerted over both him and his father. He wanted to drop his mother out of his life completely.

An additional number of individual sessions between Rich and the therapist were needed before he was ready to meet with his mother to work out difficulties with her. Rich requested the presence of his father when he met with his mother, as he felt powerless to deal with her without his father being present. In two sessions with Rich, his parents and the therapist, which lasted four and six hours respectively, Rich presented to his mother how it had not only been the seemingly aloof and un-caring attitude of his father that had contributed to his condition but also the role she had played in giving him that image of his father. He provided several factual happenings from his child-hood in which this had occurred. The mother tried to rational-ize what was presented and used many defenses to protect herself. It took about a year of weekly sessions to work out Rich's relationship with his mother. Several of those sessions were with Rich, his mother, and the therapist.

At this stage of the treatment process, in a three-way meeting with Rich, the spiritual director, and the therapist, it was de-cided that even if Rich's relationship with his mother had not been completely healed, she would remain as part of the process. Work with her would continue until Rich had developed enough ego strength and independence from her to prevent any setbacks in treatment.

The fact that Rich was progressing in his psychosexual devel-opment and feeling better was evidenced by the following:

1. Within six to seven months of treatment, he had com-pletely stopped any kind of sexual-genital acting out.

2. After nine months of treatment he completely stopped in-teracting with his two closest friends who had a homo-sexual condition. They did not approve of Rich's treatment or his desire to work through his homosexual condition.

After one and a half years of treatment:

3. There were physical movement and postural changes in him. He reported how he experienced his body in a differ-

ent way and had spontaneously assumed a more manly demeanor.

4. His fantasy level had dropped to about twice a month and remained that way for the next eight months. After that, it was no longer reported.

5. He did not watch sexually stimulating movies, and he threw away magazines and literature pertaining to homosexuality.

After thirteen months of treatment he started a friendship with a heterosexual male who greatly supported him in his journey. This friendship has lasted to date. Rich returned to the seminary after seventeen months of treatment, and he was ordained a priest two and a half years after treatment had been initiated. There was another year of treatment after ordination. When Rich completed treatment, there was an agreement to have three-way meetings with Rich, the spiritual director, and the therapist every three months for the following year. During the second year there would be two of those meetings, and then one every year for the next five years. Rich learned at this point that if he ever needed to he could call on both parties for a meeting.

Rich continued to enjoy a very good relationship with his father until the latter's death, ten years after Rich had commenced treatment. At the time of his father's death we met once a week for about two months. Four months later his spiritual director died, and we met for four sessions. Rich remains a strong, effective, and compassionate priest to this day. He has developed many good, meaningful, and beautiful relationships with both men and women. Rich suffered much during his journey, but he has turned his sufferings into love and service of God's people.

Some Therapeutic Considerations

Homosexuality can be approached in two almost opposite ways. One can treat it as an incurable condition or consider it as a condition subject to healing. In over thirty years of clinical practice I have worked with a good number of people who have sought and attained healing.

During this time I have noticed several important elements about those with a homosexual condition. In every incidence, psychosexual development and gender identification have not been completed. They have also lacked identification with the parent of the same sex. The need to meet this deficit and lack of gender identification in these individuals with a homosexual condition has remained. Many contemporary theorists and clinicians have also found this to be true. In addition, I have found that many times the parent of the opposite sex has played a significant role in the establishment of this deficit and in the development of the homosexual condition.

Researchers and therapists have long debated whether homosexuality should be classified as a neurosis or a personality disorder. If it is classified as a neurosis, one kind of treatment would be given; if it is a personality disorder, another kind of treatment would follow. It seems that homosexuality should not be classified as a neurosis. The neurosis appears to develop from conflicts resulting from superimposed ways of dealing with anxiety. Generally speaking, a person with a neurosis has attained basic gender identity; but in every instance of homosexuality, gender identity has not been attained.

In homosexuality there is a disidentification with self, with the person one is. The person is body and soul at once with a specific physiological sex, either male or female. If the gender is not developed and integrated with the physical sex, a basic unmet need is established in the individual for which he is not responsible at all. This need for gender identity will remain until it is met.

Sexual acting out to fulfill the unmet needs of gender identification has a negative effect. It does not heal the condition but rather perpetuates it and makes it even more addictive. Also, relating only to members of the same sex who exhibit a similar condition will not satisfy the gender identity unmet need because they have the same kind of deficit. When the individual establishes several relationships with heterosexuals of the same sex, he has a much better opportunity for attaining gender identity.

An individual's success at healing his condition largely depends on how he views his condition. When individuals believe (1) that they can make free choices and (2) that they can change their lives, and when (3) they are willing to take responsibility for their lives, I have found that they have the power to overcome their condition. On the other hand, when individuals accept their condition and take a deterministic outlook, their chances for completing psychosexual development are very limited. Those individuals who have been successful in overcoming their condition are those who have taken responsibility to work through their condition and have made specific choices to do so.

All individuals in pursuit of psychological integration have to reconcile their thoughts and feelings with their behavior. In their quest for moral integration another factor has to be included: that the behavior be in agreement with the person's value system. When an individual has difficulty in recognizing the condition as an objective disorder, whether morally or psychologically, then moral integration is not attained.

I see a need to take a holistic approach to the treatment of homosexuality. This includes the physical, psychological, and spiritual aspects of a person's life. I do not have sufficient evidence for concluding that the condition is genetic, hereditary, congenital, hormonal, and so on. Rather, when the individual is helped to meet the basic unmet needs of gender identity and to make free choices to combat helplessness and to pursue full psychosexual development, he is able to change his condition. Also the spiritual values of the individual become a part of his psychological and moral integration. The spiritual concerns are an integral part of the picture, and their denial only delays the individual's full realization of his human development. The person has to be treated within his life frame. Life cannot be put on hold in order to treat the homosexual condition or any other condition in a therapeutic process.

Respect and care for the individual should characterize our approach to homosexuality. This respect and care would be manifested by allowing those who choose to remain in their condition to do so but also by allowing those who wish to complete their psychosexual development to do so. When an individual recognizes a conflict and wants to resolve it, we should cooperate with him in his search for human growth.

Homosexuality can and has been healed. Sincere trust, hope, prayer, and hard work are required from all involved in this process.

CONTRIBUTORS

JEFFREY KEEFE, a Conventual Franciscan friar, was ordained a priest in 1952 with a licentiate in theology from Catholic University and obtained a doctorate in clinical psychology from Fordham University in 1965. He interned at Bellevue Psychiatric Hospital in New York City. Father Keefe has worked in clinical settings at Staten Island Mental Health and St. Vincent Medical Center, Staten Island, at the Onondaga Pastoral Counseling Center and as director of the Personal Resource Center in Syracuse, New York. He was an associate professor of psychology at the University of Notre Dame and an adjunct professor of pastoral psychology at the Franciscan theologate, St. Anthony on Hudson, Rensselaer, New York. Currently he is in private practice in Syracuse and serves as consultant on candidates for that diocese and several religious communities. Father Keefe has contributed to various periodicals and has a monthly column on developmental psychology in *Catechist* magazine.

RICHARD P. FITZGIBBONS, M.D., director of the Comprehensive Counseling Services, West Conshohocken, Pennsylvania, since 1988, completed his residency in psychiatry at the hospital of the University of Pennsylvania in 1976. Engaged in the private practice of psychiatry for almost two decades, he has spoken to a great variety of clients. From his extensive research and clinical practice he has developed insights and published material on the "origins, masks, and treatment of anger" that have benefited a large audience of priests, religious, and laity, as well as business

professionals, throughout America. He has also lectured on addictive disorders, seeking to trace their emotional roots. He has
integrated a gospel perspective into clinical practice, concentrating particularly on establishing in his clients a sense of the love
that our heavenly Father has for each one of us.

MARIA VALDES, Ph.D., earned her doctorate in clinical psychology from the University of Villanueva, Havana, Cuba, in 1965.
Besides being a licensed practicing psychologist, she is certified
by the Biofeedback Certification Institute of America (1982) and
by the Academy of Certified Neurotherapists (1994). Too numerous to mention here are her publications, oral presentations,
academic programming, professional consultations, and accomplishments. She has been involved in academic programs at
Baruch College of City University of New York and at Passaic
County Community College with the rank of professor of psychology. There are two areas in particular where she has made
significant contributions to both psychotherapy and religion.
First, for more than thirty years she has worked to bring psychotherapists and spiritual directors together in their common concern for the individual. Second, in her work concerning the
treatment of persons with homosexual tendencies, she has developed a truly creative approach, drawing upon the principles of
Catholic philosophy and sound pastoral theology together with
the valuable insights of psychotherapy, biofeedback, and neuro-
therapy. Her approach has helped many individuals toward a
fully integrated sexuality. In September 1993, she founded
HAPI, which is dedicated to the development and pursuit of the
integration of psychology and spirituality with remembrance of
the Passion of Jesus Christ.

INDEX OF PERSONS